Machine Learning for Cybersecurity Cookbook

Over 80 recipes on how to implement machine learning algorithms for building security systems using Python

Emmanuel Tsukerman

BIRMINGHAM - MUMBAI

Machine Learning for Cybersecurity Cookbook

Commissioning Editor: Sunith Shetty
Acquisition Editor: Ali Abidi
Content Development Editor: Roshan Kumar
Senior Editor: Jack Cummings
Technical Editor: Dinesh Chaudhary
Copy Editor: Safis Editing
Project Coordinator: Aishwarya Mohan
Proofreader: Safis Editing
Indexer: Tejal Daruwale Soni
Production Designer: Shraddha Falebhai

First published: November 2019

Production reference: 1221119

Published by Packt Publishing Ltd.
Livery Place
35 Livery Street
Birmingham
B3 2PB, UK.

ISBN 978-1-78961-467-1

www.packt.com

Packt>

Subscribe to our online digital library for full access to over 7,000 books and videos, as well as industry leading tools to help you plan your personal development and advance your career. For more information, please visit our website.

Why subscribe?

- Spend less time learning and more time coding with practical eBooks and Videos from over 4,000 industry professionals

- Improve your learning with Skill Plans built especially for you

- Get a free eBook or video every month

- Fully searchable for easy access to vital information

- Copy and paste, print, and bookmark content

Did you know that Packt offers eBook versions of every book published, with PDF and ePub files available? You can upgrade to the eBook version at www.packt.com and as a print book customer, you are entitled to a discount on the eBook copy. Get in touch with us at customercare@packtpub.com for more details.

At www.packt.com, you can also read a collection of free technical articles, sign up for a range of free newsletters, and receive exclusive discounts and offers on Packt books and eBooks.

Contributors

About the author

Emmanuel Tsukerman graduated from Stanford University and obtained his Ph.D. from UC Berkeley. In 2017, Dr. Tsukerman's anti-ransomware product was listed in the Top 10 ransomware products of 2018 by *PC Magazine*. In 2018, he designed an ML-based, instant-verdict malware detection system for Palo Alto Networks' WildFire service of over 30,000 customers. In 2019, Dr. Tsukerman launched the first cybersecurity data science course.

About the reviewers

Alexander Osipenko graduated *cum laude* with a degree in computational chemistry. He worked in the oil and gas industry for 4 years, working with real-time data streaming and large network data. Then, he moved to the FinTech industry and cybersecurity. He is currently a machine learning leading expert in the company, utilizing the full potential of AI for intrusion detection and insider threat detection.

Yasser Ali is a cybersecurity consultant at Thales, in the Middle East. He has extensive experience in providing consultancy and advisory services to enterprises on implementing cybersecurity best practices, critical infrastructure protection, red teaming, penetration testing, and vulnerability assessment, managing bug bounty programs, and web and mobile application security assessment. He is also an advocate speaker and participant in information security industry discussions, panels, committees, and conferences, and is a specialized trainer, featuring regularly on different media platforms around the world.

Packt is searching for authors like you

If you're interested in becoming an author for Packt, please visit authors.packtpub.com and apply today. We have worked with thousands of developers and tech professionals, just like you, to help them share their insight with the global tech community. You can make a general application, apply for a specific hot topic that we are recruiting an author for, or submit your own idea.

Table of Contents

Preface

Cyber threats today are one of the key problems every organization faces. This book uses various Python libraries, such as TensorFlow, Keras, scikit-learn, and others, to uncover common and not-so-common challenges faced by cybersecurity researchers.

The book will help readers to implement intelligent solutions to existing cybersecurity challenges and build cutting edge implementations that cater to increasingly complex organizational needs. By the end of this book, you will be able to build and use **machine learning (ML)** algorithms to curb cybersecurity threats using a recipe-based approach.

Who this book is for

This book is for cybersecurity professionals and security researchers who want to take their skills to the next level by implementing machine learning algorithms and techniques to upskill computer security. This recipe-based book will also appeal to data scientists and machine learning developers who are now looking to bring in smart techniques into the cybersecurity domain. Having a working knowledge of Python and being familiar with the basics of cybersecurity fundamentals will be required.

What this book covers

Chapter 1, *Machine Learning for Cybersecurity*, covers the fundamental techniques of machine learning for cybersecurity.

Chapter 2, *Machine Learning-Based Malware Detection*, shows how to perform static and dynamic analysis on samples. You will also learn how to tackle important machine learning challenges that occur in the domain of cybersecurity, such as class imbalance and **false positive rate (FPR)** constraints.

Chapter 3, *Advanced Malware Detection*, covers more advanced concepts for malware analysis. We will also discuss how to approach obfuscated and packed malware, how to scale up the collection of N-gram features, and how to use deep learning to detect and even create malware.

Chapter 4, *Machine Learning for Social Engineering*, explains how to build a Twitter spear-phishing bot using machine learning. You'll also learn how to use deep learning to have a recording of a target saying whatever you want them to say. The chapter also runs through a lie detection cycle and shows you how to train a **Recurrent Neural Network (RNN)** so that it is able to generate new reviews, similar to the ones in the training dataset.

Chapter 5, *Penetration Testing Using Machine Learning*, covers a wide selection of machine learning technologies for penetration testing and security countermeasures. It also covers more specialized topics, such as deanonymizing Tor traffic, recognizing unauthorized access via keystroke dynamics, and detecting malicious URLs.

Chapter 6, *Automatic Intrusion Detection*, looks at designing and implementing several intrusion detection systems using machine learning. It also addresses the example-dependent, cost-sensitive, radically-imbalanced, challenging problem of credit card fraud.

Chapter 7, *Securing and Attacking Data with Machine Learning*, covers recipes for employing machine learning to secure and attack data. It also covers an application of ML for hardware security by attacking **physically unclonable functions (PUFs)** using AI.

Chapter 8, *Secure and Private AI*, explains how to use a federated learning model using the TensorFlow Federated framework. It also includes a walk-through of the basics of encrypted computation and shows how to implement and train a differentially private deep neural network for MNIST using Keras and TensorFlow Privacy.

Appendix offers you a guide to creating infrastructure to handle the challenges of machine learning on cybersecurity data. This chapter also provides a guide to using virtual Python environments, which allow you to seamlessly work on different Python projects while avoiding package conflicts.

To get the most out of this book

You will need a basic knowledge of Python and cybersecurity.

Download the example code files

You can download the example code files for this book from your account at www.packt.com. If you purchased this book elsewhere, you can visit www.packtpub.com/support and register to have the files emailed directly to you.

You can download the code files by following these steps:

1. Log in or register at `www.packt.com`.
2. Select the **Support** tab.
3. Click on **Code Downloads**.
4. Enter the name of the book in the **Search** box and follow the onscreen instructions.

Once the file is downloaded, please make sure that you unzip or extract the folder using the latest version of:

- WinRAR/7-Zip for Windows
- Zipeg/iZip/UnRarX for Mac
- 7-Zip/PeaZip for Linux

The code bundle for the book is also hosted on GitHub at `https://github.com/PacktPublishing/Machine-Learning-for-Cybersecurity-Cookbook`. In case there's an update to the code, it will be updated on the existing GitHub repository.

We also have other code bundles from our rich catalog of books and videos available at `https://github.com/PacktPublishing/`. Check them out!

Download the color images

We also provide a PDF file that has color images of the screenshots/diagrams used in this book. You can download it here: `https://static.packt-cdn.com/downloads/9781789614671_ColorImages.pdf`.

Conventions used

There are a number of text conventions used throughout this book.

`CodeInText`: Indicates code words in text, database table names, folder names, filenames, file extensions, pathnames, dummy URLs, user input, and Twitter handles. Here is an example: "Append the labels to `X_outliers`."

A block of code is set as follows:

```
from sklearn.model_selection import train_test_split
import pandas as pd
```

Any command-line input or output is written as follows:

```
pip install sklearn pandas
```

Bold: Indicates a new term, an important word, or words that you see onscreen. For example, words in menus or dialog boxes appear in the text like this. Here is an example: "The most basic approach to hyperparameter tuning is called a **grid search**."

 Warnings or important notes appear like this.

 Tips and tricks appear like this.

Sections

In this book, you will find several headings that appear frequently (*Getting ready*, *How to do it...*, *How it works...*, *There's more...*, and *See also*).

To give clear instructions on how to complete a recipe, use these sections as follows:

Getting ready

This section tells you what to expect in the recipe and describes how to set up any software or any preliminary settings required for the recipe.

How to do it...

This section contains the steps required to follow the recipe.

How it works...

This section usually consists of a detailed explanation of what happened in the previous section.

There's more...

This section consists of additional information about the recipe in order to make you more knowledgeable about the recipe.

See also

This section provides helpful links to other useful information for the recipe.

Get in touch

Feedback from our readers is always welcome.

General feedback: If you have questions about any aspect of this book, mention the book title in the subject of your message and email us at customercare@packtpub.com.

Errata: Although we have taken every care to ensure the accuracy of our content, mistakes do happen. If you have found a mistake in this book, we would be grateful if you would report this to us. Please visit www.packt.com/submit-errata, selecting your book, clicking on the Errata Submission Form link, and entering the details.

Piracy: If you come across any illegal copies of our works in any form on the Internet, we would be grateful if you would provide us with the location address or website name. Please contact us at copyright@packt.com with a link to the material.

If you are interested in becoming an author: If there is a topic that you have expertise in and you are interested in either writing or contributing to a book, please visit authors.packtpub.com.

Reviews

Please leave a review. Once you have read and used this book, why not leave a review on the site that you purchased it from? Potential readers can then see and use your unbiased opinion to make purchase decisions, we at Packt can understand what you think about our products, and our authors can see your feedback on their book. Thank you!

For more information about Packt, please visit `packt.com`.

1
Machine Learning for Cybersecurity

In this chapter, we will cover the fundamental techniques of machine learning. We will use these throughout the book to solve interesting cybersecurity problems. We will cover both foundational algorithms, such as clustering and gradient boosting trees, and solutions to common data challenges, such as imbalanced data and false-positive constraints. A machine learning practitioner in cybersecurity is in a unique and exciting position to leverage enormous amounts of data and create solutions in a constantly evolving landscape.

This chapter covers the following recipes:

- Train-test-splitting your data
- Standardizing your data
- Summarizing large data using **principal component analysis (PCA)**
- Generating text using Markov chains
- Performing clustering using scikit-learn
- Training an XGBoost classifier
- Analyzing time series using statsmodels
- Anomaly detection using Isolation Forest
- **Natural language processing (NLP)** using hashing vectorizer and tf-idf with scikit-learn
- Hyperparameter tuning with scikit-optimize

Technical requirements

In this chapter, we will be using the following:

- scikit-learn
- Markovify
- XGBoost
- statsmodels

The installation instructions and code can be found at `https://github.com/PacktPublishing/Machine-Learning-for-Cybersecurity-Cookbook/tree/master/Chapter01`.

Train-test-splitting your data

In machine learning, our goal is to create a program that is able to perform tasks it has never been explicitly taught to perform. The way we do that is to use data we have collected to *train* or *fit* a mathematical or statistical model. The data used to fit the model is referred to as *training data*. The resulting trained model is then used to predict future, previously-unseen data. In this way, the program is able to manage new situations without human intervention.

One of the major challenges for a machine learning practitioner is the danger of *overfitting* – creating a model that performs well on the training data but is not able to generalize to new, previously-unseen data. In order to combat the problem of overfitting, machine learning practitioners set aside a portion of the data, called *test data*, and use it only to assess the performance of the trained model, as opposed to including it as part of the training dataset. This careful setting aside of testing sets is key to training classifiers in cybersecurity, where overfitting is an omnipresent danger. One small oversight, such as using only benign data from one locale, can lead to a poor classifier.

There are various other ways to validate model performance, such as cross-validation. For simplicity, we will focus mainly on train-test splitting.

Getting ready

Preparation for this recipe consists of installing the scikit-learn and `pandas` packages in `pip`. The command for this is as follows:

```
pip install sklearn pandas
```

In addition, we have included the `north_korea_missile_test_database.csv` dataset for use in this recipe.

How to do it...

The following steps demonstrate how to take a dataset, consisting of features x and labels y, and split these into a training and testing subset:

1. Start by importing the `train_test_split` module and the `pandas` library, and read your features into x and labels into y:

```
from sklearn.model_selection import train_test_split
import pandas as pd

df = pd.read_csv("north_korea_missile_test_database.csv")
y = df["Missile Name"]
X = df.drop("Missile Name", axis=1)
```

2. Next, randomly split the dataset and its labels into a training set consisting 80% of the size of the original dataset and a testing set 20% of the size:

```
X_train, X_test, y_train, y_test = train_test_split(
    X, y, test_size=0.2, random_state=31
)
```

3. We apply the `train_test_split` method once more, to obtain a validation set, `X_val` and `y_val`:

```
X_train, X_val, y_train, y_val = train_test_split(
    X_train, y_train, test_size=0.25, random_state=31
)
```

4. We end up with a training set that's 60% of the size of the original data, a validation set of 20%, and a testing set of 20%.

The following screenshot shows the output:

```
print(len(X_train))
print(len(y_train))
print(len(X_val))
print(len(y_val))
print(len(X_test))
print(len(y_test))

81
81
27
27
27
27
```

How it works...

We start by reading in our dataset, consisting of historical and continuing missile experiments in North Korea. We aim to predict the type of missile based on remaining features, such as facility and time of launch. This concludes step 1. In step 2, we apply scikit-learn's `train_test_split` method to subdivide X and y into a training set, `X_train` and `y_train`, and also a testing set, `X_test` and `y_test`. The `test_size = 0.2` parameter means that the testing set consists of 20% of the original data, while the remainder is placed in the training set. The `random_state` parameter allows us to reproduce the same *randomly generated* split. Next, concerning step 3, it is important to note that, in applications, we often want to compare several different models. The danger of using the testing set to select the best model is that we may end up overfitting the testing set. This is similar to the statistical sin of data fishing. In order to combat this danger, we create an additional dataset, called the validation set. We train our models on the training set, use the validation set to compare them, and finally use the testing set to obtain an accurate indicator of the performance of the model we have chosen. So, in step 3, we choose our parameters so that, mathematically speaking, the end result consists of a training set of 60% of the original dataset, a validation set of 20%, and a testing set of 20%. Finally, we double-check our assumptions by employing the `len` function to compute the length of the arrays (step 4).

Standardizing your data

For many machine learning algorithms, performance is highly sensitive to the relative scale of features. For that reason, it is often important to *standardize* your features. To standardize a feature means to shift all of its values so that their mean = 0 and to scale them so that their variance = 1.

One instance when normalizing is useful is when featuring the PE header of a file. The PE header contains extremely large values (for example, the `SizeOfInitializedData` field) and also very small ones (for example, the number of sections). For certain ML models, such as neural networks, the large discrepancy in magnitude between features can reduce performance.

Getting ready

Preparation for this recipe consists of installing the `scikit-learn` and `pandas` packages in `pip`. Perform the following steps:

```
pip install sklearn pandas
```

In addition, you will find a dataset named `file_pe_headers.csv` in the repository for this recipe.

How to do it...

In the following steps, we utilize scikit-learn's `StandardScaler` method to standardize our data:

1. Start by importing the required libraries and gathering a dataset, X:

```
import pandas as pd

data = pd.read_csv("file_pe_headers.csv", sep=",")
X = data.drop(["Name", "Malware"], axis=1).to_numpy()
```

Dataset X looks as follows:

```
[[2.31170e+04 1.44000e+02 3.00000e+00 ... 7.78240e+04 7.37280e+04
  0.00000e+00]
 [2.31170e+04 1.44000e+02 3.00000e+00 ... 2.94912e+05 0.00000e+00
  3.46112e+05]
 [2.31170e+04 1.44000e+02 3.00000e+00 ... 4.09600e+04 0.00000e+00
  0.00000e+00]
 ...
 [2.31170e+04 0.00000e+00 0.00000e+00 ... 6.14400e+04 0.00000e+00
  0.00000e+00]
 [2.31170e+04 1.44000e+02 3.00000e+00 ... 1.02400e+05 0.00000e+00
  0.00000e+00]
 [2.31170e+04 1.44000e+02 3.00000e+00 ... 5.57056e+05 0.00000e+00
  0.00000e+00]]
```

2. Next, standardize X using a `StandardScaler` instance:

```
from sklearn.preprocessing import StandardScaler

X_standardized = StandardScaler().fit_transform(X)
```

The standardized dataset looks like the following:

```
[[ 0.         -0.03506542 -0.04751096 ... -0.07054894 -0.0198525
  -0.04066791]
 [ 0.         -0.03506542 -0.04751096 ... -0.03849221 -0.02110877
  -0.02469983]
 [ 0.         -0.03506542 -0.04751096 ... -0.07599254 -0.02110877
  -0.04066791]
 ...
 [ 0.         -0.18093613 -0.04958686 ... -0.07296832 -0.02110877
  -0.04066791]
 [ 0.         -0.03506542 -0.04751096 ... -0.06691988 -0.02110877
  -0.04066791]
 [ 0.         -0.03506542 -0.04751096 ...  0.00021781 -0.02110877
  -0.04066791]]
```

How it works...

We begin by reading in our dataset (step 1), which consists of the PE header information for a collection of PE files. These vary greatly, with some columns reaching hundreds of thousands of files, and others staying in the single digits. Consequently, certain models, such as neural networks, will perform poorly on such unstandardized data. In step 2, we instantiate `StandardScaler()` and then apply it to rescale X using `.fit_transform(X)`. As a result, we obtained a rescaled dataset, whose columns (corresponding to features) have a mean of 0 and a variance of 1.

Summarizing large data using principal component analysis

Suppose that you would like to build a predictor for an individual's expected net fiscal worth at age 45. There are a huge number of variables to be considered: IQ, current fiscal worth, marriage status, height, geographical location, health, education, career state, age, and many others you might come up with, such as number of LinkedIn connections or SAT scores.

The trouble with having so many features is several-fold. First, the amount of data, which will incur high storage costs and computational time for your algorithm. Second, with a large feature space, it is critical to have a large amount of data for the model to be accurate. That's to say, it becomes harder to distinguish the signal from the noise. For these reasons, when dealing with high-dimensional data such as this, we often employ dimensionality reduction techniques, such as PCA. More information on the topic can be found at https:/ /en.wikipedia.org/wiki/Principal_component_analysis.

PCA allows us to take our features and return a smaller number of new features, formed from our original ones, with maximal explanatory power. In addition, since the new features are linear combinations of the old features, this allows us to anonymize our data, which is very handy when working with financial information, for example.

Getting ready

The preparation for this recipe consists of installing the scikit-learn and pandas packages in pip. The command for this is as follows:

```
pip install sklearn pandas
```

In addition, we will be utilizing the same dataset, malware_pe_headers.csv, as in the previous recipe.

How to do it...

In this section, we'll walk through a recipe showing how to use PCA on data:

1. Start by importing the necessary libraries and reading in the dataset:

```
from sklearn.decomposition import PCA
import pandas as pd

data = pd.read_csv("file_pe_headers.csv", sep=",")
X = data.drop(["Name", "Malware"], axis=1).to_numpy()
```

2. Standardize the dataset, as is necessary before applying PCA:

```
from sklearn.preprocessing import StandardScaler

X_standardized = StandardScaler().fit_transform(X)
```

3. Instantiate a `PCA` instance and use it to reduce the dimensionality of our data:

```
pca = PCA()
pca.fit_transform(X_standardized)
```

4. Assess the effectiveness of your dimensionality reduction:

```
print(pca.explained_variance_ratio_)
```

The following screenshot shows the output:

```
[1.13714096e-01 6.04526312e-02 5.35847638e-02 4.95286930e-02
 4.08242868e-02 3.43687925e-02 3.32004002e-02 3.01112226e-02
 2.86901095e-02 2.81624164e-02 2.54807940e-02 2.38845548e-02
 2.22696648e-02 2.05755591e-02 1.82485433e-02 1.73648310e-02
 1.66649078e-02 1.63647194e-02 1.52683994e-02 1.46357930e-02
 1.45790542e-02 1.45535760e-02 1.44699413e-02 1.44154480e-02
 1.42948516e-02 1.39221004e-02 1.35338124e-02 1.33766277e-02
 1.32896667e-02 1.23472302e-02 1.20507834e-02 1.15452214e-02
 1.13731313e-02 1.10939084e-02 1.07062189e-02 1.01649154e-02
 9.90148375e-03 9.61478385e-03 9.17627698e-03 9.04802544e-03
 8.66332999e-03 6.94752252e-03 6.84216033e-03 6.48244001e-03
 5.95005317e-03 5.91335216e-03 5.41615029e-03 5.10640740e-03
 4.83543074e-03 4.45888820e-03 4.29104432e-03 3.82076025e-03
 3.79864324e-03 3.24146447e-03 3.18558571e-03 2.67004617e-03
 2.03201471e-03 1.73591476e-03 1.65758475e-03 1.56708821e-03
 1.38839592e-03 1.20694096e-03 8.20896559e-04 6.92520065e-04
 2.79632267e-04 1.36614783e-04 6.56001071e-06 3.22441346e-07
 1.26534195e-10 5.64125607e-34 5.64125607e-34 5.64125607e-34
 5.64125607e-34 5.64125607e-34 5.64125607e-34 5.64125607e-34
 5.63722303e-34]
```

How it works...

We begin by reading in our dataset and then standardizing it, as in the recipe on standardizing data (steps 1 and 2). (It is necessary to work with standardized data before applying PCA). We now instantiate a new PCA transformer instance, and use it to both learn the transformation (fit) and also apply the transform to the dataset, using `fit_transform` (step 3). In step 4, we analyze our transformation. In particular, note that the elements of `pca.explained_variance_ratio_` indicate how much of the variance is accounted for in each direction. The sum is 1, indicating that all the variance is accounted for if we consider the full space in which the data lives. However, just by taking the first few directions, we can account for a large portion of the variance, while limiting our dimensionality. In our example, the first 40 directions account for 90% of the variance:

```
sum(pca.explained_variance_ratio_[0:40])
```

This produces the following output:

```
0.9068522354673663
```

This means that we can reduce our number of features to 40 (from 78) while preserving 90% of the variance. The implications of this are that many of the features of the PE header are closely correlated, which is understandable, as they are not designed to be independent.

Generating text using Markov chains

Markov chains are simple stochastic models in which a system can exist in a number of states. To know the probability distribution of where the system will be next, it suffices to know where it currently is. This is in contrast with a system in which the probability distribution of the subsequent state may depend on the past history of the system. This simplifying assumption allows Markov chains to be easily applied in many domains, surprisingly fruitfully.

In this recipe, we will utilize Markov chains to generate fake reviews, which is useful for pen-testing a review system's spam detector. In a later recipe, you will upgrade the technology from Markov chains to RNNs.

Getting ready

Preparation for this recipe consists of installing the `markovify` and `pandas` packages in `pip`. The command for this is as follows:

```
pip install markovify pandas
```

In addition, the directory in the repository for this chapter includes a CSV dataset, `airport_reviews.csv`, which should be placed alongside the code for the chapter.

How to do it...

Let's see how to generate text using Markov chains by performing the following steps:

1. Start by importing the `markovify` library and a text file whose style we would like to imitate:

   ```
   import markovify
   import pandas as pd

   df = pd.read_csv("airport_reviews.csv")
   ```

   As an illustration, I have chosen a collection of airport reviews as my text:

   ```
   "The airport is certainly tiny! ..."
   ```

2. Next, join the individual reviews into one large text string and build a Markov chain model using the airport review text:

   ```
   from itertools import chain

   N = 100
   review_subset = df["content"][0:N]
   text = "".join(chain.from_iterable(review_subset))
   markov_chain_model = markovify.Text(text)
   ```

   Behind the scenes, the library computes the transition word probabilities from the text.

3. Generate five sentences using the Markov chain model:

   ```
   for i in range(5):
       print(markov_chain_model.make_sentence())
   ```

4. Since we are using airport reviews, we will have the following as the output after executing the previous code:

```
On the positive side it's a clean airport transfer from A to C
gates and outgoing gates is truly enormous - but why when we
arrived at about 7.30 am for our connecting flight to Venice on
TAROM.
The only really bother: you may have to wait in a polite manner.
Why not have bus after a short wait to check-in there were a lots
of shops and less seating.
Very inefficient and hostile airport. This is one of the time easy
to access at low price from city center by train.
The distance between the incoming gates and ending with dirty and
always blocked by never ending roadworks.
```

Surprisingly realistic! Although the reviews would have to be filtered down to the best ones.

5. Generate 3 sentences with a length of no more than 140 characters:

```
for i in range(3):
    print(markov_chain_model.make_short_sentence(140))
```

With our running example, we will see the following output:

```
However airport staff member told us that we were put on a
connecting code share flight.
Confusing in the check-in agent was friendly.
I am definitely not keen on coming to the lack of staff . Lack of
staff . Lack of staff at boarding pass at check-in.
```

How it works...

We begin the recipe by importing the Markovify library, a library for Markov chain computations, and reading in text, which will inform our Markov model (step 1). In step 2, we create a Markov chain model using the text. The following is a relevant snippet from the text object's initialization code:

```
class Text(object):

    reject_pat = re.compile(r"(^')|('$)|\s'|'\s|[\"(\(\)\[\])]")

    def __init__(self, input_text, state_size=2, chain=None,
parsed_sentences=None, retain_original=True, well_formed=True,
reject_reg=''):
        """
```

```
            input_text: A string.
            state_size: An integer, indicating the number of words in the
    model's state.
            chain: A trained markovify.Chain instance for this text, if pre-
    processed.
            parsed_sentences: A list of lists, where each outer list is a "run"
                of the process (e.g. a single sentence), and each inner list
                contains the steps (e.g. words) in the run. If you want to
    simulate
                an infinite process, you can come very close by passing just
    one, very
                long run.
            retain_original: Indicates whether to keep the original corpus.
            well_formed: Indicates whether sentences should be well-formed,
    preventing
                unmatched quotes, parenthesis by default, or a custom regular
    expression
                can be provided.
            reject_reg: If well_formed is True, this can be provided to
    override the
                standard rejection pattern.
            """
```

The most important parameter to understand is `state_size = 2`, which means that the Markov chains will be computing transitions between consecutive pairs of words. For more realistic sentences, this parameter can be increased, at the cost of making sentences appear less original. Next, we apply the Markov chains we have trained to generate a few example sentences (steps 3 and 4). We can see clearly that the Markov chains have captured the tone and style of the text. Finally, in step 5, we create a few `tweets` in the style of the airport reviews using our Markov chains.

Performing clustering using scikit-learn

Clustering is a collection of unsupervised machine learning algorithms in which parts of the data are grouped based on similarity. For example, clusters might consist of data that is close together in n-dimensional Euclidean space. Clustering is useful in cybersecurity for distinguishing between normal and anomalous network activity, and for helping to classify malware into families.

Getting ready

Preparation for this recipe consists of installing the `scikit-learn`, `pandas`, and `plotly` packages in `pip`. The command for this is as follows:

```
pip install sklearn plotly pandas
```

In addition, a dataset named `file_pe_header.csv` is provided in the repository for this recipe.

How to do it...

In the following steps, we will see a demonstration of how scikit-learn's K-means clustering algorithm performs on a toy PE malware classification:

1. Start by importing and plotting the dataset:

```
import pandas as pd
import plotly.express as px

df = pd.read_csv("file_pe_headers.csv", sep=",")
fig = px.scatter_3d(
    df,
    x="SuspiciousImportFunctions",
    y="SectionsLength",
    z="SuspiciousNameSection",
    color="Malware",
)
fig.show()
```

The following screenshot shows the output:

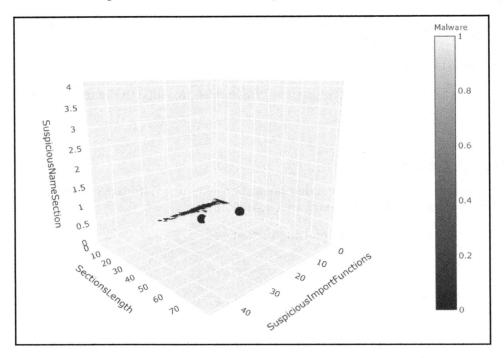

2. Extract the features and target labels:

```
y = df["Malware"]
X = df.drop(["Name", "Malware"], axis=1).to_numpy()
```

3. Next, import scikit-learn's clustering module and fit a K-means model with two clusters to the data:

```
from sklearn.cluster import KMeans

estimator = KMeans(n_clusters=len(set(y)))
estimator.fit(X)
```

4. Predict the cluster using our trained algorithm:

```
y_pred = estimator.predict(X)
df["pred"] = y_pred
df["pred"] = df["pred"].astype("category")
```

5. To see how the algorithm did, plot the algorithm's clusters:

```
fig = px.scatter_3d(
    df,
    x="SuspiciousImportFunctions",
    y="SectionsLength",
    z="SuspiciousNameSection",
    color="pred",
)
fig.show()
```

The following screenshot shows the output:

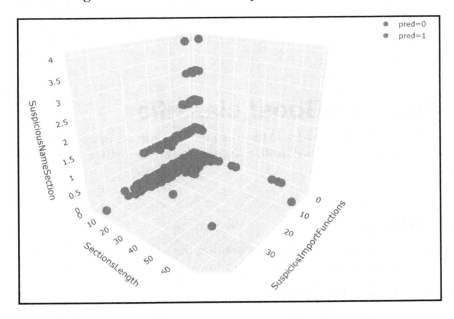

The results are not perfect, but we can see that the clustering algorithm captured much of the structure in the dataset.

How it works...

We start by importing our dataset of PE header information from a collection of samples (step 1). This dataset consists of two classes of PE files: malware and benign. We then use plotly to create a nice-looking interactive 3D graph (step 1). We proceed to prepare our dataset for machine learning. Specifically, in step 2, we set X as the features and y as the classes of the dataset. Based on the fact that there are two classes, we aim to cluster the data into two groups that will match the sample classification. We utilize the K-means algorithm (step 3), about which you can find more information at: https://en.wikipedia.org/wiki/K-means_clustering. With a thoroughly trained clustering algorithm, we are ready to predict on the testing set. We apply our clustering algorithm to predict to which cluster each of the samples should belong (step 4). Observing our results in step 5, we see that clustering has captured a lot of the underlying information, as it was able to fit the data well.

Training an XGBoost classifier

Gradient boosting is widely considered the most reliable and accurate algorithm for generic machine learning problems. We will utilize XGBoost to create malware detectors in future recipes.

Getting ready

The preparation for this recipe consists of installing the scikit-learn, pandas, and xgboost packages in pip. The command for this is as follows:

```
pip install sklearn xgboost pandas
```

In addition, a dataset named file_pe_header.csv is provided in the repository for this recipe.

How to do it...

In the following steps, we will demonstrate how to instantiate, train, and test an XGBoost classifier:

1. Start by reading in the data:

```
import pandas as pd

df = pd.read_csv("file_pe_headers.csv", sep=",")
y = df["Malware"]
X = df.drop(["Name", "Malware"], axis=1).to_numpy()
```

2. Next, train-test-split a dataset:

```
from sklearn.model_selection import train_test_split

X_train, X_test, y_train, y_test = train_test_split(X, y,
test_size=0.3)
```

3. Create one instance of an XGBoost model and train it on the training set:

```
from xgboost import XGBClassifier

XGB_model_instance = XGBClassifier()
XGB_model_instance.fit(X_train, y_train)
```

4. Finally, assess its performance on the testing set:

```
from sklearn.metrics import accuracy_score

y_test_pred = XGB_model_instance.predict(X_test)
accuracy = accuracy_score(y_test, y_test_pred)
print("Accuracy: %.2f%%" % (accuracy * 100))
```

The following screenshot shows the output:

```
Accuracy: 99.08%
```

How it works...

We begin by reading in our data (step 1). We then create a train-test split (step 2). We proceed to instantiate an XGBoost classifier with default parameters and fit it to our training set (step 3). Finally, in step 4, we use our XGBoost classifier to predict on the testing set. We then produce the measured accuracy of our XGBoost model's predictions.

Analyzing time series using statsmodels

A time series is a series of values obtained at successive times. For example, the price of the stock market sampled every minute forms a time series. In cybersecurity, time series analysis can be very handy for predicting a cyberattack, such as an insider employee exfiltrating data, or a group of hackers colluding in preparation for their next hit.

Let's look at several techniques for making predictions using time series.

Getting ready

Preparation for this recipe consists of installing the `matplotlib`, `statsmodels`, and `scipy` packages in `pip`. The command for this is as follows:

```
pip install matplotlib statsmodels scipy
```

How to do it...

In the following steps, we demonstrate several methods for making predictions using time series data:

1. Begin by generating a time series:

```
from random import random

time_series = [2 * x + random() for x in range(1, 100)]
```

2. Plot your data:

```
%matplotlib inline
import matplotlib.pyplot as plt

plt.plot(time_series)
plt.show()
```

The following screenshot shows the output:

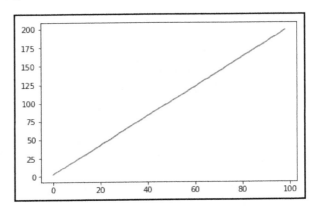

3. There is a large variety of techniques we can use to predict the consequent value of a time series:

- **Autoregression (AR):**

```
from statsmodels.tsa.ar_model import AR

model = AR(time_series)
model_fit = model.fit()
y = model_fit.predict(len(time_series), len(time_series))
```

- **Moving average (MA):**

```
from statsmodels.tsa.arima_model import ARMA

model = ARMA(time_series, order=(0, 1))
model_fit = model.fit(disp=False)
y = model_fit.predict(len(time_series), len(time_series))
```

- **Simple exponential smoothing (SES)**:

```
from statsmodels.tsa.holtwinters import SimpleExpSmoothing

model = SimpleExpSmoothing(time_series)
model_fit = model.fit()
y = model_fit.predict(len(time_series), len(time_series))
```

The resulting predictions are as follows:

```
from statsmodels.tsa.ar_model import AR

model = AR(time_series)
model_fit = model.fit()
y = model_fit.predict(len(time_series), len(time_series))
print(y)

[200.46051296]

model_fit.params

array([13.52904896,  0.0387842 ,  0.20658747,  0.2626664 , -0.23256276,
        0.1341352 ,  0.13259913,  0.17487147, -0.13811329, -0.02630609,
        0.06267792,  0.13943178,  0.24528964])

from statsmodels.tsa.arima_model import ARMA

model = ARMA(time_series, order=(0, 1))
model_fit = model.fit(disp=False)
y = model_fit.predict(len(time_series), len(time_series))
print(y)

[150.594829]

model_fit.params

array([100.52900385,    0.99994647])

from statsmodels.tsa.holtwinters import SimpleExpSmoothing

model = SimpleExpSmoothing(time_series)
model_fit = model.fit()
y = model_fit.predict(len(time_series), len(time_series))
print(y)

[198.58106655]
```

How it works...

In the first step, we generate a simple toy time series. The series consists of values on a line sprinkled with some added noise. Next, we plot our time series in step 2. You can see that it is very close to a straight line and that a sensible prediction for the value of the time series at time t is $2t$. To create a forecast of the value of the time series, we consider three different schemes (step 3) for predicting the future values of the time series. In an autoregressive model, the basic idea is that the value of the time series at time t is a linear function of the values of the time series at the previous times. More precisely, there are some constants, $c_0, c_1, \ldots, c_k$, and a number, k, such that:

$$y_t = c_0 + c_1 y_{t-1} + c_2 y_{t-2} + \ldots + c_k y_{t-k}$$

As a hypothetical example, k may be 3, meaning that the value of the time series can be easily computed from knowing its last 3 values.

In the moving-average model, the time series is modeled as fluctuating about a mean. More precisely, let w_t be a sequence of i.i.d normal variables and let θ_1 be a constant. Then, the time series is modeled by the following formula:

$$y_t = \mu + w_t + \theta_1 w_{t-1}$$

For that reason, it performs poorly in predicting the noisy linear time series we have generated.

Finally, in simple exponential smoothing, we propose a smoothing parameter, $0 < \alpha < 1$. Then, our model's estimate, s_t, is computed from the following equations:

$$s_0 = x_0$$

$$s_t = \alpha y_t + (1 - \alpha) s_{t-1}$$

In other words, we keep track of an estimate, s_t, and adjust it slightly using the current time series value, y_t. How strongly the adjustment is made is regulated by the α parameter.

Anomaly detection with Isolation Forest

Anomaly detection is the identification of events in a dataset that do not conform to the expected pattern. In applications, these events may be of critical importance. For instance, they may be occurrences of a network intrusion or of fraud. We will utilize Isolation Forest to detect such anomalies. Isolation Forest relies on the observation that it is easy to isolate an outlier, while more difficult to describe a normal data point.

Getting ready

The preparation for this recipe consists of installing the `matplotlib`, `pandas`, and `scipy` packages in `pip`. The command for this is as follows:

```
pip install matplotlib pandas scipy
```

How to do it...

In the next steps, we demonstrate how to apply the Isolation Forest algorithm to detecting anomalies:

1. Import the required libraries and set a random seed:

```
import numpy as np
import pandas as pd

random_seed = np.random.RandomState(12)
```

2. Generate a set of normal observations, to be used as training data:

```
X_train = 0.5 * random_seed.randn(500, 2)
X_train = np.r_[X_train + 3, X_train]
X_train = pd.DataFrame(X_train, columns=["x", "y"])
```

3. Generate a testing set, also consisting of normal observations:

```
X_test = 0.5 * random_seed.randn(500, 2)
X_test = np.r_[X_test + 3, X_test]
X_test = pd.DataFrame(X_test, columns=["x", "y"])
```

4. Generate a set of outlier observations. These are generated from a different distribution than the normal observations:

```
X_outliers = random_seed.uniform(low=-5, high=5, size=(50, 2))
X_outliers = pd.DataFrame(X_outliers, columns=["x", "y"])
```

5. Let's take a look at the data we have generated:

```
%matplotlib inline
import matplotlib.pyplot as plt

p1 = plt.scatter(X_train.x, X_train.y, c="white", s=50,
edgecolor="black")
p2 = plt.scatter(X_test.x, X_test.y, c="green", s=50,
edgecolor="black")
p3 = plt.scatter(X_outliers.x, X_outliers.y, c="blue", s=50,
edgecolor="black")
plt.xlim((-6, 6))
plt.ylim((-6, 6))
plt.legend(
    [p1, p2, p3],
    ["training set", "normal testing set", "anomalous testing
set"],
    loc="lower right",
)

plt.show()
```

The following screenshot shows the output:

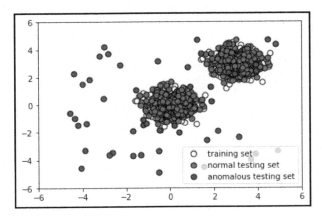

6. Now train an Isolation Forest model on our training data:

```
from sklearn.ensemble import IsolationForest

clf = IsolationForest()
clf.fit(X_train)
y_pred_train = clf.predict(X_train)
y_pred_test = clf.predict(X_test)
y_pred_outliers = clf.predict(X_outliers)
```

7. Let's see how the algorithm performs. Append the labels to X_outliers:

```
X_outliers = X_outliers.assign(pred=y_pred_outliers)
X_outliers.head()
```

The following is the output:

	x	y	pred
0	3.947504	2.891003	1
1	0.413976	-2.025841	-1
2	-2.644476	-3.480783	-1
3	-0.518212	-3.386443	-1
4	2.977669	2.215355	1

8. Let's plot the Isolation Forest predictions on the outliers to see how many it caught:

```
p1 = plt.scatter(X_train.x, X_train.y, c="white", s=50,
edgecolor="black")
p2 = plt.scatter(
    X_outliers.loc[X_outliers.pred == -1, ["x"]],
    X_outliers.loc[X_outliers.pred == -1, ["y"]],
    c="blue",
    s=50,
    edgecolor="black",
)
p3 = plt.scatter(
    X_outliers.loc[X_outliers.pred == 1, ["x"]],
    X_outliers.loc[X_outliers.pred == 1, ["y"]],
    c="red",
    s=50,
    edgecolor="black",
)

plt.xlim((-6, 6))
plt.ylim((-6, 6))
plt.legend(
```

```
    [p1, p2, p3],
    ["training observations", "detected outliers", "incorrectly
labeled outliers"],
    loc="lower right",
)

plt.show()
```

The following screenshot shows the output:

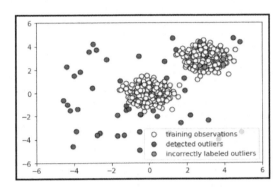

9. Now let's see how it performed on the normal testing data. Append the predicted label to X_test:

```
X_test = X_test.assign(pred=y_pred_test)
X_test.head()
```

The following is the output:

	x	y	pred
0	3.944575	3.866919	-1
1	2.984853	3.142150	1
2	3.501735	2.168262	1
3	2.906300	3.233826	1
4	3.273225	3.261790	1

10. Now let's plot the results to see whether our classifier labeled the normal testing data correctly:

```
p1 = plt.scatter(X_train.x, X_train.y, c="white", s=50,
edgecolor="black")
p2 = plt.scatter(
    X_test.loc[X_test.pred == 1, ["x"]],
    X_test.loc[X_test.pred == 1, ["y"]],
```

```
        c="blue",
        s=50,
        edgecolor="black",
    )
    p3 = plt.scatter(
        X_test.loc[X_test.pred == -1, ["x"]],
        X_test.loc[X_test.pred == -1, ["y"]],
        c="red",
        s=50,
        edgecolor="black",
    )

    plt.xlim((-6, 6))
    plt.ylim((-6, 6))
    plt.legend(
        [p1, p2, p3],
        [
            "training observations",
            "correctly labeled test observations",
            "incorrectly labeled test observations",
        ],
        loc="lower right",
    )

    plt.show()
```

The following screenshot shows the output:

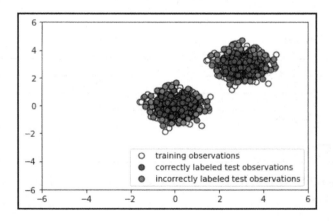

Evidently, our Isolation Forest model performed quite well at capturing the anomalous points. There were quite a few false negatives (instances where normal points were classified as outliers), but by tuning our model's parameters, we may be able to reduce these.

How it works...

The first step involves simply loading the necessary libraries that will allow us to manipulate data quickly and easily. In steps 2 and 3, we generate a training and testing set consisting of normal observations. These have the same distributions. In step 4, on the other hand, we generate the remainder of our testing set by creating outliers. This anomalous dataset has a different distribution from the training data and the rest of the testing data. Plotting our data, we see that some outlier points look indistinguishable from normal points (step 5). This guarantees that our classifier will have a significant percentage of misclassifications, due to the nature of the data, and we must keep this in mind when evaluating its performance. In step 6, we fit an instance of Isolation Forest with default parameters to the training data.

Note that the algorithm is fed no information about the anomalous data. We use our trained instance of Isolation Forest to predict whether the testing data is normal or anomalous, and similarly to predict whether the anomalous data is normal or anomalous. To examine how the algorithm performs, we append the predicted labels to X_outliers (step 7) and then plot the predictions of the Isolation Forest instance on the outliers (step 8). We see that it was able to capture most of the anomalies. Those that were incorrectly labeled were indistinguishable from normal observations. Next, in step 9, we append the predicted label to X_test in preparation for analysis and then plot the predictions of the Isolation Forest instance on the normal testing data (step 10). We see that it correctly labeled the majority of normal observations. At the same time, there was a significant number of incorrectly classified normal observations (shown in red).

Depending on how many false alarms we are willing to tolerate, we may need to fine-tune our classifier to reduce the number of false positives.

Natural language processing using a hashing vectorizer and tf-idf with scikit-learn

We often find in data science that the objects we wish to analyze are textual. For example, they might be tweets, articles, or network logs. Since our algorithms require numerical inputs, we must find a way to convert such text into numerical features. To this end, we utilize a sequence of techniques.

A *token* is a unit of text. For example, we may specify that our tokens are words, sentences, or characters. A count vectorizer takes textual input and then outputs a vector consisting of the counts of the textual tokens. A **hashing vectorizer** is a variation on the count vectorizer that sets out to be faster and more scalable, at the cost of interpretability and hashing collisions. Though it can be useful, just having the counts of the words appearing in a document corpus can be misleading. The reason is that, often, unimportant words, such as *the* and *a* (known as *stop words*) have a high frequency of occurrence, and hence little informative content. For reasons such as this, we often give words different weights to offset this. The main technique for doing so is **tf-idf**, which stands for **Term-Frequency, Inverse-Document-Frequency**. The main idea is that we account for the number of times a term occurs, but discount it by the number of documents it occurs in.

In cybersecurity, text data is omnipresent; event logs, conversational transcripts, and lists of function names are just a few examples. Consequently, it is essential to be able to work with such data, something you'll learn in this recipe.

Getting ready

The preparation for this recipe consists of installing the scikit-learn package in `pip`. The command for this is as follows:

```
pip install sklearn
```

In addition, a log file, `anonops_short.log`, consisting of an excerpt of conversations taking place on the IRC channel, `#Anonops`, is included in the repository for this chapter.

How to do it...

In the next steps, we will convert a corpus of text data into numerical form, amenable to machine learning algorithms:

1. First, import a textual dataset:

```
with open("anonops_short.txt", encoding="utf8") as f:
    anonops_chat_logs = f.readlines()
```

2. Next, count the words in the text using the hash vectorizer and then perform weighting using tf-idf:

```
from sklearn.feature_extraction.text import HashingVectorizer
from sklearn.feature_extraction.text import TfidfTransformer

my_vector = HashingVectorizer(input="content", ngram_range=(1, 2))
X_train_counts = my_vector.fit_transform(anonops_chat_logs,)
tf_transformer =
TfidfTransformer(use_idf=True,).fit(X_train_counts)
X_train_tf = tf_transformer.transform(X_train_counts)
```

3. The end result is a sparse matrix with each row being a vector representing one of the texts:

```
X_train_tf

<180830 x 1048576 sparse matrix of type <class 'numpy.float64'>'
with 3158166 stored elements in Compressed Sparse Row format>

print(X_train_tf)
```

The following is the output:

```
(0,  938273)     0.10023429482560929
(0,  871172)    -0.33044470291777067
(0,  755834)    -0.2806123960092745
(0,  556974)    -0.2171490773135763
(0,  548264)    -0.09851435603064428
(0,  531189)    -0.2566310842337745
(0,  522961)    -0.3119912982467716
(0,  514190)    -0.2527659565181208
(0,  501800)    -0.33044470291777067
(0,  499727)    -0.18952297847436425
(0,  488876)     0.13502094828386488
(0,  377854)     0.22710724511856722
(0,  334594)    -0.25581186158424035
(0,  256577)     0.20949022238574433
(0,  197273)    -0.30119674850360456
(0,  114899)     0.09713499033205285
(0,  28523)     -0.3060506288368513
(1,  960098)     0.09780838928665199
(1,  955748)    -0.2747271490090429
(1,  952302)     0.26070217969901804
(1,  938273)     0.12095603891963835
(1,  937092)    -0.2947114257264502
(1,  927866)     0.21727726371674563
(1,  820768)    -0.11065660403137358
(1,  772066)    -0.14344517367198276
  :      :
(180828,  329790)       0.06808618130417012
(180828,  312887)      -0.08249409552977467
(180828,  209871)       0.17685927011939476
(180828,  193711)      -0.14127016157231428
(180828,  181881)      -0.11885031537539834
(180828,  180525)      -0.06925490785130799
(180828,  156500)      -0.20787461071537122
(180828,  148568)       0.1963433059906426
(180828,  82508)       -0.1289257787752738
(180828,  79994)        0.23121076025389292
(180828,  78098)       -0.18205107240120946
(180828,  47738)        0.23121076025389292
(180828,  46353)        0.1045181919567425
(180828,  45900)       -0.09537730182105167
(180828,  45419)       -0.11189579574426382
(180828,  11712)       -0.16947494737589616
(180829,  1026910)      0.4082112914772047
(180829,  975831)      -0.18401193506169794
(180829,  936283)       0.2472007199039777
(180829,  856299)      -0.15436175878438183
(180829,  473183)      -0.41092004816695277
(180829,  464504)       0.2928849862993687
(180829,  251872)      -0.4714000763194845
(180829,  189128)       0.44418614795477124
(180829,  45900)       -0.20102520636796686
```

How it works...

We started by loading in the #Anonops text dataset (step 1). The Anonops IRC channel has been affiliated with the Anonymous hacktivist group. In particular, chat participants have in the past planned and announced their future targets on Anonops. Consequently, a well-engineered ML system would be able to predict cyber attacks by training on such data. In step 2, we instantiated a hashing vectorizer. The hashing vectorizer gave us counts of the 1- and 2-grams in the text, in other words, singleton and consecutive pairs of words (tokens) in the articles. We then applied a tf-idf transformer to give appropriate weights to the counts that the hashing vectorizer gave us. Our final result is a large, sparse matrix representing the occurrences of 1- and 2-grams in the texts, weighted by importance. Finally, we examined the frontend of a sparse matrix representation of our featured data in Scipy.

Hyperparameter tuning with scikit-optimize

In machine learning, a **hyperparameter** is a parameter whose value is set before the training process begins. For example, the choice of learning rate of a gradient boosting model and the size of the hidden layer of a multilayer perceptron, are both examples of hyperparameters. By contrast, the values of other parameters are derived via training. Hyperparameter selection is important because it can have a huge effect on the model's performance.

The most basic approach to hyperparameter tuning is called a **grid search**. In this method, you specify a range of potential values for each hyperparameter, and then try them all out, until you find the best combination. This brute-force approach is comprehensive but computationally intensive. More sophisticated methods exist. In this recipe, you will learn how to use *Bayesian optimization* over hyperparameters using `scikit-optimize`. In contrast to a basic grid search, in Bayesian optimization, not all parameter values are tried out, but rather a fixed number of parameter settings is sampled from specified distributions. More details can be found at `https://scikit-optimize.github.io/notebooks/bayesian-optimization.html`.

Getting ready

The preparation for this recipe consists of installing a specific version of `scikit-learn`, installing `xgboost`, and installing `scikit-optimize` in `pip`. The command for this is as follows:

```
pip install scikit-learn==0.20.3 xgboost scikit-optimize pandas
```

How to do it...

In the following steps, you will load the standard `wine` dataset and use Bayesian optimization to tune the hyperparameters of an XGBoost model:

1. Load the `wine` dataset from scikit-learn:

```
from sklearn import datasets

wine_dataset = datasets.load_wine()
X = wine_dataset.data
y = wine_dataset.target
```

2. Import XGBoost and stratified K-fold:

```
import xgboost as xgb
from sklearn.model_selection import StratifiedKFold
```

3. Import `BayesSearchCV` from `scikit-optimize` and specify the number of parameter settings to test:

```
from skopt import BayesSearchCV

n_iterations = 50
```

4. Specify your estimator. In this case, we select XGBoost and set it to be able to perform multi-class classification:

```
estimator = xgb.XGBClassifier(
    n_jobs=-1,
    objective="multi:softmax",
    eval_metric="merror",
    verbosity=0,
    num_class=len(set(y)),
)
```

5. Specify a parameter search space:

```
search_space = {
    "learning_rate": (0.01, 1.0, "log-uniform"),
    "min_child_weight": (0, 10),
    "max_depth": (1, 50),
    "max_delta_step": (0, 10),
    "subsample": (0.01, 1.0, "uniform"),
    "colsample_bytree": (0.01, 1.0, "log-uniform"),
    "colsample_bylevel": (0.01, 1.0, "log-uniform"),
    "reg_lambda": (1e-9, 1000, "log-uniform"),
    "reg_alpha": (1e-9, 1.0, "log-uniform"),
    "gamma": (1e-9, 0.5, "log-uniform"),
    "min_child_weight": (0, 5),
    "n_estimators": (5, 5000),
    "scale_pos_weight": (1e-6, 500, "log-uniform"),
}
```

6. Specify the type of cross-validation to perform:

```
cv = StratifiedKFold(n_splits=3, shuffle=True)
```

7. Define `BayesSearchCV` using the settings you have defined:

```
bayes_cv_tuner = BayesSearchCV(
    estimator=estimator,
    search_spaces=search_space,
    scoring="accuracy",
    cv=cv,
    n_jobs=-1,
    n_iter=n_iterations,
    verbose=0,
    refit=True,
)
```

8. Define a `callback` function to print out the progress of the parameter search:

```
import pandas as pd
import numpy as np

def print_status(optimal_result):
    """Shows the best parameters found and accuracy attained of the
search so far."""
    models_tested = pd.DataFrame(bayes_cv_tuner.cv_results_)
    best_parameters_so_far = pd.Series(bayes_cv_tuner.best_params_)
    print(
        "Model #{}\nBest accuracy so far: {}\nBest parameters so
```

```
far: {}\n".format(
        len(models_tested),
        np.round(bayes_cv_tuner.best_score_, 3),
        bayes_cv_tuner.best_params_,
    )
)

clf_type = bayes_cv_tuner.estimator.__class__.__name__
models_tested.to_csv(clf_type + "_cv_results_summary.csv")
```

9. Perform the parameter search:

```
result = bayes_cv_tuner.fit(X, y, callback=print_status)
```

As you can see, the following shows the output:

```
Model #1
 Best accuracy so far: 0.972
 Best parameters so far: {'colsample_bylevel':
0.019767840658391753, 'colsample_bytree': 0.5812505808116454,
'gamma': 1.7784704701058755e-05, 'learning_rate':
0.9050859661329937, 'max_delta_step': 3, 'max_depth': 42,
'min_child_weight': 1, 'n_estimators': 2334, 'reg_alpha':
0.02886003776717955, 'reg_lambda': 0.0008507166793122457,
'scale_pos_weight': 4.801764874750116e-05, 'subsample':
0.7188797743009225}

 Model #2
 Best accuracy so far: 0.972
 Best parameters so far: {'colsample_bylevel':
0.019767840658391753, 'colsample_bytree': 0.5812505808116454,
'gamma': 1.7784704701058755e-05, 'learning_rate':
0.9050859661329937, 'max_delta_step': 3, 'max_depth': 42,
'min_child_weight': 1, 'n_estimators': 2334, 'reg_alpha':
0.02886003776717955, 'reg_lambda': 0.0008507166793122457,
'scale_pos_weight': 4.801764874750116e-05, 'subsample':
0.7188797743009225}

<snip>

Model #50
 Best accuracy so far: 0.989
 Best parameters so far: {'colsample_bylevel':
0.013417868502558758, 'colsample_bytree': 0.463490250419848,
'gamma': 2.2823050161337873e-06, 'learning_rate':
0.34006478878384533, 'max_delta_step': 9, 'max_depth': 41,
'min_child_weight': 0, 'n_estimators': 1951, 'reg_alpha':
```

```
1.8321791726476395e-08, 'reg_lambda': 13.098734837402576,
'scale_pos_weight': 0.6188077759379964, 'subsample':
0.7970035272497132}
```

How it works...

In steps 1 and 2, we import a standard dataset, the `wine` dataset, as well as the libraries needed for classification. A more interesting step follows, in which we specify how long we would like the hyperparameter search to be, in terms of a number of combinations of parameters to try. The longer the search, the better the results, at the risk of overfitting and extending the computational time. In step 4, we select XGBoost as the model, and then specify the number of classes, the type of problem, and the evaluation metric. This part will depend on the type of problem. For instance, for a regression problem, we might set `eval_metric = 'rmse'` and drop `num_class` together.

Other models than XGBoost can be selected with the hyperparameter optimizer as well. In the next step, (step 5), we specify a probability distribution over each parameter that we will be exploring. This is one of the advantages of using `BayesSearchCV` over a simple grid search, as it allows you to explore the parameter space more intelligently. Next, we specify our cross-validation scheme (step 6). Since we are performing a classification problem, it makes sense to specify a stratified fold. However, for a regression problem, `StratifiedKFold` should be replaced with `KFold`.

Also note that a larger splitting number is preferred for the purpose of measuring results, though it will come at a computational price. In step 7, you can see additional settings that can be changed. In particular, `n_jobs` allows you to parallelize the task. The verbosity and the method used for scoring can be altered as well. To monitor the search process and the performance of our hyperparameter tuning, we define a callback function to print out the progress in step 8. The results of the grid search are also saved in a CSV file. Finally, we run the hyperparameter search (step 9). The output allows us to observe the parameters and the performance of each iteration of the hyperparameter search.

In this book, we will refrain from tuning the hyperparameters of classifiers. The reason is in part brevity, and in part because hyperparameter tuning here would be *premature optimization*, as there is no specified requirement or goal for the performance of the algorithm from the end user. Having seen how to perform it here, you can easily adapt this recipe to the application at hand.

Another prominent library for hyperparameter tuning to keep in mind is `hyperopt`.

2
Machine Learning-Based Malware Detection

In this chapter, we begin to get serious about applying data science to cybersecurity. We will begin by learning how to perform static and dynamic analysis on samples. Building on this knowledge, we will learn how to featurize samples in order to construct a dataset with informative features. The highlight of the chapter is learning how to build a static malware detector using the featurization skills we have learned. Finally, you will learn how to tackle important machine learning challenges that occur in the domain of cybersecurity, such as class imbalance and **false positive rate** (**FPR**) constraints.

The chapter covers the following recipes:

- Malware static analysis
- Malware dynamic analysis
- Using machine learning to detect the file type
- Measuring the similarity between two strings
- Measuring the similarity between two files
- Extracting N-grams
- Selecting the best N-grams
- Building a static malware detector
- Tackling class imbalance
- Handling type I and type II errors

Technical requirements

In this chapter, we will be using the following:

- YARA
- `pefile`
- `PyGitHub`
- Cuckoo Sandbox
- **Natural Language Toolkit (NLTK)**
- `imbalanced-learn`

The code and datasets can be found at `https://github.com/PacktPublishing/Machine-Learning-for-Cybersecurity-Cookbook/tree/master/Chapter02`.

Malware static analysis

In static analysis, we examine a sample without executing it. The amount of information that can be obtained this way is large, ranging from something as simple as the name of the file to the more complex, such as specialized YARA signatures. We will be covering a selection of the large variety of features you could obtain by statically analyzing a sample. Despite its power and convenience, static analysis is no silver bullet, mainly because software can be obfuscated. For this reason, we will be employing dynamic analysis and other techniques in later chapters.

Computing the hash of a sample

Without delving into the intricacies of hashing, a hash is essentially a short and unique string signature. For example, we may hash the sequence of bytes of a file to obtain an essentially unique code for that file. This allows us to quickly compare two files to see whether they are identical.

There exist many hash procedures out there, so we will focus on the most important ones, namely, SHA256 and MD5. Note that MD5 is known to exhibit vulnerabilities due to hash collisions—instances where two different objects have the same hash and, therefore, should be used with caution. In this recipe, we take an executable file and compute its MD5 and SHA256 hashes.

Getting ready

Preparation for this recipe consists of downloading a test file, which is the Python executable from `https://www.python.org/ftp/python/3.7.2/python-3.7.2-amd64.exe`.

How to do it...

In the following steps, we will see how to obtain the hash of a file:

1. Begin by importing the libraries and selecting the desired file you wish to hash:

```python
import sys
import hashlib

filename = "python-3.7.2-amd64.exe"
```

2. Instantiate the MD5 and SHA256 objects, and specify the size of the chunks we will be reading:

```python
BUF_SIZE = 65536
md5 = hashlib.md5()
sha256 = hashlib.sha256()
```

3. We then read in the file in chunks of 64 KB and incrementally construct our hashes:

```python
with open(filename, "rb") as f:
    while True:
        data = f.read(BUF_SIZE)
        if not data:
            break
        md5.update(data)
        sha256.update(data)
```

4. Finally, print out the resulting hashes:

```python
print("MD5: {0}".format(md5.hexdigest()))
print("SHA256: {0}".format(sha256.hexdigest()))
```

This results in the following output:

```
MD5: ff258093f0b3953c886192dec9f52763
SHA256:
0fe2a696f5a3e481fed795ef6896ed99157bcef273ef3c4a96f2905cbdb3aa13
```

How it works...

This section will explain the steps that have been provided in the previous section:

- In step 1, we import `hashlib`, a standard Python library for hash computation. We also specify the file we will be hashing—in this case, the file is `python-3.7.2-amd64.exe`.
- In step 2, we instantiate an `md5` object and an `sha256` object and specify the size of the chunks we will be reading.
- In step 3, we utilize the `.update(data)` method. This method allows us to compute the hash incrementally because it computes the hash of the concatenation. In other words, `hash.update(a)` followed by `hash.update(b)` is equivalent to `hash.update(a+b)`.
- In step 4, we print out the hashes in hexadecimal digits.

We can also verify that our computation is consistent with the hash calculations given by other sources, such as VirusTotal and the official Python website. The MD5 hash is displayed on the Python web page (`https://www.python.org/downloads/release/python-372/`):

| Windows x86-64 executable install | Windows | for AMD64/EM64T/x64 | ff258093f0b3953c886192dec9f52763 | 26140976 | SIG |

The SHA256 hash is computed by uploading the file to VirusTotal (`https://www.virustotal.com/gui/home`):

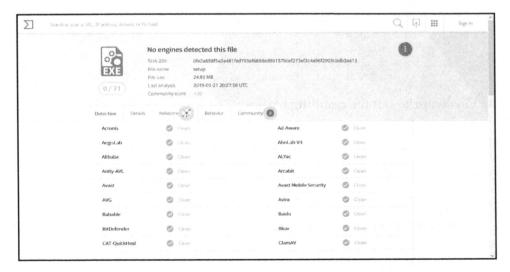

YARA

YARA is a computer language that allows a security expert to conveniently specify a rule that will then be used to classify all samples matching the rule. A minimal rule consists of a name and a condition, for example, the following:

```
rule my_rule_name { condition: false }
```

This rule will not match any file. Conversely, the following rule will match every sample:

```
Rule my_rule_name { condition: true }
```

A more useful example will match any file over 100 KB:

```
Rule over_100kb { condition: filesize > 100KB }
```

Another example is checking whether a particular file is a PDF. To do so, we check if the magic numbers of the file correspond to the PDF. Magic numbers are a sequence of several bytes that occurs at the beginning of a file and indicates the type of file it is. In the case of a PDF, the sequence is 25 50 44 46:

```
rule is_a_pdf {
strings:
  $pdf_magic = {25 50 44 46}
condition:
  $pdf_magic at 0
}
```

Now, let's see how to run our rules against files.

Getting ready

Preparation for this recipe consists of installing YARA on your device. Instructions can be found at https://yara.readthedocs.io/en/stable/. For Windows, you need to download an executable file for YARA.

How to do it...

In the following steps, we show you how to create YARA rules and test them against a file:

1. Copy your rules, as seen here, into a text file and name it `rules.yara`:

```
rule is_a_pdf
{
        strings:
                $pdf_magic = {25 50 44 46}
        condition:
                $pdf_magic at 0
}
rule dummy_rule1
{
        condition:
                false
}
rule dummy_rule2
{
        condition:
                true
}
```

2. Next, select a file you would like to check your rules against. Call it `target_file`. In a terminal, execute `Yara rules.yara target_file` as follows:

```
Yara rule.yara PythonBrochure
```

The result should be as follows:

```
is_a_pdf target_file
dummy_rule2 target_rule
```

How it works...

As you can observe, in *Step 1*, we copied several YARA rules. The first rule checks the magic numbers of a file to see if they match those of a PDF. The other two rules are trivial rules—one that matches every file, and one that matches no file. Then, in *Step 2*, we used the YARA program to run the rules against the target file. We saw from a printout that the file matched some rules but not others, as expected from an effective YARA ruleset.

Examining the PE header

Portable executable (PE) files are a common Windows file type. PE files include the .exe, .dll, and .sys files. All PE files are distinguished by having a PE header, which is a header section of the code that instructs Windows on how to parse the subsequent code. The fields from the PE header are often used as features in the detection of malware. To easily extract the multitude of values of the PE header, we will utilize the pefile Python module. In this recipe, we will parse the PE header of a file, and then print out notable portions of it.

Getting ready

Preparation for this recipe consists of installing the pefile package in pip. In a terminal of your Python environment, run the following:

```
pip install pefile
```

In addition, download the test file Python executable from https://www.python.org/ftp/python/3.7.2/python-3.7.2-amd64.exe.

How to do it...

In the following steps, we will parse the PE header of a file, and then print out notable portions of it:

1. Import the PE file and use it to parse the PE header of your desired file:

   ```
   import pefile

   desired_file = "python-3.7.2-amd64.exe"
   pe = pefile.PE(desired_file)
   ```

2. List the imports of the PE file:

   ```
   for entry in pe.DIRECTORY_ENTRY_IMPORT:
       print(entry.dll)
       for imp in entry.imports:
           print("\t", hex(imp.address), imp.name)
   ```

A small portion of the output is shown here:

```
b'ADVAPI32.dll'
          0x44b000 b'RegCloseKey'
          0x44b004 b'RegOpenKeyExW'
          0x44b008 b'OpenProcessToken'
          0x44b00c b'AdjustTokenPrivileges'
          0x44b010 b'LookupPrivilegeValueW'
          0x44b014 b'InitiateSystemShutdownExW'
          0x44b018 b'GetUserNameW'
          0x44b01c b'RegQueryValueExW'
          0x44b020 b'RegDeleteValueW'
          0x44b024 b'CloseEventLog'
          0x44b028 b'OpenEventLogW'
          0x44b02c b'ReportEventW'
          0x44b030 b'ConvertStringSecurityDescriptorToSecurityDescriptorW'
          0x44b034 b'DecryptFileW'
          0x44b038 b'CreateWellKnownSid'
          0x44b03c b'InitializeAcl'
          0x44b040 b'SetEntriesInAclW'
          0x44b044 b'ChangeServiceConfigW'
          0x44b048 b'CloseServiceHandle'
          0x44b04c b'ControlService'
          0x44b050 b'OpenSCManagerW'
          0x44b054 b'OpenServiceW'
          0x44b058 b'QueryServiceStatus'
          0x44b05c b'SetNamedSecurityInfoW'
          0x44b060 b'CheckTokenMembership'
```

3. List the sections of the PE file:

```
for section in pe.sections:
    print(
        section.Name,
        hex(section.VirtualAddress),
        hex(section.Misc_VirtualSize),
        section.SizeOfRawData,
    )
```

The output of the previous code is as follows:

```
b'.text\x00\x00\x00' 0x1000 0x49937 301568
b'.rdata\x00\x00' 0x4b000 0x1ed60 126464
b'.data\x00\x00\x00' 0x6a000 0x1730 2560
b'.wixburn' 0x6c000 0x38 512
b'.rsrc\x00\x00\x00' 0x6d000 0x165f4 91648
b'.reloc\x00\x00' 0x84000 0x3dfc 15872
```

4. Print a full dump of the parsed information:

```
print(pe.dump_info())
```

A small portion of the output is displayed here:

```
In [6]:  print(pe.dump_info())

         ----------DOS_HEADER----------

         [IMAGE_DOS_HEADER]
         0x0        0x0      e_magic:                0x5A4D
         0x2        0x2      e_cblp:                 0x90
         0x4        0x4      e_cp:                   0x3
         0x6        0x6      e_crlc:                 0x0
         0x8        0x8      e_cparhdr:              0x4
         0xA        0xA      e_minalloc:             0x0
         0xC        0xC      e_maxalloc:             0xFFFF
         0xE        0xE      e_ss:                   0x0
         0x10       0x10     e_sp:                   0xB8
         0x12       0x12     e_csum:                 0x0
         0x14       0x14     e_ip:                   0x0
         0x16       0x16     e_cs:                   0x0
         0x18       0x18     e_lfarlc:               0x40
         0x1A       0x1A     e_ovno:                 0x0
         0x1C       0x1C     e_res:
         0x24       0x24     e_oemid:                0x0
         0x26       0x26     e_oeminfo:              0x0
         0x28       0x28     e_res2:
         0x3C       0x3C     e_lfanew:               0x110


         ----------NT_HEADERS----------

         [IMAGE_NT_HEADERS]
         0x110      0x0      Signature:              0x4550

         ----------FILE_HEADER----------

         [IMAGE_FILE_HEADER]
         0x114      0x0      Machine:                0x14C
         0x116      0x2      NumberOfSections:       0x6
         0x118      0x4      TimeDateStamp:          0x5A10AD86 [Sat Nov 18 22:00:38 2017 UTC]
         0x11C      0x8      PointerToSymbolTable:   0x0
         0x120      0xC      NumberOfSymbols:        0x0
```

How it works...

We began in *step 1* by importing the `pefile` library and specifying which file we will be
analyzing. In this case, the file was `python-3.7.2-amd64.exe`, though it is just as easy to
analyze any other PE file. We then continued on to examine the DLLs being imported by
the file, in order to understand which methods the file may be using in *Step 2*. DLLs answer
this question because a DLL is a library of code that other applications may call upon. For
example, `USER32.dll` is a library that contains Windows USER, a component of the
Microsoft Windows operating system that provides core functionality for building user
interfaces. The component allows other applications to leverage the functionality for
window management, message passing, input processing, and standard controls. Logically
then, if we see that a file is importing a method such as `GetCursorPos`, then it is likely to
be looking to determine the position of the cursor. Continuing in *step 3*, we printed out the
sections of the PE file. These provide a logical and physical separation to the different parts
of a program, and therefore offer the analyst valuable information about the program.
Finally, we printed out all of the parsed PE header information from the file in preparation
for later utilizing it for feature engineering (*Step 4*).

Featurizing the PE header

In this section, we will extract features from the PE header to be used in building a `malware/benign` samples classifier. We will continue utilizing the `pefile` Python module.

Getting ready

Preparation for this recipe consists of installing the `pefile` package in `pip`. The command is as follows:

```
pip install pefile
```

In addition, benign and malicious files have been provided for you in the `PE Samples Dataset` folder in the root of the repository. Extract all archives named `Benign PE Samples*.7z` to a folder named `Benign PE Samples`. Extract all archives named `Malicious PE Samples*.7z` to a folder named `Malicious PE Samples`.

How to do it...

In the following steps, we will collect notable portions of the PE header:

1. Import `pefile` and modules for enumerating our samples:

```
import pefile
from os import listdir
from os.path import isfile, join

directories = ["Benign PE Samples", "Malicious PE Samples"]
```

2. We define a function to collect the names of the sections of a file and preprocess them for readability and normalization:

```
def get_section_names(pe):
    """Gets a list of section names from a PE file."""
    list_of_section_names = []
    for sec in pe.sections:
        normalized_name = sec.Name.decode().replace("\x00",
"").lower()
        list_of_section_names.append(normalized_name)
    return list_of_section_names
```

3. We define a convenience function to preprocess and standardize our imports:

```
def preprocess_imports(list_of_DLLs):
    """Normalize the naming of the imports of a PE file."""
    return [x.decode().split(".")[0].lower() for x in list_of_DLLs]
```

4. We then define a function to collect the imports from a file using `pefile`:

```
def get_imports(pe):
    """Get a list of the imports of a PE file."""
    list_of_imports = []
    for entry in pe.DIRECTORY_ENTRY_IMPORT:
        list_of_imports.append(entry.dll)
    return preprocess_imports(list_of_imports)
```

5. Finally, we prepare to iterate through all of our files and create lists to store our features:

```
imports_corpus = []
num_sections = []
section_names = []
for dataset_path in directories:
    samples = [f for f in listdir(dataset_path) if
isfile(join(dataset_path, f))]
    for file in samples:
        file_path = dataset_path + "/" + file
        try:
```

6. In addition to collecting the preceding features, we also collect the number of sections of a file:

```
pe = pefile.PE(file_path)
imports = get_imports(pe)
n_sections = len(pe.sections)
sec_names = get_section_names(pe)
imports_corpus.append(imports)
num_sections.append(n_sections)
section_names.append(sec_names)
```

7. In case a file's PE header cannot be parsed, we define a try-catch clause:

```
except Exception as e:
    print(e)
    print("Unable to obtain imports from " + file_path)
```

How it works...

As you can see, in *Step 1*, we imported the `pefile` module to enumerate the samples. Once that is done, we define the convenience function, as you can see in *Step 2*. The reason being that it often imports using varying cases (upper/lower). This causes the same import to appear as distinct imports.

After preprocessing the imports, we then define another function to collect all the imports of a file into a list. We will also define a function to collect the names of the sections of a file in order to standardize these names such as `.text`, `.rsrc`, and `.reloc` while containing distinct parts of the file (*Step 3*). The files are then enumerated in our folders and empty lists will be created to hold the features we will be extracting. The predefined functions will then collect the imports (*Step 4*), section names, and the number of sections of each file (*Steps 5* and *6*). Lastly, a try-catch clause will be defined in case a file's PE header cannot be parsed (*Step 7*). This can happen for many reasons. One reason being that the file is not actually a PE file. Another reason is that its PE header is intentionally or unintentionally malformed.

Malware dynamic analysis

Unlike static analysis, dynamic analysis is a malware analysis technique in which the expert executes the sample, and then studies the sample's behavior as it is being run. The main advantage of dynamic analysis over static is that it allows you to bypass obfuscation by simply observing how a sample behaves, rather than trying to decipher the sample's contents and behavior. Since malware is intrinsically unsafe, researchers resort to executing samples in a **virtual machine (VM)**. This is called **sandboxing**.

Getting ready

One of the most prominent tools for automating the analysis of samples in a VM is Cuckoo Sandbox. The initial installation of Cuckoo Sandbox is straightforward; simply run the following command:

```
pip install -U cuckoo
```

You must make sure that you also have a VM that your machine can control. Configuring the sandbox can be a challenge, but instructions are available at `https://cuckoo.sh/docs/`.

We show now how to utilize Cuckoo Sandbox to obtain a dynamic analysis of a sample.

How to do it...

Once your Cuckoo Sandbox is set up, and has a web interface running, follow these steps to gather runtime information about a sample:

1. Open up your web interface (the default location is `127.0.0.1:8000`), click **SUBMIT A FILE FOR ANALYSIS**, and select the sample you wish to analyze:

2. The following screen will appear automatically. In it, select the type of analysis you wish to perform on your sample:

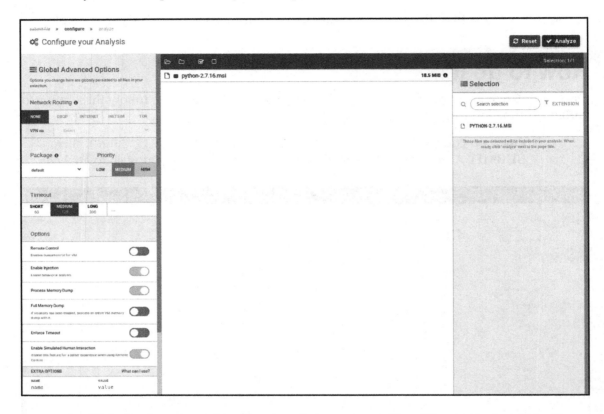

3. Click **Analyze** to analyze the sample in your sandbox. The result should look as follows:

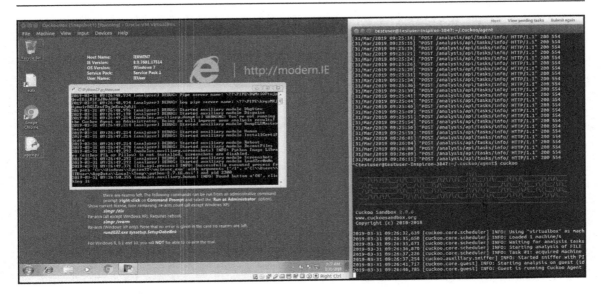

4. Next, open up the report for the sample you have analyzed:

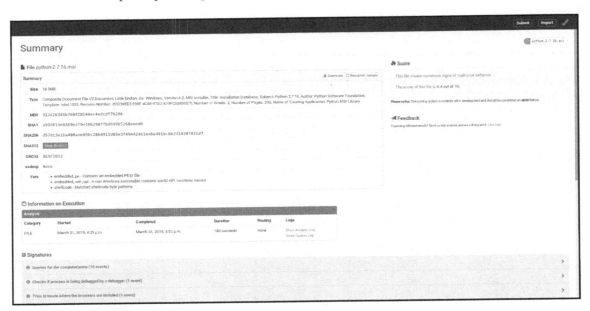

5. Select the **Behavioral Analysis** tab:

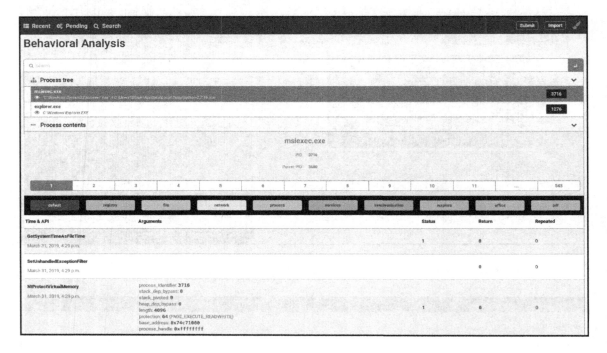

The displayed sequence of API calls, registry key changes, and other events can all be used as input to a classifier.

How it works...

At a conceptual level, obtaining dynamic analysis results consists of running samples in environments that allow the analyst to collect runtime information. Cuckoo Sandbox is a flexible framework with prebuilt modules to do just that. We began our recipe for using Cuckoo Sandbox by opening up the web portal (*Step 1*). A **command-line interface** (**CLI**) exists as well. We proceeded to submit a sample and select the type of analysis we wished to perform (*Steps 2* and *3*). These steps, too, can be performed through the Cuckoo CLI. We proceeded to examine the analysis report (*Step 4*). You can see at this stage how the many modules of Cuckoo Sandbox reflect in the final analysis output. For instance, if a module for capturing traffic is installed and used, then the report will contain the data captured in the network tab. We proceeded to focus our view of the analysis to behavioral analysis (*Step 5*), and in particular to observe the sequence of API calls. API calls are basically operations performed by the OS. This sequence makes up a fantastic feature set that we will utilize to detect malware in future recipes. Finally, note that in a production environment, it may make sense to create a custom-made sandbox with custom modules for data collection, as well as equip it with anti-VM detection software to facilitate successful analysis.

Using machine learning to detect the file type

One of the techniques hackers use to sneak their malicious files into security systems is to obfuscate their file types. For example, a (malicious) PowerShell script is expected to have an extension, .ps1. A system administrator can aim to combat the execution of all PowerShell scripts on a system by preventing the execution of all files with the .ps1 extension. However, the mischievous hacker can remove or change the extension, rendering the file's identity a mystery. Only by examining the contents of the file can it then be distinguished from an ordinary text file. For practical reasons, it is not possible for humans to examine all text files on a system. Consequently, it is expedient to resort to automated methods. In this chapter, we will demonstrate how you can use machine learning to detect the file type of an unknown file. Our first step is to curate a dataset.

Scraping GitHub for files of a specific type

To curate a dataset, we will scrape GitHub for the specific file types we are interested in.

Getting ready

Preparation for this recipe consists of installing the PyGitHub package in pip by running the following command:

```
pip install PyGitHub
```

In addition, you will need GitHub account credentials.

How to do it...

In the following steps, we curate a dataset and then use it to create a classifier to determine the file type. For demonstration purposes, we show how to obtain a collection of PowerShell scripts, Python scripts, and JavaScript files by scraping GitHub. A collection of samples obtained in this way can be found in the accompanying repository as PowerShellSamples.7z, PythonSamples.7z, and JavascriptSamples.7z. First, we will write the code for the JavaScript scraper:

1. Begin by importing the PyGitHub library in order to be able to call the GitHub API. We also import the base64 module for decoding the base64 encoded files:

```
import os
from github import Github
import base64
```

2. We must supply our credentials, and then specify a query—in this case, for JavaScript—to select our repositories:

```
username = "your_github_username"
password = "your_password"
target_dir = "/path/to/JavascriptSamples/"
g = Github(username, password)
repositories = g.search_repositories(query='language:javascript')
n = 5
i = 0
```

3. We loop over the repositories matching our criteria:

```
for repo in repositories:
    repo_name = repo.name
    target_dir_of_repo = target_dir+"\\"+repo_name
    print(repo_name)
    try:
```

4. We create a directory for each repository matching our search criteria, and then read in its contents:

```
os.mkdir(target_dir_of_repo)
i += 1
contents = repo.get_contents("")
```

5. We add all directories of the repository to a queue in order to list all of the files contained within the directories:

```
while len(contents) > 1:
    file_content = contents.pop(0)
    if file_content.type == "dir":
        contents.extend(repo.get_contents(file_content.path))
    else:
```

6. If we find a non-directory file, we check whether its extension is `.js`:

```
st = str(file_content)
filename = st.split("\"")[1].split("\"")[0]
extension = filename.split(".")[-1]
if extension == "js":
```

7. If the extension is `.js`, we write out a copy of the file:

```
file_contents = repo.get_contents(file_content.path)
file_data = base64.b64decode(file_contents.content)
filename = filename.split("/")[-1]
file_out = open(target_dir_of_repo+"/"+filename, "wb")
file_out.write(file_data)
except:
    pass
if i==n:
    break
```

8. Once finished, it is convenient to move all the JavaScript files into one folder.

   To obtain PowerShell samples, run the same code, changing the following:

```
target_dir = "/path/to/JavascriptSamples/"
repositories = g.search_repositories(query='language:javascript')
```

To the following:

```
target_dir = "/path/to/PowerShellSamples/"
repositories = g.search_repositories(query='language:powershell').
```

Similarly, for Python files, we do the following:

```
target_dir = "/path/to/PythonSamples/"
repositories = g.search_repositories(query='language:python').
```

How it works...

We start by importing the `PyGitHub` library in *Step 1* in order to be able to conveniently call the GitHub APIs. These will allow us to scrape and explore the universe of repositories. We also import the `base64` module for decoding the `base64` encoded files that we will be downloading from GitHub. Note that there is a rate limit on the number of API calls a generic user can make to GitHub. For this reason, you will find that if you attempt to download too many files in a short duration, your script will not get all of the files. Our next step is to supply our credentials to GitHub (*step 2*), and specify that we are looking for repositories with JavaScript, using the `query='language:javascript'` command. We enumerate such repositories matching our criteria of being associated with JavaScript, and if they do, we search through these for files ending with `.js` and create local copies (steps 3 to 6). Since these files are encoded in `base64`, we make sure to decode them to plaintext in step 7. Finally, we show you how to adjust the script in order to scrape other file types, such as Python and PowerShell (Step 8).

Classifying files by type

Now that we have a dataset, we would like to train a classifier. Since the files in question are scripts, we approach the problem as an NLP problem.

Getting ready

Preparation for this recipe consists of installing the `scikit-learn` package in `pip`. The instructions are as follows:

```
pip install sklearn
```

In addition, we have supplied you with samples of each file type in the `Javascript Samples.7z`, `PythonSamples.7z`, and `PowerShellSamples.7z` archives, in case you would like to supplement your own dataset. Extract these into separate folders for the following recipe.

How to do it...

The code for the following can be found on `https://github.com/PacktPublishing/Machine-Learning-for-Cybersecurity-Cookbook/blob/master/Chapter02/Classifying%20Files%20by%20Type/File%20Type%20Classifier.ipynb`. We build a classifier using this data to predict files as JavaScript, Python, or PowerShell:

1. Begin by importing the necessary libraries and specifying the paths of the samples we will be using to train and test:

```
import os
from sklearn.feature_extraction.text import HashingVectorizer,
TfidfTransformer
from sklearn.ensemble import RandomForestClassifier
from sklearn.model_selection import train_test_split
from sklearn.metrics import accuracy_score, confusion_matrix
from sklearn.pipeline import Pipeline
javascript_path = "/path/to/JavascriptSamples/"
python_path = "/path/to/PythonSamples/"
powershell_path = "/path/to/PowerShellSamples/"
```

2. Next, we read in all of the file types. We also create an array of labels with -1, 0, and 1 representing the JavaScript, Python, and PowerShell scripts, respectively:

```
corpus = []
labels = []
file_types_and_labels = [(javascript_path, -1), (python_path, 0),
(powershell_path, 1)]
for files_path, label in file_types_and_labels:
    files = os.listdir(files_path)
    for file in files:
        file_path = files_path + "/" + file
        try:
            with open(file_path, "r") as myfile:
                data = myfile.read().replace("\n", "")
        except:
            pass
        data = str(data)
        corpus.append(data)
        labels.append(label)
```

3. We go on to create a train-test split and a pipeline that will perform basic NLP on the files, followed by a random forest classifier:

```
X_train, X_test, y_train, y_test = train_test_split(
    corpus, labels, test_size=0.33, random_state=11
)
text_clf = Pipeline(
    [
        ("vect", HashingVectorizer(input="content", ngram_range=(1,
3))),
        ("tfidf", TfidfTransformer(use_idf=True,)),
        ("rf", RandomForestClassifier(class_weight="balanced")),
    ]
)
```

4. We fit the pipeline to the training data, and then use it to predict on the testing data. Finally, we print out the accuracy and the confusion matrix:

```
text_clf.fit(X_train, y_train)
y_test_pred = text_clf.predict(X_test)
print(accuracy_score(y_test, y_test_pred))
print(confusion_matrix(y_test, y_test_pred))
```

This results in the following output:

```
0.9840273816314888
[[1222    0    0]
 [  28  502    0]
 [   0    0    1]]
```

How it works...

Leveraging the dataset we built up in the *Scraping GitHub for files of a specific type* recipe, we place files in different directories, based on their file type, and then specify the paths in preparation for building our classifier (step 1). The code for this recipe assumes that the "JavascriptSamples" directory and others contain the samples, and have no subdirectories. We read in all files into a corpus, and record their labels (step 2). We train-test split the data and prepare a pipeline that will perform basic NLP on the files, followed by a random forest classifier (step 3). The choice of classifier here is meant for illustrative purposes, rather than to imply a best choice of classifier for this type of data. Finally, we perform the basic, but important, steps in the process of creating a machine learning classifier, consisting of fitting the pipeline to the training data and then assessing its performance on the testing set by measuring its accuracy and confusion matrix (step 4).

Measuring the similarity between two strings

To check whether two files are identical, we utilize standard cryptographic hash functions, such as SHA256 and MD5. However, at times, we would like to also know to what extent two files are similar. For that purpose, we utilize similarity hashing algorithms. The one we will be demonstrating here is ssdeep.

First, let's see how to use ssdeep to compare two strings. This can be useful to detect tampering in a text or script and also plagiarism.

Getting ready

Preparation for this recipe consists of installing the ssdeep package in pip. The installation is a little tricky and does not always work on Windows. Instructions can be found at https://python-ssdeep.readthedocs.io/en/latest/installation.html.

If you only have a Windows machine and installing ssdeep does not work, then one possible solution is to run ssdeep on an Ubuntu VM, and then install it in pip, using the following command:

```
pip install ssdeep
```

How to do it...

1. Begin by importing the ssdeep library and creating three strings:

```
import ssdeep

str1 = "Lorem ipsum dolor sit amet, consectetur adipiscing elit,
sed do eiusmod tempor incididunt ut labore et dolore magna aliqua."
str2 = "Lorem ipsum dolor sit amet, consectetur adipiscing elit,
sed do eiusmod tempor incididunt ut labore et dolore Magna aliqua."
str3 = "Lorem ipsum dolor sit amet, consectetur adipiscing elit,
sed do eiusmod tempor incididunt ut labore et dolore aliqua."
str4 = "Something completely different from the other strings."
```

2. Hash the strings:

```
hash1 = ssdeep.hash(str1)
hash2 = ssdeep.hash(str2)
hash3 = ssdeep.hash(str3)
hash4 = ssdeep.hash(str4)
```

As a reference,

hash1 is
`u'3:f4oo8MRwRJFGW1gC6uWv6MQ2MFSl+JuBF8BSnJi:f4kPvtHMCMuby`
`FtQ'`,

hash2 is
`u'3:f4oo8MRwRJFGW1gC6uWv6MQ2MFSl+JuBF8BS+EFECJi:f4kPvtHMC`
`MubyFIsJQ'`,

hash3 is
`u'3:f4oo8MRwRJFGW1gC6uWv6MQ2MFSl+JuBF8BS6:f4kPvtHMCMubyF0`
`'`, and

hash4 is `u'3:60QKZ+4CDTfDaRFKYLVL:ywKDC2mVL'`.

3. Next, we see what kind of similarity scores the strings have:

```
ssdeep.compare(hash1, hash1)
ssdeep.compare(hash1, hash2)
ssdeep.compare(hash1, hash3)
ssdeep.compare(hash1, hash4)
```

The numerical results are as follows:

```
100
39
37
0
```

How it works...

The basic idea behind `ssdeep` is to combine a number of traditional hashes whose boundaries are determined by the context of the input. This collection of hashes can then be used to identify modified versions of known files even when they have been modified by insertion, modification, or deletion.

For our recipe, we began by creating a set of four test strings meant as a toy example to illustrate how changes in a string will affect its similarity measures (step 1). The first, str1, is simply the first sentence of Lorem Ipsum. The second string, str2, differs in the capitalization of m in magna. The third string, str3, is missing the word magna altogether. Finally, the fourth string is an entirely different string. Our next step, step 2, is to hash the strings using the similarity hashing ssdeep library. Observe that similar strings have visibly similar similarity hashes. This should be contrasted with traditional hashes, in which even a small alteration produces a completely different hash. Next, we derive the similarity score between the various strings using ssdeep (step 3). In particular, observe that the ssdeep similarity score between two strings is an integer ranging between 0 and 100, with 100 being identical and 0 being dissimilar. Two identical strings will have a similarity score of 100. Changing the case of one letter in our string lowered the similarity score significantly to 39 because the strings are relatively short. Removing a word lowered it to 37. And two completely different strings had a similarity of 0.

Although other, in some cases better, fuzzy hashes are available, ssdeep is still a primary choice because of its speed and being a de facto standard.

Measuring the similarity between two files

Now, we are going to see how to apply ssdeep to measure the similarity between two binary files. The applications of this concept are many, but one in particular is using the similarity measure as a distance in clustering.

Getting ready

Preparation for this recipe consists of installing the ssdeep package in pip. The installation is a little tricky and does not always work on Windows. Instructions can be found at https://python-ssdeep.readthedocs.io/en/latest/installation.html.

If you only have a Windows machine and it does not work, then one possible solution is to run ssdeep on an Ubuntu VM by installing pip with this command:

```
pip install ssdeep
```

In addition, download a test file such as the Python executable from https://www.python. org/ftp/python/3.7.2/python-3.7.2-amd64.exe.

How to do it...

In the following recipe, we tamper with a binary file. We then compare it to the original to see that `ssdeep` determines that the two files are highly similar but not identical:

1. First, we download the latest version of Python, `python-3.7.2-amd64.exe`. I am going to create a copy, rename it `python-3.7.2-amd64-fake.exe`, and add a null byte at the end:

```
truncate -s +1 python-3.7.2-amd64-fake.exe
```

2. Using `hexdump`, I can verify that the operation was successful by looking at the file before and after:

```
hexdump -C python-3.7.2-amd64.exe |tail -5
```

This results in the following output:

```
018ee0f0  e3 af d6 e9 05 3f b7 15  a1 c7 2a 5f b6 ae 71 1f
|.....?....*_..q.|
018ee100  6f 46 62 1c 4f 74 f5 f5  a1 e6 91 b7 fe 90 06 3e
|oFb.Ot........>|
018ee110  de 57 a6 e1 83 4c 13 0d  b1 4a 3d e5 04 82 5e 35
|.W...L...J=...^5|
018ee120  ff b2 e8 60 2d e0 db 24  c1 3d 8b 47 b3 00 00 00  |...`-
..$.=.G....|
```

The same can be verified with a second file using the following command:

```
hexdump -C python-3.7.2-amd64-fake.exe |tail -5
```

This results in the following output:

```
018ee100  6f 46 62 1c 4f 74 f5 f5  a1 e6 91 b7 fe 90 06 3e
|oFb.Ot........>|
018ee110  de 57 a6 e1 83 4c 13 0d  b1 4a 3d e5 04 82 5e 35
|.W...L...J=...^5|
018ee120  ff b2 e8 60 2d e0 db 24  c1 3d 8b 47 b3 00 00 00  |...`-
..$.=.G....|
018ee130  00                                                |.|
018ee131
```

3. Now, I will hash the two files using `ssdeep` and compare the result:

```
import ssdeep

hash1 = ssdeep.hash_from_file("python-3.7.2-amd64.exe")
hash2 = ssdeep.hash_from_file("python-3.7.2-amd64-fake.exe")
ssdeep.compare(hash1, hash2)
```

The output to the preceding code is 99.

How it works...

This scenario simulates tampering with a file and then utilizing similarity hashing to detect the existence of tampering, as well as measuring the size of the delta. We begin with a vanilla Python executable and then tamper with it by adding a null byte at the end (step 1). In real life, a hacker may take a legitimate program and insert malicious code into the sample. We double-checked that the tempering was successful and examined its nature using a hexdump in step 2. We then ran a similarity computation using similarity hashing on the original and tempered file, to observe that a minor alteration took place (step 3). Utilizing only standard hashing, we would have no idea how the two files are related, other than to conclude that they are not the same file. Knowing how to compare files allows us to cluster malware and benign files in machine learning algorithms, as well as group them into families.

Extracting N-grams

In standard quantitative analysis of text, N-grams are sequences of N tokens (for example, words or characters). For instance, given the text *The quick brown fox jumped over the lazy dog*, if our tokens are words, then the 1-grams are *the, quick, brown, fox, jumped, over, the, lazy,* and *dog*. The 2-grams are *the quick, quick brown, brown fox,* and so on. The 3-grams are *the quick brown, quick brown fox, brown fox jumped,* and so on. Just like the local statistics of the text allowed us to build a Markov chain to perform statistical predictions and text generation from a corpus, N-grams allow us to model the local statistical properties of our corpus. Our ultimate goal is to utilize the counts of N-grams to help us predict whether a sample is malicious or benign. In this recipe, we demonstrate how to extract N-gram counts from a sample.

Getting ready

Preparation for this recipe consists of installing the `nltk` package in `pip`. The instructions are as follows:

```
pip install nltk
```

In addition, download a test file, such as the Python executable from https://www.python.org/ftp/python/3.7.2/python-3.7.2-amd64.exe.

How to do it...

In the following steps, we will enumerate all the 4-grams of a sample file and select the 50 most frequent ones:

1. We begin by importing the `collections` library to facilitate counting and the `ngrams` library from `nltk` to ease extraction of N-grams:

```
import collections
from nltk import ngrams
```

2. We specify which file we would like to analyze:

```
file_to_analyze = "python-3.7.2-amd64.exe"
```

3. We define a convenience function to read in a file's bytes:

```
def read_file(file_path):
    """Reads in the binary sequence of a binary file."""
    with open(file_path, "rb") as binary_file:
        data = binary_file.read()
    return data
```

4. We write a convenience function to take a byte sequence and obtain N-grams:

```
def byte_sequence_to_Ngrams(byte_sequence, N):
    """Creates a list of N-grams from a byte sequence."""
    Ngrams = ngrams(byte_sequence, N)
    return list(Ngrams)
```

5. We write a function to take a file and obtain its count of N-grams:

```
def binary_file_to_Ngram_counts(file, N):
    """Takes a binary file and outputs the N-grams counts of its
binary sequence."""
    filebyte_sequence = read_file(file)
    file_Ngrams = byte_sequence_to_Ngrams(filebyte_sequence, N)
    return collections.Counter(file_Ngrams)
```

6. We specify that our desired value is N=4 and obtain the counts of all 4-grams in the file:

```
extracted_Ngrams = binary_file_to_Ngram_counts(file_to_analyze, 4)
```

7. We list the 10 most common 4-grams of our file:

```
print(extracted_Ngrams.most_common(10))
```

The result is as follows:

```
[((0, 0, 0, 0), 24201), ((139, 240, 133, 246), 1920), ((32, 116,
111, 32), 1791), ((255, 255, 255, 255), 1663), ((108, 101, 100,
32), 1522), ((100, 32, 116, 111), 1519), ((97, 105, 108, 101),
1513), ((105, 108, 101, 100), 1513), ((70, 97, 105, 108), 1505),
((101, 100, 32, 116), 1503)]
```

How it works...

In the literature and industry, it has been determined that the most frequent N-grams are also the most informative ones for a malware classification algorithm. For this reason, in this recipe, we will write functions to extract them for a file. We start by importing some helpful libraries for our extraction of N-grams (step 1). In particular, we import the collections library and the ngrams library from nltk. The collections library allows us to convert a list of N-grams to a frequency count of the N-grams, while the ngrams library allows us to take an ordered list of bytes and obtain a list of N-grams. We specify the file we would like to analyze and write a function that will read all of the bytes of a given file (steps 2 and 3). We define a few more convenience functions before we begin the extraction. In particular, we write a function to take a file's sequence of bytes and output a list of its N-grams (step 4), and a function to take a file and output the counts of its N-grams (step 5). We are now ready to pass in a file and extracts its N-grams. We do so to extract the counts of 4-grams of our file (step 6) and then display the 10 most common of them, along with their counts (step 7). We see that some of the N-gram sequences, such as (0,0,0,0) and (255,255,255,255) may not be very informative. For this reason, we will utilize feature selection methods to cut out the less informative N-grams in our next recipe.

Selecting the best N-grams

The number of different N-grams grows exponentially in N. Even for a fixed tiny N, such as N=3, there are *256x256x256=16,777,216* possible N-grams. This means that the number of N-grams features is impracticably large. Consequently, we must select a smaller subset of N-grams that will be of most value to our classifiers. In this section, we show three different methods for selecting the topmost informative N-grams.

Getting ready

Preparation for this recipe consists of installing the scikit-learn and nltk packages in pip. The instructions are as follows:

```
pip install sklearn nltk
```

In addition, benign and malicious files have been provided for you in the PE Samples Dataset folder in the root of the repository. Extract all archives named Benign PE Samples*.7z to a folder named Benign PE Samples. Extract all archives named Malicious PE Samples*.7z to a folder named Malicious PE Samples.

How to do it...

In the following steps, we show three different methods for selecting the most informative N-grams. The recipe assumes that binaryFileToNgramCounts(file, N) and all other helper functions from the previous recipe have been included:

1. Begin by specifying the folders containing our samples, specifying our N, and importing modules to enumerate files:

```
from os import listdir
from os.path import isfile, join

directories = ["Benign PE Samples", "Malicious PE Samples"]
N = 2
```

2. Next, we count all the N-grams from all the files:

```
Ngram_counts_all_files = collections.Counter([])
for dataset_path in directories:
    all_samples = [f for f in listdir(dataset_path) if
isfile(join(dataset_path, f))]
    for sample in all_samples:
        file_path = join(dataset_path, sample)
        Ngram_counts_all_files +=
binary_file_to_Ngram_counts(file_path, N)
```

3. We collect the `K1=1000` most frequent N-grams into a list:

```
K1 = 1000
K1_most_frequent_Ngrams = Ngram_counts_all_files.most_common(K1)
K1_most_frequent_Ngrams_list = [x[0] for x in
K1_most_frequent_Ngrams]
```

4. A helper method, `featurize_sample`, will be used to take a sample and output the number of appearances of the most common N-grams in its byte sequence:

```
def featurize_sample(sample, K1_most_frequent_Ngrams_list):
    """Takes a sample and produces a feature vector.
    The features are the counts of the K1 N-grams we've selected.
    """
    K1 = len(K1_most_frequent_Ngrams_list)
    feature_vector = K1 * [0]
    file_Ngrams = binary_file_to_Ngram_counts(sample, N)
    for i in range(K1):
        feature_vector[i] =
file_Ngrams[K1_most_frequent_Ngrams_list[i]]
    return feature_vector
```

5. We iterate through our directories, and use the preceding `featurize_sample` function to featurize our samples. We also create a set of labels:

```
directories_with_labels = [("Benign PE Samples", 0), ("Malicious PE
Samples", 1)]
X = []
y = []
for dataset_path, label in directories_with_labels:
    all_samples = [f for f in listdir(dataset_path) if
isfile(join(dataset_path, f))]
    for sample in all_samples:
        file_path = join(dataset_path, sample)
        X.append(featurize_sample(file_path,
K1_most_frequent_Ngrams_list))
        y.append(label)
```

6. We import the libraries we will be using for feature selection and specify how many features we would like to narrow down to:

```
from sklearn.feature_selection import SelectKBest,
mutual_info_classif, chi2

K2 = 10
```

7. We perform three types of feature selections for our N-grams:

- **Frequency**—selects the most frequent N-grams:

```
X = np.asarray(X)
X_top_K2_freq = X[:,:K2]
```

- **Mutual information**—selects the N-grams ranked highest by the mutual information algorithm:

```
mi_selector = SelectKBest(mutual_info_classif, k=K2)
X_top_K2_mi = mi_selector.fit_transform(X, y)
```

- **Chi-squared**—selects the N-grams ranked highest by the chi squared algorithm:

```
chi2_selector = SelectKBest(chi2, k=K2)
X_top_K2_ch2 = chi2_selector.fit_transform(X, y)
```

How it works...

Unlike the previous recipe, in which we analyzed a single file's N-grams, in this recipe, we look at a large collection of files to understand which N-grams are the most informative features. We start by specifying the folders containing our samples, our value of N, and import some modules to enumerate files (step 1). We proceed to count *all* N-grams from *all* files in our dataset (step 2). This allows us to find the *globally* most frequent N-grams. Of these, we filter down to the K1=1000 most frequent ones (step 3). Next, we introduce a helper method, featurizeSample, to be used to take a sample and output the number of appearances of the K1 most common N-grams in its byte sequence (step 4). We then iterate through our directories of files, and use the previous featurizeSample function to featurize our samples, as well as record their labels, as malicious or benign (step 5). The importance of the labels is that the assessment of whether an N-gram is informative depends on being able to discriminate between the malicious and benign classes based on it.

We import the `SelectKBest` library to select the best features via a score function, and the two score functions, mutual information and chi-squared (step 6). Finally, we apply the three different feature selection schemes to select the best N-grams and apply this knowledge to transform our features (step 7). In the first method, we simply select the K2 most frequent N-grams. Note that the selection of this method is often recommended in the literature, and is easier because of not requiring labels or extensive computation. In the second method, we use mutual information to narrow down the K2 features, while in the third, we use chi-squared to do so.

Building a static malware detector

In this section, we will see how to put together the recipes we discussed in prior sections to build a malware detector. Our malware detector will take in both features extracted from the PE header as well as features derived from N-grams.

Getting ready

Preparation for this recipe consists of installing the `scikit-learn`, `nltk`, and `pefile` packages in `pip`. The instructions are as follows:

```
pip install sklearn nltk pefile
```

In addition, benign and malicious files have been provided for you in the `"PE Samples Dataset"` folder in the root of the repository. Extract all archives named `"Benign PE Samples*.7z"` to a folder named `"Benign PE Samples"`. Extract all archives named `"Malicious PE Samples*.7z"` to a folder named `"Malicious PE Samples"`.

How to do it...

In the following steps, we will demonstrate a complete workflow in which we begin with raw samples, featurize them, vectorize their results, put them together, and finally train and test a classifier:

1. Begin by enumerating our samples and assigning their labels:

```
import os
from os import listdir

directories_with_labels = [("Benign PE Samples", 0), ("Malicious PE
Samples", 1)]
```

```
list_of_samples = []
labels = []
for dataset_path, label in directories_with_labels:
    samples = [f for f in listdir(dataset_path)]
    for sample in samples:
        file_path = os.path.join(dataset_path, sample)
        list_of_samples.append(file_path)
        labels.append(label)
```

2. We perform a stratified train-test split:

```
from sklearn.model_selection import train_test_split

samples_train, samples_test, labels_train, labels_test =
train_test_split(
    list_of_samples, labels, test_size=0.3, stratify=labels,
random_state=11
)
```

3. We introduce convenience functions from prior sections in order to obtain features:

```
import collection
from nltk import ngrams
import numpy as np
import pefile


def read_file(file_path):
    """Reads in the binary sequence of a binary file."""
    with open(file_path, "rb") as binary_file:
        data = binary_file.read()
    return data


def byte_sequence_to_Ngrams(byte_sequence, N):
    """Creates a list of N-grams from a byte sequence."""
    Ngrams = ngrams(byte_sequence, N)
    return list(Ngrams)


def binary_file_to_Ngram_counts(file, N):
    """Takes a binary file and outputs the N-grams counts of its
binary sequence."""
    filebyte_sequence = read_file(file)
    file_Ngrams = byte_sequence_to_Ngrams(filebyte_sequence, N)
    return collections.Counter(file_Ngrams)
```

```
def get_NGram_features_from_sample(sample,
K1_most_frequent_Ngrams_list):
    """Takes a sample and produces a feature vector.
    The features are the counts of the K1 N-grams we've selected.
    """
    K1 = len(K1_most_frequent_Ngrams_list)
    feature_vector = K1 * [0]
    file_Ngrams = binary_file_to_Ngram_counts(sample, N)
    for i in range(K1):
        feature_vector[i] =
file_Ngrams[K1_most_frequent_Ngrams_list[i]]
    return feature_vector


def preprocess_imports(list_of_DLLs):
    """Normalize the naming of the imports of a PE file."""
    temp = [x.decode().split(".")[0].lower() for x in list_of_DLLs]
    return " ".join(temp)


def get_imports(pe):
    """Get a list of the imports of a PE file."""
    list_of_imports = []
    for entry in pe.DIRECTORY_ENTRY_IMPORT:
        list_of_imports.append(entry.dll)
    return preprocess_imports(list_of_imports)


def get_section_names(pe):
    """Gets a list of section names from a PE file."""
    list_of_section_names = []
    for sec in pe.sections:
        normalized_name = sec.Name.decode().replace("\x00",
"").lower()
        list_of_section_names.append(normalized_name)
    return "".join(list_of_section_names)
```

4. We select the 100 most frequent 2-grams as our features:

```
N = 2
Ngram_counts_all = collections.Counter([])
for sample in samples_train:
    Ngram_counts_all += binary_file_to_Ngram_counts(sample, N)
K1 = 100
K1_most_frequent_Ngrams = Ngram_counts_all.most_common(K1)
K1_most_frequent_Ngrams_list = [x[0] for x in
K1_most_frequent_Ngrams]
```

5. We extract the N-gram counts, section names, imports, and number of sections of each sample in our training test, and skip over samples whose PE header cannot be parsed:

```
imports_corpus_train = []
num_sections_train = []
section_names_train = []
Ngram_features_list_train = []
y_train = []
for i in range(len(samples_train)):
    sample = samples_train[i]
    try:
        NGram_features = get_NGram_features_from_sample(
            sample, K1_most_frequent_Ngrams_list
        )
        pe = pefile.PE(sample)
        imports = get_imports(pe)
        n_sections = len(pe.sections)
        sec_names = get_section_names(pe)
        imports_corpus_train.append(imports)
        num_sections_train.append(n_sections)
        section_names_train.append(sec_names)
        Ngram_features_list_train.append(NGram_features)
        y_train.append(labels_train[i])
    except Exception as e:
        print(sample + ":")
        print(e)
```

6. We use a hashing vectorizer followed by `tfidf` to convert the imports and section names, both of which are text features, into a numerical form:

```
from sklearn.feature_extraction.text import HashingVectorizer,
TfidfTransformer
from sklearn.pipeline import Pipeline

imports_featurizer = Pipeline(
    [
        ("vect", HashingVectorizer(input="content", ngram_range=(1,
2))),
        ("tfidf", TfidfTransformer(use_idf=True,)),
    ]
)
section_names_featurizer = Pipeline(
    [
        ("vect", HashingVectorizer(input="content", ngram_range=(1,
2))),
        ("tfidf", TfidfTransformer(use_idf=True,)),
    ]
```

```
)
imports_corpus_train_transformed =
imports_featurizer.fit_transform(
    imports_corpus_train
)
section_names_train_transformed =
section_names_featurizer.fit_transform(
    section_names_train
)
```

7. We combine the vectorized features into a single array:

```
from scipy.sparse import hstack, csr_matrix

X_train = hstack(
    [
        Ngram_features_list_train,
        imports_corpus_train_transformed,
        section_names_train_transformed,
        csr_matrix(num_sections_train).transpose(),
    ]
)
```

8. We train a Random Forest classifier on the training set and print out its score:

```
from sklearn.ensemble import RandomForestClassifier

clf = RandomForestClassifier(n_estimators=100)
clf = clf.fit(X_train, y_train)
```

9. We collect the features of the testing set, just as we did for the training set:

```
imports_corpus_test = []
num_sections_test = []
section_names_test = []
Ngram_features_list_test = []
y_test = []
for i in range(len(samples_test)):
    file = samples_test[i]
    try:
        NGram_features = get_NGram_features_from_sample(
            sample, K1_most_frequent_Ngrams_list
        )
        pe = pefile.PE(file)
        imports = get_imports(pe)
        n_sections = len(pe.sections)
        sec_names = get_section_names(pe)
        imports_corpus_test.append(imports)
```

```
                num_sections_test.append(n_sections)
                section_names_test.append(sec_names)
                Ngram_features_list_test.append(NGram_features)
                y_test.append(labels_test[i])
        except Exception as e:
            print(sample + ":")
            print(e)
```

10. We apply the previously trained transformers to vectorize the text features and then test our classifier on the resulting test set:

```
imports_corpus_test_transformed =
imports_featurizer.transform(imports_corpus_test)
section_names_test_transformed =
section_names_featurizer.transform(section_names_test)
X_test = hstack(
    [
        Ngram_features_list_test,
        imports_corpus_test_transformed,
        section_names_test_transformed,
        csr_matrix(num_sections_test).transpose(),
    ]
)
print(clf.score(X_test, y_test))
```

The score of our classifier is as follows:

```
0.8859649122807017
```

How it works...

There are several notable new ideas in this section. We start by enumerating our samples and assigning them their respective labels (step 1). Because our dataset is imbalanced, it makes sense to use a stratified train-test split (step 2). In a stratified train-test split, a train-test split is created in which the proportion of each class is the same in the training set, testing set, and original set. This ensures that there is no possibility that our training set, for example, will consist of only one class due to a chance event. Next, we load the functions we will be using to featurize our samples. We employ our feature extraction techniques, as in previous recipes, to compute the best N-gram features (step 4) and then iterate through all of the files to extract all of the features (step 5). We then take the PE header features we obtained previously, such as section names and imports, and vectorize them using a basic NLP approach (step 6).

Having obtained all these different features, we are now ready to combine them, which we do using the `scipy` hstack, to merge the different features into one large sparse `scipy` array (step 7). We continue on to train a Random Forest classifier with default parameters (step 8) and then repeat the extraction process for our testing set (step 9). In step 10, we finally test out our trained classifier, obtaining a promising starting score. Overall, this recipe provides the foundations for a malware classifier that can be expanded into a high-powered solution.

Tackling class imbalance

Often in applying machine learning to cybersecurity, we are faced with highly imbalanced datasets. For instance, it may be much easier to access a large collection of benign samples than it is to collect malicious samples. Conversely, you may be working at an enterprise that, for legal reasons, is prohibited from saving benign samples. In either case, your dataset will be highly skewed toward one class. As a consequence, naive machine learning aimed at maximizing accuracy will result in a classifier that predicts almost all samples as coming from the overrepresented class. There are several techniques that can be used to tackle the challenge of class imbalance.

Getting ready

Preparation for this recipe consists of installing the `scikit-learn` and `imbalanced-learn` pip packages. The instructions are as follows:

```
pip install sklearn imbalanced-learn
```

How to do it...

In the following steps, we will demonstrate several methods for dealing with imbalanced data:

1. Begin by loading the training and testing data, importing a decision tree, as well as some libraries we will be using to score performance:

```
from sklearn import tree
from sklearn.metrics import balanced_accuracy_score
import numpy as np
import scipy.sparse
import collections
```

```
X_train = scipy.sparse.load_npz("training_data.npz")
y_train = np.load("training_labels.npy")
X_test = scipy.sparse.load_npz("test_data.npz")
y_test = np.load("test_labels.npy")
```

2. Train and test a simple Decision Tree classifier:

```
dt = tree.DecisionTreeClassifier()
dt.fit(X_train, y_train)
dt_pred = dt.predict(X_test)
print(collections.Counter(dt_pred))
print(balanced_accuracy_score(y_test, dt_pred))
```

This results in the following output:

```
Counter({0: 121, 1: 10})
0.8333333333333333
```

Next, we test several techniques to improve performance.

3. **Weighting:** We set the class weights of our classifier to `"balanced"` and train and test this new classifier:

```
dt_weighted = tree.DecisionTreeClassifier(class_weight="balanced")
dt_weighted.fit(X_train, y_train)
dt_weighted_pred = dt_weighted.predict(X_test)
print(collections.Counter(dt_weighted_pred))
print(balanced_accuracy_score(y_test, dt_weighted_pred))
```

This results in the following output:

```
Counter({0: 114, 1: 17})
0.9913793103448276
```

4. **Upsampling the minor class:** We extract all test samples from class 0 and class 1:

```
from sklearn.utils import resample

X_train_np = X_train.toarray()
class_0_indices = [i for i, x in enumerate(y_train == 0) if x]
class_1_indices = [i for i, x in enumerate(y_train == 1) if x]
size_class_0 = sum(y_train == 0)
X_train_class_0 = X_train_np[class_0_indices, :]
y_train_class_0 = [0] * size_class_0
X_train_class_1 = X_train_np[class_1_indices, :]
```

5. We upsample the elements of class 1 with replacements until the number of samples of class 1 and class 0 are equal:

```
X_train_class_1_resampled = resample(
    X_train_class_1, replace=True, n_samples=size_class_0
)
y_train_class_1_resampled = [1] * size_class_0
```

6. We combine the newly upsampled samples into a single training set:

```
X_train_resampled = np.concatenate([X_train_class_0,
X_train_class_1_resampled])
y_train_resampled = y_train_class_0 + y_train_class_1_resampled
```

7. We train and test a Random Forest classifier on our upsampled training set:

```
from scipy import sparse

X_train_resampled = sparse.csr_matrix(X_train_resampled)
dt_resampled = tree.DecisionTreeClassifier()
dt_resampled.fit(X_train_resampled, y_train_resampled)
dt_resampled_pred = dt_resampled.predict(X_test)
print(collections.Counter(dt_resampled_pred))
print(balanced_accuracy_score(y_test, dt_resampled_pred))
```

This results in the following output:

```
Counter({0: 114, 1: 17})
0.9913793103448276
```

8. **Downsampling the major class:** We perform similar steps to the preceding upsampling, except this time we down-sample the major class until it is of the same size as the minor class:

```
X_train_np = X_train.toarray()
class_0_indices = [i for i, x in enumerate(y_train == 0) if x]
class_1_indices = [i for i, x in enumerate(y_train == 1) if x]
size_class_1 = sum(y_train == 1)
X_train_class_1 = X_train_np[class_1_indices, :]
y_train_class_1 = [1] * size_class_1
X_train_class_0 = X_train_np[class_0_indices, :]
X_train_class_0_downsampled = resample(
    X_train_class_0, replace=False, n_samples=size_class_1
)
y_train_class_0_downsampled = [0] * size_class_1
```

9. We create a new training set from the downsampled data:

```
X_train_downsampled = np.concatenate([X_train_class_1,
X_train_class_0_downsampled])
y_train_downsampled = y_train_class_1 + y_train_class_0_downsampled
```

10. We train a Random Forest classifier on this dataset:

```
X_train_downsampled = sparse.csr_matrix(X_train_downsampled)
dt_downsampled = tree.DecisionTreeClassifier()
dt_downsampled.fit(X_train_downsampled, y_train_downsampled)
dt_downsampled_pred = dt_downsampled.predict(X_test)
print(collections.Counter(dt_downsampled_pred))
print(balanced_accuracy_score(y_test, dt_downsampled_pred))
```

This results in the following output:

```
Counter({0: 100, 1: 31})
0.9310344827586207
```

11. **Classifier including inner balancing samplers:** We utilize the imbalanced-learn package classifiers that resample subsets of data before the training estimators:

```
from imblearn.ensemble import BalancedBaggingClassifier

balanced_clf = BalancedBaggingClassifier(
    base_estimator=tree.DecisionTreeClassifier(),
    sampling_strategy="auto",
    replacement=True,
)
balanced_clf.fit(X_train, y_train)
balanced_clf_pred = balanced_clf.predict(X_test)
print(collections.Counter(balanced_clf_pred))
print(balanced_accuracy_score(y_test, balanced_clf_pred))
```

This results in the following output:

```
Counter({0: 113, 1: 18})
0.9494252873563218
```

How it works...

We start by loading in a predefined dataset (step 1) using the `scipy.sparse.load_npz` loading function to load previously saved sparse matrices. Our next step is to train a basic Decision Tree model on our data (step 2). To measure performance, we utilize the balanced accuracy score, a measure that is often used in classification problems with imbalanced datasets. By definition, balanced accuracy is the average of recall obtained on each class. The best value is 1, whereas the worst value is 0.

In the following steps, we employ different techniques to tackle the class imbalance. Our first approach is to utilize class weights to adjust our Decision Tree to an imbalanced dataset (step 3). The balanced mode uses the values of *y* to automatically adjust weights inversely proportional to the class frequencies in the input data as *n_samples / (n_classes * np.bincount(y))*. In steps 4 to 7, we utilize upsampling to tackle class imbalance. This is the process of randomly duplicating observations from the minority class in order to reinforce the minority class's signal.

There are several methods for doing so, but the most common way is to simply resample with replacements as we have done. The two main concerns with upsampling are that it increases the size of the dataset and that it can lead to overfitting due to training on the same sample numerous times. In steps 8 to 10, we down-sample our major class. This simply means that we don't use all of the samples we have, but just enough so that we balance our classes.

The main issue with this technique is that we are forced to use a smaller training set. Our final approach, and the most sophisticated one, is to utilize a classifier that includes inner balancing samplers, namely the `BalancedBaggingClassifier` from `imbalanced-learn` (step 11). Overall, we see that every single one of our methods for tackling class imbalance increased the balanced accuracy score.

Handling type I and type II errors

In many situations in machine learning, one type of error may be more important than another. For example, in a multilayered defense system, it may make sense to require a layer to have a low false alarm (low false positive) rate, at the cost of some detection rate. In this section, we provide a recipe for ensuring that the FPR does not exceed a desired limit by using thresholding.

Getting ready

Preparation for this recipe consists of installing scikit-learn and xgboost in pip. The instructions are as follows:

```
pip install sklearn xgboost
```

How to do it...

In the following steps, we will load a dataset, train a classifier, and then tune a threshold to satisfy a false positive rate constraint:

1. We load a dataset and specify that the desired FPR is at or below 1%:

```
import numpy as np
from scipy import sparse
import scipy

X_train = scipy.sparse.load_npz("training_data.npz")
y_train = np.load("training_labels.npy")
X_test = scipy.sparse.load_npz("test_data.npz")
y_test = np.load("test_labels.npy")
desired_FPR = 0.01
```

2. We write methods to calculate FPR and TPR:

```
from sklearn.metrics import confusion_matrix


def FPR(y_true, y_pred):
    """Calculate the False Positive Rate."""
    CM = confusion_matrix(y_true, y_pred)
    TN = CM[0][0]
    FP = CM[0][1]
    return FP / (FP + TN)


def TPR(y_true, y_pred):
    """Calculate the True Positive Rate."""
    CM = confusion_matrix(y_true, y_pred)
    TP = CM[1][1]
    FN = CM[1][0]
    return TP / (TP + FN)
```

3. We write a method to convert a vector of probabilities into a Boolean vector using thresholding:

```
def perform_thresholding(vector, threshold):
    """Threshold a vector."""
    return [0 if x >= threshold else 1 for x in vector]
```

4. We train an XGBoost model and calculate a probability prediction on the training data:

```
from xgboost import XGBClassifier

clf = XGBClassifier()
clf.fit(X_train, y_train)
clf_pred_prob = clf.predict_proba(X_train)
```

5. Let's examine our prediction probability vectors:

```
print("Probabilities look like so:")
print(clf_pred_prob[0:5])
print()
```

This results in the following output:

```
Probabilities look like so:
[[0.9972162  0.0027838 ]
 [0.9985584  0.0014416 ]
 [0.9979202  0.00207978]
 [0.96858877 0.03141126]
 [0.91427565 0.08572436]]
```

6. We loop over 1,000 different threshold values, calculate the FPR for each, and when we satisfy our FPR<=desiredFPR, we select that threshold:

```
M = 1000
print("Fitting threshold:")
for t in reversed(range(M)):
    scaled_threshold = float(t) / M
    thresholded_prediction = perform_thresholding(clf_pred_prob[:,
0], scaled_threshold)
    print(t, FPR(y_train, thresholded_prediction), TPR(y_train,
thresholded_prediction))
    if FPR(y_train, thresholded_prediction) <= desired_FPR:
        print()
        print("Selected threshold: ")
        print(scaled_threshold)
        break
```

This results in the following output:

```
Fitting threshold:
999 1.0 1.0
998 0.6727272727272727 1.0
997 0.4590909090909091 1.0
996 0.33181818181818185 1.0
 <snip>
 649 0.05454545454545454 1.0
648 0.004545454545454545 0.7857142857142857
Selected threshold: 0.648
```

How it works...

We begin this recipe by loading in a previously featurized dataset and specifying a desired FPR constraint of 1% (step 1). The value to be used in practice depends highly on the situation and type of file being considered. There are a few considerations to follow: if the file is extremely common, but rarely malicious, such as a PDF, the desired FPR will have to be set very low, for example, 0.01%.

If the system is supported by additional systems that will double-check its verdict without human effort, then a high FPR might not be detrimental. Finally, a customer may have a preference, which will suggest a recommended value. We define a pair of convenience functions for FPR and TPR in step 2—these functions are very handy and reusable. Another convenience function we define is a function that will take our threshold value and use it to threshold a numerical vector (step 3).

In step 4, we train a model on the training data, and determine prediction probabilities on the training set as well. You can see what these look like in step 5. When a large dataset is available, using a validation set for determining the proper threshold will reduce the likelihood of overfitting. Finally, we compute the threshold to be used in future classification in order to ensure that the FPR constraint will be satisfied (step 6).

Advanced Malware Detection 3

In this chapter, we will be covering more advanced concepts for malware analysis. In the previous chapter, we covered general methods for attacking malware classification. Here, we will discuss more specific approaches and cutting-edge technologies. In particular, we will cover how to approach obfuscated and packed malware, how to scale up the collection of N-gram features, and how to use deep learning to detect and even create malware.

This chapter comprises the following recipes:

- Detecting obfuscated JavaScript
- Featurizing PDF files
- Extracting N-grams quickly using the hash-gram algorithm
- Building a dynamic malware classifier
- MalConv – end-to-end deep learning for malicious PE detection
- Using packers
- Assembling a packed sample dataset
- Building a classifier for packers
- MalGAN – creating evasive malware
- Tracking malware drift

Technical requirements

The following are the technical prerequisites for this chapter:

- Keras
- TensorFlow
- XGBoost
- UPX
- Statsmodels

Code and datasets may be found at `https://github.com/PacktPublishing/Machine-Learning-for-Cybersecurity-Cookbook/tree/master/Chapter03`.

Detecting obfuscated JavaScript

In this section, we will see how to use machine learning to detect when a JavaScript file is obfuscated. Doing so can serve to create a binary feature, obfuscated or not, to be used in benign/malicious classification, and can serve also as a prerequisite step to deobfuscating the scripts.

Getting ready

Preparation for this recipe involves installing the `scikit-learn` package in `pip`. The command is as follows:

```
pip install sklearn
```

In addition, obfuscated and non-obfuscated JavaScript files have been provided for you in the repository. Extract `JavascriptSamplesNotObfuscated.7z` to a folder named `JavaScript Samples`. Extract `JavascriptSamplesObfuscated.7z` to a folder named `JavaScript Samples Obfuscated`.

How to do it...

In the following steps, we will demonstrate how a binary classifier can detect obfuscated JavaScript files:

1. Begin by importing the libraries we will be needing to process the JavaScript's content, prepare the dataset, classify it, and measure the performance of our classifier:

```
import os
from sklearn.feature_extraction.text import HashingVectorizer,
TfidfTransformer
from sklearn.ensemble import RandomForestClassifier
from sklearn.model_selection import train_test_split
from sklearn.metrics import accuracy_score, confusion_matrix
from sklearn.pipeline import Pipeline
```

2. We specify the paths of our obfuscated and non-obfuscated JavaScript files and assign the two types of file different labels:

```
js_path = "path\\to\\JavascriptSamples"
obfuscated_js_path = "path\\to\\ObfuscatedJavascriptSamples"

corpus = []
labels = []
file_types_and_labels = [(js_path, 0), (obfuscated_js_path, 1)]
```

3. We then read our files into a corpus and prepare labels:

```
for files_path, label in file_types_and_labels:
    files = os.listdir(files_path)
    for file in files:
        file_path = files_path + "/" + file
        try:
            with open(file_path, "r") as myfile:
                data = myfile.read().replace("\n", "")
                data = str(data)
                corpus.append(data)
                labels.append(label)
        except:
            pass
```

4. We split our dataset into a training and testing set, and prepare a pipeline to perform basic NLP, followed by a random forest classifier:

```
X_train, X_test, y_train, y_test = train_test_split(
    corpus, labels, test_size=0.33, random_state=42
```

```
    )
    text_clf = Pipeline(
        [
            ("vect", HashingVectorizer(input="content", ngram_range=(1,
3))),
            ("tfidf", TfidfTransformer(use_idf=True,)),
            ("rf", RandomForestClassifier(class_weight="balanced")),
        ]
    )
```

5. Finally, we fit our pipeline to the training data, predict the testing data, and then print out our results:

```
text_clf.fit(X_train, y_train)
y_test_pred = text_clf.predict(X_test)

print(accuracy_score(y_test, y_test_pred))
print(confusion_matrix(y_test, y_test_pred))
```

The accuracy and confusion matrix is shown here:

```
0.9605911330049262
[[405  18]
 [ 14 375]]
```

How it works...

We begin by importing standard Python libraries to analyze the files and set up machine learning pipelines (*Step 1*). In *Steps 2* and *3*, we collect the non-obfuscated and obfuscated JavaScript files into arrays and assign them their respective labels. This is preparation for our binary classification problem. Note that the main challenge in producing this classifier is producing a large and useful dataset. Ideas for solving this hurdle include collecting a large number of JavaScript samples and then using different tools to obfuscate these. Consequently, your classifier will likely be able to avoid overfitting to one type of obfuscation. Having collected the data, we separate it into training and testing subsets (*Step 4*). In addition, we set up a pipeline to apply NLP methods to the JavaScript code itself, and then train a classifier (*Step 4*). Finally, we measure the performance of our classifier in *Step 5*. You will notice that besides the challenge of constructing an appropriate dataset, the recipe is similar to the one we used to detect the file type.

Featurizing PDF files

In this section, we will see how to featurize PDF files in order to use them for machine learning. The tool we will be utilizing is the PDFiD Python script designed by *Didier Stevens* (https://blog.didierstevens.com/). Stevens selected a list of 20 features that are commonly found in malicious files, including whether the PDF file contains JavaScript or launches an automatic action. It is suspicious to find these features in a file, hence, the appearance of these can be indicative of malicious behavior.

Essentially, the tool scans through a PDF file, and counts the number of occurrences of each of the ~20 features. A run of the tool appears as follows:

```
PDFiD 0.2.5 PythonBrochure.pdf

PDF Header: %PDF-1.6
obj                 1096
endobj              1095
stream              1061
endstream           1061
xref                   0
trailer                0
startxref              2
/Page                 32
/Encrypt               0
/ObjStm               43
/JS                    0
/JavaScript            0
/AA                    1
/OpenAction            0
/AcroForm              1
/JBIG2Decode           0
/RichMedia             0
/Launch                0
/EmbeddedFile          0
/XFA                   0
/URI                   0
/Colors > 2^24         0
```

Getting ready

The requisite files for this recipe are in the pdfid and PDFSamples folders included in the repository.

How to do it...

In the following steps, you will featurize a collection of PDF files using the PDFiD script:

1. Download the tool and place all accompanying code in the same directory as featurizing PDF Files.ipynb.

2. Import IPython's io module so as to capture the output of an external script:

```
from IPython.utils import io
```

3. Define a function to featurize a PDF:

```
def PDF_to_FV(file_path):
    """Featurize a PDF file using pdfid."""
```

4. Run pdfid against a file and capture the output of the operation:

```
with io.capture_output() as captured:
    %run -i pdfid $file_path
out = captured.stdout
```

5. Next, parse the output so that it is a numerical vector:

```
out1 = out.split("\n")[2:-2]
return [int(x.split()[-1]) for x in out1]
```

6. Import listdir to enumerate the files of a folder and specify where you have placed your collection of PDFs:

```
from os import listdir

PDFs_path = "PDFSamples\\"
```

7. Iterate through each file in the directory, featurize it, and then collect all the feature vectors into X:

```
X = []
files = listdir(PDFs_path)
for file in files:
    file_path = PDFs_path + file
    X.append(PDF_to_FV(file_path))
```

How it works...

We start our preparation by downloading the PDFiD tool and placing our PDF files in a convenient location for analysis (*Step 1*). Note that the tool is free and simple to use. Continuing, we import the very useful IPython's io module in order to capture the results of an external program, namely, PDFiD (*Step 2*). In the following steps, *Step 3* and *Step 5*, we define a function PDF to FV that takes a PDF file and featurizes it. In particular, it utilizes the PDFiD tool, and then parses its output into a convenient form. When we run on the PDFSamples\PythonBrochure.pdf file, our functions output the following vector:

```
[1096, 1095, 1061, 1061, 0, 0, 2, 32, 0, 43, 0, 0, 1, 0, 1, 0, 0, 0, 0, 0,
0, 0]
```

Now that we are able to featurize a single PDF file, why not featurize all of our PDF files to make these amenable to machine learning (*Steps 6* and *7*). In particular, in *Step 6*, we provide a path containing the PDF files we would like to featurize, and, in *Step 7*, we perform the actual featurization of the files.

Extracting N-grams quickly using the hash-gram algorithm

In this section, we demonstrate a technique for extracting the most frequent N-grams quickly and memory-efficiently. This allows us to make the challenges that come with the immense number of N-grams easier. The technique is called **Hash-Grams**, and relies on hashing the N-grams as they are extracted. A property of N-grams is that they follow a power law that ensures that hash collisions have an insignificant impact on the quality of the features thus obtained.

Getting ready

Preparation for this recipe involves installing nltk in pip. The command is as follows:

```
pip install nltk
```

In addition, benign and malicious files have been provided for you in the PE Samples Dataset folder in the root of the repository. Extract all archives named Benign PE Samples*.7z to a folder named Benign PE Samples, and extract all archives named Malicious PE Samples*.7z to a folder named Malicious PE Samples.

How to do it...

In the following steps, we will demonstrate how the hash-gram algorithm works:

1. Begin by specifying the folders containing our samples, the parameter N, and importing a library for hashing and a library to extract N-grams from a string:

```
from os import listdir
from nltk import ngrams
import hashlib

directories = ["Benign PE Samples", "Malicious PE Samples"]
N = 2
```

2. We create a function to read in the bytes of a file and turn these into N-grams:

```
def read_file(file_path):
    """Reads in the binary sequence of a binary file."""
    with open(file_path, "rb") as binary_file:
        data = binary_file.read()
    return data

def byte_sequence_to_Ngrams(byte_sequence, N):
    """Creates a list of N-grams from a byte sequence."""
    return ngrams(byte_sequence, N)
```

3. Now, we will want to hash the N-grams:

```
def hash_input(inp):
    """Compute the MD5 hash of an input."""
    return int(hashlib.md5(inp).hexdigest(), 16)

def make_ngram_hashable(Ngram):
    """Convert N-gram into bytes to be hashable."""
    return bytes(Ngram)
```

4. The `hash_file_Ngrams_into_dictionary` function takes an N-gram, hashes it, and then increments the count in the dictionary for the hash. The reduction module B (%B) ensures that there can be no more than B keys in the dictionary:

```
def hash_file_Ngrams_into_dictionary(file_Ngrams, T):
    """Hashes N-grams in a list and then keeps track of the counts
in a dictionary."""
    for Ngram in file_Ngrams:
        hashable_Ngram = make_ngram_hashable(Ngram)
        hashed_and_reduced = hash_input(hashable_Ngram) % B
        T[hashed_and_reduced] = T.get(hashed_and_reduced, 0) + 1
```

5. We specify a value for B, the largest prime number smaller than 2^16, and create an empty dictionary:

```
B = 65521
T = {}
```

6. We iterate over our files and count their hashed N-grams:

```
for dataset_path in directories:
    samples = [f for f in listdir(dataset_path)]
    for file in samples:
        file_path = dataset_path + "/" + file
        file_byte_sequence = read_file(file_path)
        file_Ngrams = byte_sequence_to_Ngrams(file_byte_sequence,
N)
        hash_file_Ngrams_into_dictionary(file_Ngrams, T)
```

7. We select the most frequent K1=1000 using heapq:

```
K1 = 1000
import heapq

K1_most_common_Ngrams_Using_Hash_Grams = heapq.nlargest(K1, T)
```

8. Once the top-hashed N-grams have been selected, these make up the feature set. In order to featurize a sample, one iterates over its N-grams, hashes, and reduces them, and, if the result is one of the selected top-hashed N-grams, increments the feature vector at that index:

```
def featurize_sample(file, K1_most_common_Ngrams_Using_Hash_Grams):
    """Takes a sample and produces a feature vector.
    The features are the counts of the K1 N-grams we've selected.
    """
    K1 = len(K1_most_common_Ngrams_Using_Hash_Grams)
    fv = K1 * [0]
    file_byte_sequence = read_file(file_path)
    file_Ngrams = byte_sequence_to_Ngrams(file_byte_sequence, N)
    for Ngram in file_Ngrams:
        hashable_Ngram = make_ngram_hashable(Ngram)
        hashed_and_reduced = hash_input(hashable_Ngram) % B
        if hashed_and_reduced in
K1_most_common_Ngrams_Using_Hash_Grams:
            index =
K1_most_common_Ngrams_Using_Hash_Grams.index(hashed_and_reduced)
            fv[index] += 1
    return fv
```

9. Finally, we featurize our dataset:

```
X = []
for dataset_path in directories:
    samples = [f for f in listdir(dataset_path)]
    for file in samples:
        file_path = dataset_path + "/" + file
        X.append(featurize_sample(file_path,
K1_most_common_Ngrams_Using_Hash_Grams))
```

How it works...

The initial steps in the hash-gram recipe are similar to the ordinary extraction of N-grams. First, we prepare by specifying the folders containing our samples, our value of N (as in N-grams). In addition, we import a hashing library, which is an action different from the ordinary extraction of N-grams (*Step 1*). Continuing our preparation, we define a function to read in all the bytes of a file (as opposed to reading in its content) and turn these into N-grams (*Step 2*). We define a function to compute the MD5 hash of an N-gram and return the result as a hexadecimal number. Additionally, we define a function to convert an N-gram to its byte constituents in order to be able to hash it (*Step 3*).

Next, we define a function to iterate through the hashed N-grams of a file, reduce these to modulo B, and then increase the count in the dictionary for the reduced hash (*Step 4*). The parameter B controls the limit on how many different keys the dictionary will have. By hashing, we are able to randomize the buckets that count the N-grams. Now, as we are about to run our functions, it's time to specify the value of B. We select the value for B to be the largest prime number smaller than 2^{16} (*Step 5*).

It is standard to select a prime to ensure that the number of hash collisions is minimal. We now iterate through our directory of files and apply the functions we have defined previously to each file (*Step 6*). The result is a large dictionary, *T*, that contains counts of hashed N-grams. This dictionary is not too big, and we easily select the top K1 most common reduced hashes of N-grams from it (*Step 7*). By doing so, the probability is high that we select the top most frequent N-grams, although there may be more than K1 due to hash collisions. At this point, we have our feature set, which is N-grams that get mapped by hashing to the K1 hashed N-grams we have selected. We now featurize our dataset (*Steps 8* and *9*). In particular, we iterate through our files, computing their N-grams. If an N-gram has a reduced hash that is one of the K1 selected ones, we consider it to be a frequent N-gram, and use it as part of our feature set.

It is important to note that the hash-grams algorithm will not always be faster, but it is expected to be whenever the datasets under consideration are large. In many cases, in a situation where a naive approach to extracting N-grams leads to memory error, hash-grams is able to terminate successfully.

See also

For additional details on the hash-gram algorithm, see `https://www.edwardraff.com/publications/hash-grams-faster.pdf`.

Building a dynamic malware classifier

In certain situations, there is a considerable advantage to being able to detect malware based on its behavior. In particular, it is much more difficult for a malware to hide its intentions when it is being analyzed in a dynamic situation. For this reason, classifiers that operate on dynamic information can be much more accurate than their static counterparts. In this section, we provide a recipe for a dynamic malware classifier. The dataset we use is part of a VirusShare repository from android applications. The dynamic analysis was performed by Johannes Thon on several LG Nexus 5 devices with Android API 23, (over 4,000 malicious apps were dynamically analyzed on the LG Nexus 5 device farm (API 23), and over 4,300 benign apps were dynamically analyzed on the LG Nexus 5 device farm (API 23) by goorax, used under CC BY / unmodified from the original).

Our approach will be to use N-grams on the sequence of API calls.

Getting ready

Preparation for this recipe involves installing `scikit-learn`, `nltk`, and `xgboost` in `pip`. The command is as follows:

```
pip install sklearn nltk xgboost
```

In addition, benign and malicious dynamic analysis files have been provided for you in the repository. Extract all archives named `DA Logs Benign*.7z` to a folder named `DA Logs Benign`, and extract all archives named `DA Logs Malware*.7z` to a folder named `DA Logs Malicious`.

How to do it...

In the following steps, we demonstrate how a classifier can detect malware based on an observed sequence of API calls.

1. Our logs are in JSON format, so we begin by importing the JSON library.

```
import numpy as np
import os
import json

directories_with_labels = [("DA Logs Benign", 0), ("DA Logs
Malware", 1)]
```

2. Write a function to parse the JSON logs:

```
def get_API_class_method_type_from_log(log):
    """Parses out API calls from behavioral logs."""
    API_data_sequence = []
    with open(log) as log_file:
        json_log = json.load(log_file)
        api_calls_array = "[" + json_log["api_calls"] + "]"
```

3. We choose to extract the class, method, and type of the API call:

```
    api_calls = json.loads(api_calls_array)
    for api_call in api_calls:
        data = api_call["class"] + ":" + api_call["method"] +
":" + api_call["type"]
        API_data_sequence.append(data)
    return API_data_sequence
```

4. We read our logs into a corpus and collect their labels:

```
data_corpus = []
labels = []
for directory, label in directories_with_labels:
    logs = os.listdir(directory)
    for log_path in logs:
        file_path = directory + "/" + log_path
        try:
data_corpus.append(get_API_class_method_type_from_log(file_path))
            labels.append(label)
        except:
            pass
```

5. Now, let's take a look at what the data in our corpus looks like:

```
print(data_corpus[0])
```

```
['android.os.SystemProperties:get:content',
 'android.os.SystemProperties:get:content',
 'android.os.SystemProperties:get:content',
 'android.os.SystemProperties:get:content',
 'android.os.SystemProperties:get:content',
 'android.os.SystemProperties:get:content',
 'android.os.SystemProperties:get:content',
 'android.os.SystemProperties:get:content',
 'android.os.SystemProperties:get:content',
 'android.os.SystemProperties:get:content',
 'android.os.SystemProperties:get:content',
 'android.os.SystemProperties:get:content',
 'android.app.ContextImpl:registerReceiver:binder',
 'android.app.ContextImpl:registerReceiver:binder',
 'android.os.SystemProperties:get:content',
 'android.os.SystemProperties:get:content']
```

6. We proceed to perform a train-test split:

```
from sklearn.model_selection import train_test_split

corpus_train, corpus_test, y_train, y_test = train_test_split(
    data_corpus, labels, test_size=0.2, random_state=11
)
```

7. Our approach is to use N-grams, so we load our N-gram extraction functions, with a slight modification for the current data format:

```
import collections
from nltk import ngrams
import numpy as np


def read_file(file_path):
    """Reads in the binary sequence of a binary file."""
    with open(file_path, "rb") as binary_file:
        data = binary_file.read()
    return data


def text_to_Ngrams(text, n):
    """Produces a list of N-grams from a text."""
    Ngrams = ngrams(text, n)
    return list(Ngrams)
```

```
def get_Ngram_counts(text, N):
    """Get a frequency count of N-grams in a text."""
    Ngrams = text_to_Ngrams(text, N)
    return collections.Counter(Ngrams)
```

8. We specify N=4 and collect all N-grams:

```
N = 4
total_Ngram_count = collections.Counter([])
for file in corpus_train:
    total_Ngram_count += get_Ngram_counts(file, N)
```

9. Next, we narrow down to the K1 = 3000 most frequent N-grams:

```
K1 = 3000
K1_most_frequent_Ngrams = total_Ngram_count.most_common(K1)
K1_most_frequent_Ngrams_list = [x[0] for x in
K1_most_frequent_Ngrams]

[('java.lang.reflect.Method:invoke:reflection',
 'java.lang.reflect.Method:invoke:reflection',
 'java.lang.reflect.Method:invoke:reflection',
 'java.lang.reflect.Method:invoke:reflection'),

('java.io.FileInputStream:read:runtime',
 'java.io.FileInputStream:read:runtime',
 'java.io.FileInputStream:read:runtime',
 'java.io.FileInputStream:read:runtime'),

 <snip>

 ('android.os.SystemProperties:get:content',
 'android.os.SystemProperties:get:content',
 'android.os.SystemProperties:get:content',
 'javax.crypto.spec.SecretKeySpec:javax.crypto.spec.SecretKeySpec:cr
ypto')
```

10. We then write a method to featurize a sample into a vector of N-gram counts:

```
def featurize_sample(file, Ngrams_list):
    """Takes a sample and produces a feature vector.
    The features are the counts of the K1 N-grams we've selected.
    """
    K1 = len(Ngrams_list)
    feature_vector = K1 * [0]
    fileNgrams = get_Ngram_counts(file, N)
    for i in range(K1):
        feature_vector[i] = fileNgrams[Ngrams_list[i]]
    return feature_vector
```

11. We apply this function to featurize our training and testing samples:

```
X_train = []
for sample in corpus_train:
    X_train.append(featurize_sample(sample,
K1_most_frequent_Ngrams_list))
X_train = np.asarray(X_train)
X_test = []
for sample in corpus_test:
    X_test.append(featurize_sample(sample,
K1_most_frequent_Ngrams_list))
X_test = np.asarray(X_test)
```

12. We use mutual information to further narrow the K1=3000 most frequent N-grams to K2=500 most informative N-grams. We then set up a pipeline to subsequently run an XGBoost classifier:

```
from sklearn.feature_selection import SelectKBest,
mutual_info_classif
from sklearn.pipeline import Pipeline
from xgboost import XGBClassifier

K2 = 500
mi_pipeline = Pipeline(
    [
        ("mutual_information", SelectKBest(mutual_info_classif,
k=K2)),
        ("xgb", XGBClassifier()),
    ]
)
```

13. We train our pipeline and evaluate its accuracy on the training and testing sets:

```
mi_pipeline.fit(X_train, y_train)
print("Training accuracy:")
print(mi_pipeline.score(X_train, y_train))
print("Testing accuracy:")
print(mi_pipeline.score(X_test, y_test))
```

The following output gives us the training and testing accuracies:

```
Training accuracy:
0.8149428743235118
Testing accuracy:
0.8033674082982561
```

How it works...

In this recipe, we perform something exciting, namely, classification of malware and benign samples based on their runtime behavior. Our first three steps are to define a function to read in and parse the JSON logs that contain information about the samples runtime behavior. As an aside, JSON is a useful file format whenever your data might have a variable number of attributes. We make the strategic choice to extract the API call class, method, and content. Other features are available as well, such as the time at which the API call was made and what arguments were called. The trade-off is that the dataset will be larger and these features might cause a slowdown or overfit. Investigation is recommended as regards selecting additional features for a classifier.

With our function defined, we proceed with performing parsing and collecting all of our parsed data in one place (*Step 4*). In *Step 5*, we take a peek at our corpus. We see a sample of the quadruples of API calls that make up our data. Next is the standard step of performing a training-testing split. In *Steps 7* and *8*, we load our N-gram extraction functions and use these to extract N-grams from our dataset. These extraction methods are similar to the ones used for binary files, but adjusted for the text format at hand. Initially, we collect the K1=3000 most frequent N-grams in order to reduce the computational load. By increasing the numbers K1 and, later on, K2, we can expect the accuracy of our classifier to improve, but the memory and computational requirements to increase (*Step 9*). In *Step 10*, we define a function to featurize the samples into their N-gram feature vectors, and then, in *Step 11*, we apply this function to featurize our training and testing samples. We would like to narrow down our feature set further. We choose to use mutual information to select the K2=500 most informative N-grams from the K1=3000 most frequent ones (*Step 12*)—there are many options, as discussed in the recipe on selecting the best N-grams.

For instance, an alternative choice would have been to use chi-squared. In addition, other classifiers aside from XGBoost can be chosen. Finally, we see that the accuracy obtained suggests that the approach of using N-grams on the sequence of API calls to be promising.

MalConv – end-to-end deep learning for malicious PE detection

One of the new developments in static malware detection has been the use of deep learning for end-to-end machine learning for malware detection. In this setting, we completely skip all feature engineering; we need not have any knowledge of the PE header or other features that may be indicative of PE malware. We simply feed a stream of raw bytes into our neural network and train. This idea was first suggested in https://arxiv.org/pdf/1710.09435.pdf. This architecture has come to be known as **MalConv**, as shown in the following screenshot:

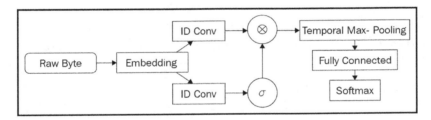

Getting ready

Preparation for this recipe involves installing a number of packages in pip, namely, keras, tensorflow, and tqdm. The command is as follows:

```
pip install keras tensorflow tqdm
```

In addition, benign and malicious files have been provided for you in the PE Samples Dataset folder in the root of the repository. Extract all archives named Benign PE Samples*.7z to a folder named Benign PE Samples, and extract all archives named Malicious PE Samples*.7z to a folder named Malicious PE Samples.

How to do it...

In this recipe, we detail how to train MalConv on raw PE files:

1. We import numpy for vector operations and tqdm to keep track of progress in our loops:

```
import numpy as np
from tqdm import tqdm
```

2. Define a function to embed a byte as a vector:

```
def embed_bytes(byte):
    binary_string = "{0:08b}".format(byte)
    vec = np.zeros(8)
    for i in range(8):
        if binary_string[i] == "1":
            vec[i] = float(1) / 16
        else:
            vec[i] = -float(1) / 16
    return vec
```

3. Read in the locations of your raw PE samples and create a list of their labels:

```
import os
from os import listdir

directories_with_labels = [("Benign PE Samples", 0), ("Malicious PE
Samples", 1)]
list_of_samples = []
labels = []
for dataset_path, label in directories_with_labels:
    samples = [f for f in listdir(dataset_path)]
    for file in samples:
        file_path = os.path.join(dataset_path, file)
        list_of_samples.append(file_path)
        labels.append(label)
```

4. Define a convenience function to read in the byte sequence of a file:

```
def read_file(file_path):
    """Read the binary sequence of a file."""
    with open(file_path, "rb") as binary_file:
        return binary_file.read()
```

5. Set a maximum length, `maxSize`, of bytes to read in per sample, embed all the bytes of the samples, and gather the result in X:

```
max_size = 15000
num_samples = len(list_of_samples)
X = np.zeros((num_samples, 8, max_size))
Y = np.asarray(labels)
file_num = 0
for file in tqdm(list_of_samples):
    sample_byte_sequence = read_file(file)
    for i in range(min(max_size, len(sample_byte_sequence))):
        X[file_num, :, i] = embed_bytes(sample_byte_sequence[i])
    file_num += 1
```

6. Prepare an optimizer:

```
from keras import optimizers

my_opt = optimizers.SGD(lr=0.01, decay=1e-5, nesterov=True)
```

7. Utilize the Keras functional API to set up the deep neural network architecture:

```
from keras import Input
from keras.layers import Conv1D, Activation, multiply,
GlobalMaxPool1D, Dense
from keras import Model

inputs = Input(shape=(8, maxSize))
conv1 = Conv1D(kernel_size=(128), filters=32, strides=(128),
padding='same')(inputs)
conv2 = Conv1D(kernel_size=(128), filters=32, strides=(128),
padding='same')(inputs)
a = Activation('sigmoid', name='sigmoid')(conv2)
mul = multiply([conv1, a])
b = Activation('relu', name='relu')(mul)
p = GlobalMaxPool1D()(b)
d = Dense(16)(p)
predictions = Dense(1, activation='sigmoid')(d)
model = Model(inputs=inputs, outputs=predictions)
```

8. Compile the model and choose a batch size:

```
model.compile(optimizer=my_opt, loss="binary_crossentropy",
metrics=["acc"])
batch_size = 16
num_batches = int(num_samples / batch_size)
```

9. Train the model on batches:

```
for batch_num in tqdm(range(num_batches)):
    batch = X[batch_num * batch_size : (batch_num + 1) *
batch_size]
    model.train_on_batch(
        batch, Y[batch_num * batch_size : (batch_num + 1) *
batch_size]
    )
```

How it works...

We begin by importing `numpy` and `tqdm` (*Step 1*), a package that allows you to keep track of progress in a loop by showing a percentage progress bar. As part of feeding the raw bytes of a file into our deep neural network, we use a simple embedding of bytes in an 8-dimensional space, in which each bit of the byte corresponds to a coordinate of the vector (*Step 2*). A bit equal to 1 means that the corresponding coordinate is set to 1/16, whereas a bit value of 0 corresponds to a coordinate equal to -1/16. For example, 10010001 is embedded as the vector (1/16, -1/16, -1/16, 1/16, -1/16, -1/16, -1/16, 1/16). Other ways to perform embeddings, such as ones that are trained along with the neural network, are possible.

The MalConv architecture makes a simple, but computationally fast, choice. In *Step 3*, we list our samples and their labels, and, in *Step 4*, we define a function to read the bytes of a file. Note the `rb` setting in place of `r`, so as to read the file as a byte sequence. In *Step 5*, we use `tqdm` to track the progress of the loop. For each file, we read in the byte sequence and embed each byte into an 8-dimensional space. We then gather all of these into X. If the number of bytes exceeds `maxSize=15000`, then we stop. If the number of bytes is smaller than maxSize, then the bytes are assumed to be 0's. The `maxSize` parameter, which controls how many bytes we read per file, can be tuned according to memory capacity, the amount of computation available, and the size of the samples. In the following steps (*Steps 6 and 7*), we define a standard optimizer, namely, a stochastic gradient descent with a selection of parameters, and define the architecture of our neural network to match closely with that of MalConv. Note that we have used the Keras functional API here, which allows us to create non-trivial, input-output relations in our model.

Finally, note that better architectures and choices of parameters are an open area of research. Continuing, we are now free to select a batch size and begin training (*Steps 8 and 9*). The batch size is an important parameter that can affect both speed and stability of the learning process. For our purposes, we have made a simple choice. We feed in a batch at a time, and train our neural network.

Tackling packed malware

Packing is the compression or encryption of an executable file, distinguished from ordinary compression in that it is typically decompressed during runtime, in memory, as opposed to being decompressed to disk, prior to execution. Packers pose an obfuscation challenge to analysts.

A packer called VMProtect, for example, protects its content from analyst eyes by executing in a virtual environment with a unique architecture, making it a great challenge for anyone to analyze the software.

Amber is a reflective PE packer for bypassing security products and mitigations. It can pack regularly compiled PE files into reflective payloads that can load and execute themselves like a shellcode. It enables stealthy in-memory payload deployment that can be used to bypass anti-virus, firewall, IDS, IPS products, and application whitelisting mitigations. The most commonly used packer is UPX.

Since packing obfuscates code, it can often result in a decrease in the performance of a machine learning classifier. By determining which packer was used to pack an executable, we can then utilize the same packer to unpack the code, that is, revert the code to its original, non-obfuscated version. Then, it becomes simpler for both antivirus and machine learning to detect whether the file is malicious.

Using packers

In this recipe, we will show how to obtain a packer, namely UPX, and how to use it. The purpose of having a collection of packers is, firstly, to perform data augmentation as will be detailed in the remainder of the recipe, and, secondly, to be able to unpack a sample once the packer used to pack it is determined.

Getting ready

There are no packages required for the following recipe. You may find `upx.exe` in the `Packers` folder of the repository for this book.

How to do it...

In this recipe, you will utilize the UPX packer to pack a file:

1. Download and unarchive the latest version of UPX from `https://github.com/upx/upx/releases/`

2. Execute `upx.exe` against the file you wish to pack by running `upx.exe` and `foofile.exe`. The result of a successful packing appears as follows:

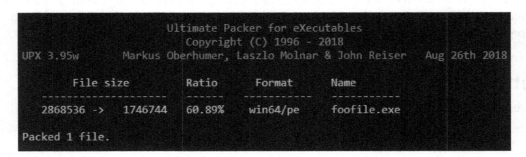

The file remains an executable, unlike in the case of archives, which become zipped.

How it works...

As you can see, using a packer is very simple. One of the benefits of most packers is that they reduce the size of the file, in addition to obfuscating its content. Many hackers utilize custom-made packers. The advantage of these is that they are difficult to unpack. From the standpoint of detecting malicious files, a file that is packed using a custom packer is highly suspicious.

Assembling a packed sample dataset

One obvious way in which to assemble a dataset for a packer classifier is to collect samples that have been packed and whose packing has been labeled. Another fruitful way in which to assemble packed samples is to collect a large dataset of files and then pack these yourself.

Getting ready

There are no packages required for the following recipe. You may find upx.exe in the Packers folder of the repository for this book.

How to do it...

In this recipe, you will use UPX to pack a directory of files.

1. Place upx.exe in a directory, A, and place a collection of samples in a directory, B, in A. For this example, B is Benign PE Samples UPX.

2. List the files of directory B:

```
import os

files_path = "Benign PE Samples UPX/"
files = os.listdir(files_path)
file_paths = [files_path+x for x in files]
```

3. Run upx against each file in B:

```
from subprocess import Popen, PIPE

cmd = "upx.exe"
for path in file_paths:
    cmd2 = cmd+" \""+path+"\""
    res = Popen(cmd2, stdout=PIPE).communicate()
    print(res)
```

4. Whenever an error occurs in packing, remove the original sample:

```
if "error" in str(res[0]):
    print(path)
    os.remove(path)
```

How it works...

The first two steps are preparation for running our UPX packer. In *Step 3*, we use a subprocess to call an external command, namely UPX, in Python. As we pack our samples (*Step 4*), whenever an error occurs, we remove the sample, as it cannot be packed successfully. This ensures that our directory contains nothing but packed samples, so that we can feed in clean and organized data to our classifier.

Building a classifier for packers

Having assembled the labeled data, consisting of packed samples in directories labeled according to the packer, we are ready to train a classifier to determine whether a sample was packed, and, if so, by which packer.

Getting ready

Preparation for this recipe involves installing `scikit-learn` and `nltk` in `pip`. The command is as follows:

```
pip install sklearn nltk
```

In addition, packed and non-packed files have been provided for you in the repository. In this recipe, three types of samples are used: unpacked, UPX packed, and Amber packed. Extract all archives named `Benign PE Samples*.7z` from `PE Samples Dataset` in the root of the repository to a folder named `Benign PE Samples`, extract `Benign PE Samples UPX.7z` to a folder named `Benign PE Samples UPX`, and extract `Benign PE Samples Amber.7z` to a folder named `Benign PE Samples Amber`.

How to do it...

In this recipe, you will build a classifier to determine which packer was used to pack a file:

1. Read in the names of the files to be analyzed along with their labels, corresponding to the packer used:

```python
import os
from os import listdir

directories_with_labels = [
    ("Benign PE Samples", 0),
    ("Benign PE Samples UPX", 1),
    ("Benign PE Samples Amber", 2),
]
list_of_samples = []
labels = []
for dataset_path, label in directories_with_labels:
    samples = [f for f in listdir(dataset_path)]
    for file in samples:
        file_path = os.path.join(dataset_path, file)
        list_of_samples.append(file_path)
        labels.append(label)
```

2. Create a train-test split:

```python
from sklearn.model_selection import train_test_split

samples_train, samples_test, labels_train, labels_test = train_test_split(
    list_of_samples, labels, test_size=0.3, stratify=labels,
random_state=11
)
```

3. Define the imports needed to extract N-grams:

```python
import collections
from nltk import ngrams
import numpy as np
```

4. Define the functions to be used in extracting N-grams:

```python
def read_file(file_path):
    """Reads in the binary sequence of a binary file."""
    with open(file_path, "rb") as binary_file:
        data = binary_file.read()
    return data
```

```
def byte_sequence_to_Ngrams(byte_sequence, N):
    """Creates a list of N-grams from a byte sequence."""
    Ngrams = ngrams(byte_sequence, N)
    return list(Ngrams)


def extract_Ngram_counts(file, N):
    """Takes a binary file and outputs the N-grams counts of its
binary sequence."""
    filebyte_sequence = read_file(file)
    file_Ngrams = byte_sequence_to_Ngrams(filebyte_sequence, N)
    return collections.Counter(file_Ngrams)


def featurize_sample(sample, K1_most_frequent_Ngrams_list):
    """Takes a sample and produces a feature vector.
    The features are the counts of the K1 N-grams we've selected.
    """
    K1 = len(K1_most_frequent_Ngrams_list)
    feature_vector = K1 * [0]
    file_Ngrams = extract_Ngram_counts(sample, N)
    for i in range(K1):
        feature_vector[i] =
file_Ngrams[K1_most_frequent_Ngrams_list[i]]
    return feature_vector
```

5. Pass through the data, and select the N-grams you wish to utilize as your features:

```
N = 2
total_Ngram_count = collections.Counter([])
for file in samples_train:
    total_Ngram_count += extract_Ngram_counts(file, N)
K1 = 100
K1_most_common_Ngrams = total_Ngram_count.most_common(K1)
K1_most_common_Ngrams_list = [x[0] for x in K1_most_common_Ngrams]
```

6. Featurize the training set:

```
Ngram_features_list_train = []
y_train = []
for i in range(len(samples_train)):
    file = samples_train[i]
    NGram_features = featurize_sample(file,
K1_most_common_Ngrams_list)
    Ngram_features_list_train.append(NGram_features)
    y_train.append(labels_train[i])
X_train = Ngram_features_list_train
```

7. Train a random forest model on the training data:

```
from sklearn.ensemble import RandomForestClassifier

clf = RandomForestClassifier(n_estimators=100)
clf = clf.fit(X_train, y_train)
```

8. Featurize the testing set:

```
Ngram_features_list_test = []
y_test = []
for i in range(len(samples_test)):
    file = samples_test[i]
    NGram_features = featurize_sample(file,
K1_most_common_Ngrams_list)
    Ngram_features_list_test.append(NGram_features)
    y_test.append(labels_test[i])
X_test = Ngram_features_list_test
```

9. Utilize the trained classifier to predict on the testing set, and assess the performance using a confusion matrix:

```
y_pred = clf.predict(X_test)
from sklearn.metrics import confusion_matrix

confusion_matrix(y_test, y_pred)
```

The output is as follows:

```
[25]:  from sklearn.metrics import confusion_matrix
       confusion_matrix(y_test, y_pred)

[25]:  array([[64,  2,  0],
              [ 0, 66,  0],
              [ 0,  0, 66]], dtype=int64)
```

How it works...

We start simply by organizing our data and labels into arrays (*Step 1*). In particular, we read in our samples and give them the label corresponding to the packer with which they have been packed. In *Step 2*, we train-test split our data. We are now ready to featurize our data, so we import the requisite libraries for N-gram extraction, as well as define our N-gram functions (*Steps 3* and *4*), which are discussed in other recipes, and, making a simplifying choice of $N=2$ and the $K1=100$ most frequent N-grams as our features, featurize our data (*Steps 5* and *6*). Different values of N and other methods of selecting the most informative N-grams can yield superior results, while increasing the need for computational resources. Having featurized the data, we train-test split it (*Step 7*) and then train a random forest classifier (a simple first choice) on the data (*Step 8*). Judging by the confusion matrix in *Step 9*, we see that a machine learning classifier performs very accurately on this type of problem.

MalGAN – creating evasive malware

Using **Generative Adversarial Networks (GANs)**, we can create adversarial malware samples to train and improve our detection methodology, as well as to identify gaps before an adversary does. The code here is based on **j40903272/MalConv-keras**. The adversarial malware samples are malware samples that have been modified by padding them with a small, but carefully calculated, sequence of bytes, selected so as to fool the neural network (in this case, MalConv) being used to classify the samples.

Getting ready

Preparation for this recipe involves installing the `pandas`, `keras`, `tensorflow`, and `scikit-learn` packages in `pip`. The command is as follows:

```
pip install pandas keras tensorflow sklearn
```

The associated code and resource files for `MalGan` have been included in the repository for this book, in the `MalGan` directory. In addition, assemble a collection of PE samples and then place their paths in the first column of the file:

```
"MalGAN_input/samplesIn.csv"
```

In the second column, type in these samples' verdicts (1 for benign and 0 for malicious).

How to do it...

In this recipe, you will learn how to create adversarial malware:

1. Begin by importing the code for MalGAN, as well as some utility libraries.

   ```
   import os
   import pandas as pd
   from keras.models import load_model
   import MalGAN_utils
   import MalGAN_gen_adv_examples
   ```

2. Specify the input and output paths:

   ```
   save_path = "MalGAN_output"
   model_path = "MalGAN_input/malconv.h5"
   log_path = "MalGAN_output/adversarial_log.csv"
   pad_percent = 0.1
   threshold = 0.6
   step_size = 0.01
   limit = 0.
   input_samples = "MalGAN_input/samplesIn.csv"
   ```

3. Set whether you'd like to use a GPU for adversarial sample generation:

   ```
   MalGAN_utils.limit_gpu_memory(limit)
   ```

4. Read in the csv file containing the names and labels of your samples into a data frame:

   ```
   df = pd.read_csv(input_samples, header=None)
   fn_list = df[0].values
   ```

5. Load the pre-computed MalConv model:

   ```
   model = load_model(model_path)
   ```

6. Use the **Fast Gradient Step Method (FGSM)** to generate adversarial malware:

   ```
   adv_samples, log = MalGAN_gen_adv_examples.gen_adv_samples(model,
   fn_list, pad_percent, step_size, threshold)
   ```

7. Save a log of the results and write the samples to disk:

```
log.save(log_path)
for fn, adv in zip(fn_list, adv_samples):
    _fn = fn.split('/')[-1]
    dst = os.path.join(save_path, _fn)
    print(dst)
    with open(dst, 'wb') as f:
        f.write(adv)
```

How it works...

We start by importing all the MalGAN code that we will be using (*Step 1*). We must specify a few arguments (*Step 2*), to be explained now. The `savePath` parameter is the location into which the adversarial examples will be saved. The `modelPath` variable is the path to the pre-computed weights of MalConv. The `logPath` parameter is where data pertaining to the application of the **Fast Gradient Signed Method** (**FGSM**) to the sample is recorded. For example, a log file may appear as follows:

filename	original score	file length	pad length	loss	predict score
0778...b916	0.001140	235	23	1	0.912

Observe that the original score is close to 0, indicating that the original sample is considered malicious by MalConv. After selecting which bytes to use to pad, the final prediction score is close to 1, indicating that the modified sample is now considered benign. The `padPercent` parameter determines how many bytes are appended to the end of a sample. The `threshold` parameter determines how certain the neural network should be in the adversarial example being benign for it to be written to disk. `stepSize` is a parameter used in the FGSM. That's all for parameters at this stage. We still have another choice to make, which is whether to use a CPU or GPU (*Step 3*). We make the choice of using a CPU in this recipe for simplicity. Obviously, a GPU would make computations faster. The `limit` parameter here indicates how much GPU to use in the computation, and is set to 0. In the next step, *Step 4*, we read in the `.csv` file pointed to by the `inputSamples` parameter. This input log takes a format such as the following:

2b5137a1658c...8	1
0778a070b28...6	0

Here, in the first column, the path of a sample is given, and, in the second column, a label is provided (1 for benign and 0 for malicious). We now load the precomputed MalGAN model (*Step 5*), generate adversarial malware samples (*Step 6*), and then save them onto disk (*Step 7*).

Tracking malware drift

The distribution of malware is ever-changing. Not only are new samples released, but new types of viruses as well. For example, cryptojackers are a relatively recent breed of malware unknown until the advent of cryptocurrency. Interestingly, from a machine learning perspective, it's not only the types and distribution of malware that are evolving, but also their definitions, something known as **concept drift**. To be more specific, a 15 year-old virus is likely no longer executable in the systems currently in use. Consequently, it cannot harm a user, and is therefore no longer an instance of malware.

By tracking the drift of malware, and even predicting it, an organization is better able to channel its resources to the correct type of defense, inoculating itself from future threats.

Getting ready

Preparation for this recipe involves installing the `matplotlib`, `statsmodels`, and `scipy` packages in `pip`. The command is as follows:

```
pip install matplotlib statsmodels scipy
```

How to do it...

In this recipe, you will use a regression on time series to predict the distribution of malware based on historical data:

1. Collect historical data on the distribution of malware in your domain of interest:

```
month0 = {"Trojan": 24, "CryptoMiner": 11, "Other": 36, "Worm": 29}
month1 = {"Trojan": 28, "CryptoMiner": 25, "Other": 22, "Worm": 25}
month2 = {"Trojan": 18, "CryptoMiner": 36, "Other": 41, "Worm": 5}
month3 = {"CryptoMiner": 18, "Trojan": 33, "Other": 44, "Worm": 5}
months = [month0, month1, month2, month3]
```

2. Convert the data into a separate time series for each class of malware:

```
trojan_time_series = []
crypto_miner_time_series = []
worm_time_series = []
other_time_series = []
for month in months:
    trojan_time_series.append(month["Trojan"])
    crypto_miner_time_series.append(month["CryptoMiner"])
    worm_time_series.append(month["Worm"])
    other_time_series.append(month["Other"])
```

The following graph shows the time series for Trojan:

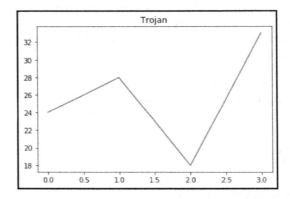

The following graph shows the time series for CryptoMiners:

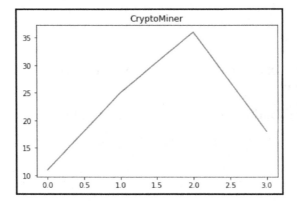

The following graph shows the time series for Worms:

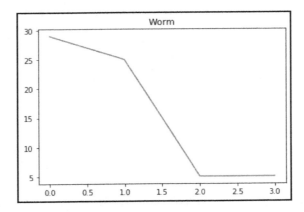

The following graph shows the time series for other types of malware:

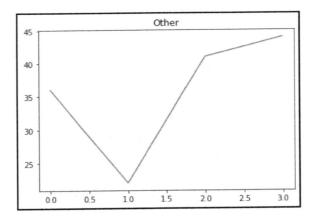

3. Import the moving average from statsmodels:

```
from statsmodels.tsa.arima_model import ARMA
```

4. Predict the following month's distribution based on the time series using the moving average.

```
ts_model = ARMA(trojan_time_series, order=(0, 1))
model_fit_to_data = ts_model.fit(disp=True)
y_Trojan = model_fit_to_data.predict(len(trojan_time_series),
len(trojan_time_series))
print("Trojan prediction for following month: " + str(y_Trojan[0])
+ "%")
```

The result for Trojans is as follows:

Trojan prediction for following month: 21.699999876315772%

We run the same method for Cryptominers:

```
ts_model = ARMA(crypto_miner_time_series, order=(0, 1))
model_fit_to_data = ts_model.fit(disp=True)
y_CryptoMiner = model_fit_to_data.predict(
    len(crypto_miner_time_series), len(crypto_miner_time_series)
)
print("CryptoMiner prediction for following month: " +
str(y_CryptoMiner[0]) + "%")
```

We obtain the following prediction:

CryptoMiner prediction for following month: 24.09999979660618%

In the case of Worms, use the following code:

```
ts_model = ARMA(worm_time_series, order=(0, 1))
model_fit_to_data = ts_model.fit(disp=True)
y_Worm = model_fit_to_data.predict(len(worm_time_series),
len(worm_time_series))
print("Worm prediction for following month: " + str(y_Worm[0]) +
"%")
```

We obtain the following prediction:

Worm prediction for following month: 14.666665384131406%

For other types of Malware, we use the following code:

```
ts_model = ARMA(other_time_series, order=(0, 1))
model_fit_to_data = ts_model.fit(disp=True)
y_Other = model_fit_to_data.predict(len(other_time_series),
len(other_time_series))
print("Other prediction for following month: " + str(y_Other[0]) +
"%")
```

We obtain the following prediction:

Other prediction for following month: 27.400000645620793%

How it works...

For instructive purposes, we produce a toy dataset representing the percentage of each type of malware in time (*Step 1*). With a larger amount of historical data, such a dataset can indicate where to channel your resources in the domain of security. We collect the data in one place and produce visualization plots (*Step 2*). We would like to perform simple forecasting, so we import ARMA, which stands for *autoregressive–moving-average model*, and is a generalization of the moving-average model. For simplicity, we specialize ARMA to **moving average (MA)**. In *Step 4*, we employ MA to make a prediction on how the percentages of malware will evolve to the next time period. With a larger dataset, it is prudent to attempt different models, as well as create a train-test split that accounts for time. This will allow you to find the most explanatory model, in other words, the model that produces the most accurate time forecasts.

4
Machine Learning for Social Engineering

There are a lot of cool new applications of **machine learning (ML)**, and nowhere do these shine as much as they do in social engineering. ML has enabled hugely successful automated spear phishing, as we will learn via a Twitter spear phishing bot recipe. It has also been used to generate fake, but realistic, videos and, at the same time, to discover when these are fake. It offers the ability to voice transfer, detect lies, and many other handy tools that you will see in this chapter's recipes, designed to step up your social engineering game.

This chapter covers the following recipes:

- Twitter spear phishing bot
- Voice impersonation
- Speech recognition for **Open Source Intelligence (OSINT)**
- Facial recognition
- Deepfake
- Deepfake recognition
- Lie detection using ML
- Personality analysis
- Social Mapper
- Training a fake review generator
- Generating fake reviews
- Fake news

Technical requirements

In this chapter, we will be using the following:

- Markovify
- Twitter developer account
- Tweepy
- PyTorch
- OpenCV
- Keras
- TensorFlow
- IBM's Watson

The code and datasets may be found at https://github.com/PacktPublishing/Machine-Learning-for-Cybersecurity-Cookbook/tree/master/Chapter04.

Twitter spear phishing bot

In this recipe, we are going to use machine learning to build a Twitter spear phishing bot. The bot will utilize artificial intelligence to mimic its targets' tweets, hence creating interesting and enticing content for its own tweets. Also, the tweets will contain embedded links, resulting in targets clicking these phishing links. Of course, we will not be utilizing this bot for malicious purpose, and our links will be dummy links. The links themselves will be obfuscated, so a target will not be able to tell what is really hidden behind them until after they click.

Experimentally, it has been shown that this form of attack has a high percentage success rate, and by simulating this form of attack, you can test and improve the security posture of your client or organization.

Getting ready

Preparation for this recipe consists of installing the tweepy and markovify packages in pip. The instructions are as follows:

```
pip install tweepy markovify
```

Also, you will need to set up a developer account on Twitter. The process is relatively simple and account creation is free.

How to do it...

In the following steps, we demonstrate how to use machine learning to create a spear phishing Twitter bot:

1. Set up a developer account on Twitter.
2. Create a new app and obtain your consumer API keys, access token, and access token secret.
3. Import the `tweepy` library and fill in your credentials to access the Twitter API:

```
import json
import tweepy

CONSUMER_API_KEY = "fill me in"
CONSUMER_API_SECRET_KEY = "fill me in"
ACCESS_TOKEN = "fill me in"
ACCESS_TOKEN_SECRET = "fill me in"

auth = tweepy.OAuthHandler(CONSUMER_API_KEY,
CONSUMER_API_SECRET_KEY)
auth.set_access_token(ACCESS_TOKEN, ACCESS_TOKEN_SECRET)

api = tweepy.API(
    auth, wait_on_rate_limit=True, wait_on_rate_limit_notify=True,
compression=True
)
```

4. We select a user we would like to target or imitate. In this case, I chose a prominent figure in technology, active on Twitter:

```
user_id = "elonmusk"
```

5. Collect the user's latest `count = 200` tweets:

```
count = 200
user_tweets = api.user_timeline(screen_name=user_id, count=count,
tweet_mode="extended")
```

6. Collect all of the user's Tweets into one large text:

```
tweet_corpus = []
for tweet in user_tweets:
    tweet_corpus.append(tweet.full_text)
tweets_text = ". ".join(tweet_corpus)
```

7. We now proceed to process the text. We define a function that will replace any found instance of a URL with a new URL:

```
import re

def replace_URLs(string, new_URL):
    """Replaces all URLs in a string with a custom URL."""
    modified_string = re.sub(
        "http[s]?://(?:[a-zA-Z]|[0-9]|[$-_@.&+]|[!*\(\),
]|(?:%[0-9a-fA-F][0-9a-fA-F]))+",
        " " + new_URL + " ",
        string,
    )
    return modified_string
```

8. Create a phishing link and insert it into the tweets. In our case, we used a URL shortener to obfuscate the fact that the link takes a user to `google.com`:

```
phishing_link = "https://urlzs.com/u8ZB"
processed_tweets_text = replace_URLs(tweets_text, phishing_link)
```

9. Train a Markov model on the processed text and generate tweets:

```
import markovify

markov_model = markovify.Text(processed_tweets_text)
```

10. Generate the desired number of tweets that contains the phishing link:

```
num_phishing_tweets_desired = 5
num_phishing_tweets_so_far = 0
generated_tweets = []
while num_phishing_tweets_so_far < num_phishing_tweets_desired:
    tweet = markov_model.make_short_sentence(140)
    if phishing_link in tweet and tweet not in generated_tweets:
        generated_tweets.append(tweet)
        num_phishing_tweets_so_far += 1
```

We will see the following output:

```
Told you AI was dangerous!! 🜂🜔🜚 https://urlzs.com/u8ZB …. @flcnhvy @WorldAndScience Sounds about right.
Area 51 https://urlzs.com/u8ZB 's rapid progress in space!
@hanktheskank34 @joerogan 😳😳. DMT FTW https://urlzs.com/u8ZB …. @flcnhvy @WorldAndScience Sounds about right.
Told you AI was dangerous!! 🜂🜔🜚 https://urlzs.com/u8ZB …. @mortchad @TheOnion I'd love to. obv.
Why aren't more people talking about this!? https://urlzs.com/u8ZB …. @mortchad @TheOnion I'd love to. obv.
```

11. Publish your tweets and target either the user, followers of the user, or friends of the user. For instance, this code obtains the user's friends:

```
user = api.get_user(user_id)
for friend in user.friends():
    print(friend.screen_name)
```

The output we'll see is as follows:

```
wonderofscience
SpaceComCC
AFSpace
Liv_Boeree
shivon
Teslarati
neiltyson
SciGuySpace
wlopwangling
Berger_SN
pewdiepie
CathieDWood
lexfridman
ccsakuras
4thFromOurStar
TheOnion
BBCScienceNews
sciencemagazine
NatureNews
TheStoicEmperor
```

How it works...

In steps 1 and 2, you will want to go onto the Twitter developer web page to create your API account, which will be free. To access the Twitter API through Python, we use the `tweepy` library (step 3). Our goal is to learn from the tweets of a target Twitter user so that our tweets have the same style and topics as that user. Such tweets then form likely bait for anyone interested in the same topics and style. We chose to imitate Elon Musk's style for our tweets (step 4). We proceed to collect the last 200 tweets that Elon has released (steps 5 and 6). Generally speaking, the more tweets from the user you can obtain, the more convincing the model will be. However, it may be important to account for time and relevancy—that is, that users are more likely to click on timely and relevant tweets than those dealing with aged topics.

We define a function to process the text so that all the URLs are replaced with the desired URL (step 7) and then apply it to our text (step 8). We used a URL shortener to hide the destination of the phishing link, which is just Google. There is great room for creativity at this stage of processing the tweets. For instance, we may customize the @ screen names so they are more relevant to our target. In steps 9 and 10, we train a Markov model on the tweets we have processed and then generate several tweets with the phishing link embedded in them. Finally, concerning step 11, keep in mind that other modifications to make the bot more effective include picking the optimal time of day, week, month, or other (for example, event-related timing) to send the tweet or adding photos with links into the tweet.

Voice impersonation

Using the new technology of voice style transfer via neural networks, it is becoming easier and easier to convincingly impersonate a target's voice. In this section, we show you how to use deep learning to have a recording of a target saying whatever you want them to say, for example, to have a target's voice used for social engineering purposes or, a more playful example, using Obama's voice to sing Beyoncé songs. We selected the architecture in `mazzystar/randomCNN-voice-transfer` that allows for fast results with high quality. In particular, there is no need to pre-train the model on a large dataset of recorded audio.

In the accompanying code for this book, you will find two versions of the voice transfer neural network code, one for GPU and one for CPU. We describe here the one for CPU, though the one for GPU is very similar.

Getting ready

Preparation for this recipe consists of installing `pytorch` and `librosa` in `pip`. The instructions are as follows:

```
pip install torch librosa
```

Also, place two files in the `voice_impersonation_input` folder. One file will be an audio recording of the message you would like to vocalize and another file will be the voice in which you would like to vocalize that message.

How to do it...

In the following steps, we provide a recipe for transferring the voice of one speaker to the recording of another speaker. The code is structured in three parts: Voice Impersonation for CPU (main), a model, and utilities. We will discuss how to run the main and explain what it is doing. Whenever a reference occurs to the other parts of the code, we will provide a high-level explanation of what the referenced method does, but leave the details out for the sake of brevity.

The following code can be found in `Voice Impersonation.ipynb`:

1. Import PyTorch utilities, the neural network model, and `math` for some basic computations:

   ```
   import math
   from torch.autograd import Variable
   from voice_impersonation_utils import *
   from voice_impersonation_model import *
   ```

2. Specify the voice we wish to use in `style_file` and the audio we wish to utter in that voice in `content_file`:

   ```
   input_files = "voice_impersonation_input/"
   content_file = input_files + "male_voice.wav"
   style_file = input_files + "Eleanor_Roosevelt.wav"
   ```

3. We extract the spectra of the content and style files and convert these into PyTorch tensors:

```
audio_content, sampling_rate = wav2spectrum(content_file)
audio_style, sampling_rate = wav2spectrum(style_file)
audio_content_torch = torch.from_numpy(audio_content)[None, None,
:, :]
audio_style_torch = torch.from_numpy(audio_style)[None, None, :, :]
```

4. We instantiate a Random CNN model and set it to `eval` mode:

```
voice_impersonation_model = RandomCNN()
voice_impersonation_model.eval()
```

5. We prepare the tensors for the upcoming training of the neural network and select the Adam optimizer and a learning rate:

```
audio_content_variable = Variable(audio_content_torch,
requires_grad=False).float()
audio_style_variable = Variable(audio_style_torch,
requires_grad=False).float()
audio_content = voice_impersonation_model(audio_content_variable)
audio_style = voice_impersonation_model(audio_style_variable)

learning_rate = 0.003
audio_G_var = Variable(
    torch.randn(audio_content_torch.shape) * 1e-3,
requires_grad=True
)
opt = torch.optim.Adam([audio_G_var])
```

6. We specify `style` and `content` parameters and how long we wish to train our model:

```
style_param = 1
content_param = 5e2

num_epochs = 500
print_frequency = 50
```

7. We train our model:

```
for epoch in range(1, num_epochs + 1):
    opt.zero_grad()
    audio_G = voice_impersonation_model(audio_G_var)

    content_loss = content_param *
compute_content_loss(audio_content, audio_G)
```

```
        style_loss = style_param *
compute_layer_style_loss(audio_style, audio_G)
        loss = content_loss + style_loss
        loss.backward()
        opt.step()
```

8. We print the ongoing progress of the training, specify the output file's name, and, finally, convert the neural network's output spectrum into an audio file:

```
if epoch % print_frequency == 0:
    print("epoch: "+str(epoch))
    print("content loss: "+str(content_loss.item()))
    print("style loss: "+str(style_loss.item()))
    print("loss: "+str(loss.item()))

gen_spectrum = audio_G_var.cpu().data.numpy().squeeze()
output_audio_name = "Eleanor_saying_there_was_a_change_now.wav"
spectrum2wav(gen_spectrum, sampling_rate, output_audio_name)
```

The final result of our computation can be seen in the audio file with the name `Eleanor_saying_there_was_a_change_now.wav`.

How it works...

We begin by importing PyTorch, the neural network model, and `math` for some basic computations (step 1). More interestingly, in step 2, we specify content and style audio. In the content file, you can utter whatever phrase you wish, for example, *you can't do cybersecurity without machine learning*. Then, in the style file, you select a recording of someone's voice, for example, a recording of a famous individual such as Elon Musk. The final result of the voice impersonation is that Elon Musk says that *you can't do cybersecurity without machine learning*. Steps 3, 4, and 5 involve some legwork to prepare our data to be fed into our model and then instantiate a Random CNN model and its optimizer. The main feature of the model is that it uses a 2D convolutional layer rather than a 1D layer for the audio spectrogram and it computes `grams` over the time axis. Setting the model to evaluation mode (to be contrasted with training mode) affects the behavior of certain layers, such as dropout and batch norm, that are used differently in training versus testing. In the next step (step 6), we define the `style` and `content` parameters, which assign relative weights to style and content. In particular, these determine how strongly the final audio will inherit the style versus content from the respective files. We are now ready to train our model, which we do in step 7 by performing forward and back propagation. We monitor the progress of the training (step 8), and then finally output an audio file to disk that pronounces the content file using the style of the style file. You may find this file in the repository for this book.

Speech recognition for OSINT

The story goes that a pen tester was performing intelligence gathering on the at-the-time director of the FBI, James Comey. By listening to footage from Comey, the pen tester noted that Comey mentioned having several social media accounts, including a Twitter account. However, at the time, no account of his was known.

Through thorough investigation, the pen tester eventually discovered Comey's secret Twitter account, screen name Reinhold Niebuhr. The goal of this recipe is to help the pen tester to automate and expedite the sifting through large amounts of audio/video footage about a target in the search of keywords. Specifically, we use machine learning to convert speech into text, collect this text, and then search for keywords of interest.

Getting ready

Preparation for this recipe consists of installing the `speechrecognition` package in `pip`. The instructions are as follows:

```
pip install speechrecognition
```

In addition, collect a number of audio files whose speech you would like to recognize.

How to do it...

In the following steps, we show how to use the speech recognition library to convert audio recordings of speech into text and then search through these texts for desired keywords:

1. Import the speech recognition library and select a list of audio files whose speech we wish to convert into text. Also, create a list of keywords you would like to automatically detect in these audio files:

```
import speech_recognition

list_of_audio_files = ["Eleanor_Roosevelt.wav", "Comey.wav"]
keywords = ["Twitter", "Linkedin", "Facebook", "Instagram",
"password", "FBI"]
```

2. Define a function that uses the Google speech recognition API to convert the audio file into text:

```
def transcribe_audio_file_to_text(audio_file):
    """Takes an audio file and produces a text transcription."""
    recognizer = speech_recognition.Recognizer()
    with speech_recognition.AudioFile(audio_file) as audio_source:
        audio = recognizer.record(audio_source)
        return recognizer.recognize_google(audio)
```

3. Convert the audio files into text and create a dictionary to remember which audio file the text came from:

```
audio_corpus = {}
for audio_file in list_of_audio_files:
    audio_corpus[transcribe_audio_file_to_text(audio_file)] =
audio_file

print(audio_corpus)
```

The corpus output is as the following:

```
{"I'm very glad to be able to take part in this celebration dim sum
Direct on human rights day": 'Eleanor_Roosevelt.wav', "have you met
read recently that I'm on Twitter I am not a tweeter I am there to
listen to read especially what's being said about the FBI and its
mission": 'Comey.wav'}
```

4. Search through the corpus of text for the keywords and print out which audio files had those keywords:

```
for keyword in keywords:
    for transcription in audio_corpus:
        if keyword in transcription:
            print(
                "keyword "
                + keyword
                + " found in audio "
                + '"'
                + audio_corpus[transcription]
                + '"'
            )
```

Our run has detected the keyword `Twitter`:

```
keyword Twitter found in audio "Comey.wav"
keyword FBI found in audio "Comey.wav"
```

How it works...

We begin by importing the speech recognition library and selecting a list of audio files whose speech we wish to convert into text. Also, we create a list of keywords we would like to automatically detect in these audio files (step 1). The approach taken, of detecting the utterance of these keywords, can be made more robust through stemming or lemmatization, which effectively accounts for variants of the keywords that have the same meaning. For example, Twitter, Twitted, and Tweet would all be detected if this approach is properly implemented. In step 2, we specify that we will use Google's Speech Recognition API to transcribe the audio. Other speech recognition services, such as pocketsphinx, are available as well. We are now ready to transcribe our audio files, which we do in step 3. Now we have our audio in text format, and it's smooth sailing from here. Simply search for the keywords of interest (step 4). An additional optimization that may be fruitful when the corpus and text grow larger is to print the sentence where the keyword was found, to make it easier to understand the context.

Facial recognition

A facial recognition system is a technology for identifying or verifying a person in images or videos. When performing OSINT on a target or potential targets, a facial recognition system can be invaluable. In this recipe, you will learn how to use the well-developed `face_recognition` Python library.

Getting ready

Preparation for this recipe consists of installing the `face_recognition` and OpenCV packages in `pip`. The instructions are as follows:

```
pip install face_recognition opencv-python
```

In addition, you will want a portrait of an individual and a collection of images through which you would like to search for that individual.

How to do it...

In the following steps, you will train `face_recognition` to find and label a given individual in a series of images:

1. Begin by importing the `face_recognition` library:

   ```
   import face_recognition
   ```

2. Start by loading in a labeled portrait of the individual on which you will perform OSINT:

   ```
   known_image =
   face_recognition.load_image_file("trump_official_portrait.jpg")
   ```

   The face of the individual must be clearly visible:

3. Next, load in an `unknown` image, in which you would like to automatically detect the face of the individual:

   ```
   unknown_image =
   face_recognition.load_image_file("trump_and_others.jpg")
   ```

The individual whose face is being searched for is present in this screenshot:

4. Encode the face of the individual:

```
trump_encoding = face_recognition.face_encodings(known_image)[0]
```

5. Encode the faces of all individuals in the unknown image:

```
unknown_faces = face_recognition.face_encodings(unknown_image)
```

6. Perform a search for the face of the individual:

```
matches = face_recognition.compare_faces(unknown_faces,
trump_encoding)
print(matches)
```

The output is as follows:

```
[False, False, False, True]
```

7. Load the locations of all faces in the unknown image and save the location of the match into a variable:

```
face_locations = face_recognition.face_locations(unknown_image)
trump_face_location = face_locations[3]
```

8. Read in the unknown image into `cv2`:

```
import cv2
unknown_image_cv2 = cv2.imread("trump_and_others.jpg")
```

9. Draw a rectangle on the unknown image for where the matching face is:

```
(top, right, bottom, left) = trump_face_location
cv2.rectangle(unknown_image_cv2, (left, top), (right, bottom), (0,
0, 255), 2)
```

10. Label the rectangle:

```
cv2.rectangle(unknown_image_cv2, (left, bottom - 35), (right,
bottom), (0, 0, 255), cv2.FILLED)
font = cv2.FONT_HERSHEY_DUPLEX
cv2.putText(unknown_image_cv2, "Trump", (left + 6, bottom - 6),
font, 1.0, (255, 255, 255), 1)
```

11. Display the image with the labeled rectangle:

```
cv2.namedWindow('image', cv2.WINDOW_NORMAL)
cv2.imshow('image',unknown_image_cv2)
cv2.waitKey(0)
cv2.destroyAllWindows()
```

The following screenshot shows us that the output has been successful:

It is straightforward to automate this searching and labeling process.

How it works...

Begin simply by importing the facial recognition library (step 1). In the next step, we load the image of the target we wish to locate in a collection of images in our pen test. Next, prepare an example image that we would like to scan for the presence of the target's face (step 3). Encode all found faces in images (steps 4 and 5) and then search for the face of the target (step 6). For convenience, we print out the results of seeking a match with the target's face. In steps 7-10, we wish to demonstrate that we have found a match. To that end, we load the image we have scanned. We then draw a rectangle and a label where our classifier has detected the target's face. Looking at the result in step 11, we see a massive success. We made a successful detection.

In passing, note that the technology behind the `face_recognition` tool is deep learning, and, as a corollary, a search process for faces can be expedited using a GPU.

Deepfake

Deepfake is the technique of using a neural network to take a video or image, superimpose some content onto it, and make the result look realistic. For example, the technique can take a video of Alice saying she supports a movement, and then, replacing Alice with Bob, create a realistic-looking video of Bob saying he supports the movement. Clearly, this technique has deep implications on the trust we can place on videos and images, while also providing a useful tool for social engineers.

In this recipe, we use a Deepfake variant to take the image of the face of one target and realistically superimpose it onto the image of another target's face. The recipe is a refactored and simplified version of the code in the GitHub repository, `wuhuikai/FaceSwap`.

Getting ready

Preparation for this recipe consists of installing `opencv`, `dlib`, and `scipy` in `pip`. The instructions are as follows:

```
pip install opencv-python dlib scipy
```

Also, you will want two images; one is a portrait of an individual and one is an image containing a face. The former face will be transferred onto the latter. A sample has been provided for you in the `deepfake_input` folder.

How to do it...

In the following steps, we provide a recipe for replacing the face of one individual in an image with that of another. The code is structured in five parts: `Deepfake.ipynb` (main), the `deepfake_config` configuration file, `deepfake_face_detection`, `deepfake_face_points_detection`, and `deepfake_face_swap`. Also, a models folder is included.

The following code can be found in `Deepfake.ipynb`:

1. Import `opencv` for image operations and the methods needed to swap faces from the associated code:

```
import os
import cv2
import numpy as np
from deepfake_face_detection import select_face
from deepfake_face_swap import (
    warp_image_2d,
    warp_image_3d,
    mask_from_points,
    apply_mask,
    correct_colours,
    transformation_from_points,
    ProcessFace,
)
```

2. Specify the image containing the face we wish to use in `content_image` and the image where we want the face to be transferred to in `target_image`. Finally, specify where you'd like the result created:

```
content_image = "deepfake_input/author.jpg"
target_image = "deepfake_input/gymnast.jpg"
result_image_path = "deepfake_results/author_gymnast.jpg"
```

In the running example, the source image is a picture of the author's face:

The destination image is a picture of a gymnast mid-performance:

3. Read in the images into `opencv` and then extract the source and destination faces:

```
content_img = cv2.imread(content_image)
destination_img = cv2.imread(target_image)
content_img_points, content_img_shape, content_img_face =
select_face(content_img)
destination_img_points, destination_img_shape, destination_img_face
= select_face(
    destination_img
)
```

4. Compute a transformed version of the source face:

```
result_image = ProcessFace(
    content_img_points, content_img_face, destination_img_points,
destination_img_face
)
```

5. Draw the transformed face into the destination image and write the file to disk:

```
x, y, w, h = destination_img_shape
destination_img_copy = destination_img.copy()
destination_img_copy[y : y + h, x : x + w] = result_image
result_image = destination_img_copy
cv2.imwrite(result_image_path, result_image)
```

The final result of the `deepfake` operation in this example is an image with the gymnast's body and author's face:

By applying the method frame by frame, it can be extended to videos.

How it works...

Begin, as usual, by importing the appropriate libraries (step 1). Specify, in step 2, the style and content images. Here, the content is the target image while the style is the face to draw in. In step 3, note that if there are several faces in the image, a screen will be presented to you asking which of the faces you would like to use. The next step is a computation to determine how to draw the superimposed face (step 4). Having completed this step, we can now draw out and display the `deepfake` superimposed face in step 5. Evidently, this implementation has room for improvement but does an OK job.

Deepfake recognition

With the advent of deepfake and similar image forgery technology, it is becoming more and more difficult to differentiate between forgery and real media. Fortunately, just as neural networks can compose fake media, they can also detect it. In this recipe, we will utilize a deep neural network to detect fake images. The recipe utilizes the MesoNet architecture, found in the GitHub repository, `DariusAf/MesoNet`.

Getting ready

Preparation for this recipe consists of installing `keras`, `tensorflow`, and `pillow` in `pip`. The instructions are as follows:

```
pip install keras tensorflow pillow
```

In addition, a collection of fake and real images has been provided for you in the `mesonet_test_images` folder, to which you may add additional images.

How to do it...

In the following steps, we provide a recipe for detecting when an image is produced by deepfake. The code is structured in four parts: Deepfake `Recognition.ipynb` (main), the `mesonet_classifiers.py` file defining the MesoNet classifier, the `mesonet_weights` folder holding the trained weights, and the `mesonet_test_images` folder containing our test images.

The following code can be found in Deepfake `Recognition.ipynb`:

1. Import the MesoNet neural network and the image data generator from `keras`:

```
from mesonet_classifiers import *
from keras.preprocessing.image import ImageDataGenerator
```

2. Instantiate MesoNet and load its weights:

```
MesoNet_classifier = Meso4()
MesoNet_classifier.load("mesonet_weights/Meso4_DF")
```

3. Create an image data generator to read in images from a directory and specify the path where the unknown images are stored:

```
image_data_generator = ImageDataGenerator(rescale=1.0 / 255)
data_generator = image_data_generator.flow_from_directory(
    "", classes=["mesonet_test_images"]
)
```

The following is the output:

```
Found 3 images belonging to 1 classes.
```

4. Define a dictionary to translate numerical labels to the text labels, `"real"` and `"fake"`:

```
num_to_label = {1: "real", 0: "fake"}
```

In our example, we place three images in the folder, one real and two fake:

Can you tell which ones are which?

5. Running MesoNet reveals the following output:

```
X, y = data_generator.next()
probabilistic_predictions = MesoNet_classifier.predict(X)
predictions = [num_to_label[round(x[0])] for x in
probabilistic_predictions]
print(predictions)
```

The following is the output:

```
['real', 'fake', 'fake']
```

How it works...

As for most recipes, we begin by importing the necessary libraries. We then load up a MesoNet model in step 2, that is, load up its structure and pre-trained weights. For clarity, the architecture may be found in the MesoNet_classifiers file and is given by the following:

```
x = Input(shape = (IMGWIDTH, IMGWIDTH, 3))
x1 = Conv2D(8, (3, 3), padding='same', activation = 'relu')(x)
x1 = BatchNormalization()(x1)
x1 = MaxPooling2D(pool_size=(2, 2), padding='same')(x1)
x2 = Conv2D(8, (5, 5), padding='same', activation = 'relu')(x1)
x2 = BatchNormalization()(x2)
x2 = MaxPooling2D(pool_size=(2, 2), padding='same')(x2)
x3 = Conv2D(16, (5, 5), padding='same', activation = 'relu')(x2)
x3 = BatchNormalization()(x3)
x3 = MaxPooling2D(pool_size=(2, 2), padding='same')(x3)
x4 = Conv2D(16, (5, 5), padding='same', activation = 'relu')(x3)
x4 = BatchNormalization()(x4)
x4 = MaxPooling2D(pool_size=(4, 4), padding='same')(x4)
y = Flatten()(x4)
y = Dropout(0.5)(y)
y = Dense(16)(y)
y = LeakyReLU(alpha=0.1)(y)
y = Dropout(0.5)(y)
y = Dense(1, activation = 'sigmoid')(y)
```

In step 3, we define and use an ImageDataGenerator, a convenient keras object that allows us to perform image processing in one place—in the case at hand, to rescale and normalize the numerical values of pixels. It is hard to tell what the labels 0 and 1 represent. For that reason, for readability purposes, we define a dictionary to translate 0s and 1s into the words, real and fake (step 4). Finally, in step 5, we see that the MesoNet model was able to correctly predict the labels of the test images.

Lie detection using machine learning

When gathering intelligence for social engineering purposes, it is crucial to be able to tell when an individual is telling the truth and when they are lying. To this end, machine learning can come to our aid. By analyzing a video for microexpressions and vocal quality, a machine learning system can help to identify untruthful actors. In this recipe, we will be running through a lie detection cycle, using a slightly modified version of Lie To Me, a lie detection system that uses facial and vocal recognition.

Getting ready

Preparation for this recipe consists of installing several packages in `pip`. The list of packages can be found in the `requirements.txt` file. To install all of these at once, run the following:

```
pip install -r requirements.txt
```

You will need one video file with audio to analyze.

How to do it...

In the following steps, we provide a recipe for analyzing a video for lying behavior:

1. Run the Lie To Me application:

    ```
    Python application.py
    ```

2. Open the portal for Lie To Me by going to the IP address specified, for example, `127.0.0.1:5000`, by opening a web browser and typing this address.

3. Click on **UPLOAD** and select a video you would like to analyze:

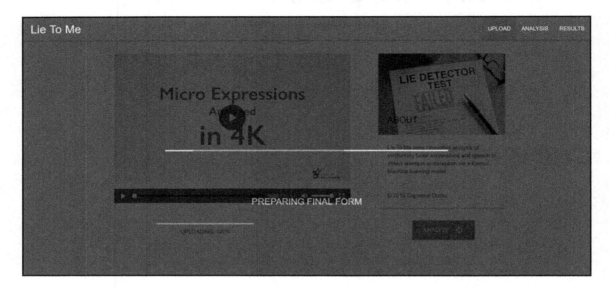

4. Once the analysis is complete, you will notice the following.

The following screenshot shows the variation happening in the **Blink Analysis** graph:

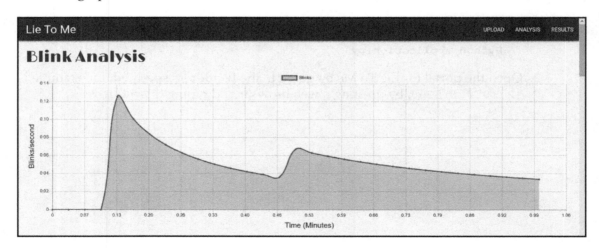

The following screenshot shows the variation happening in the **Micro Expression Analysis** graph:

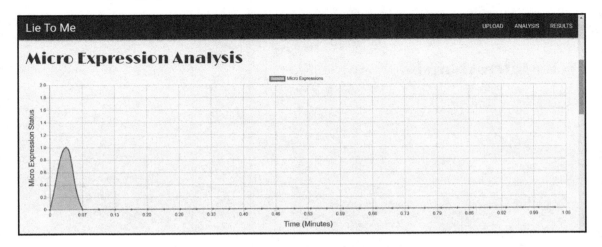

The following screenshot shows the variation happening in the **Voice Energy Analysis** graph:

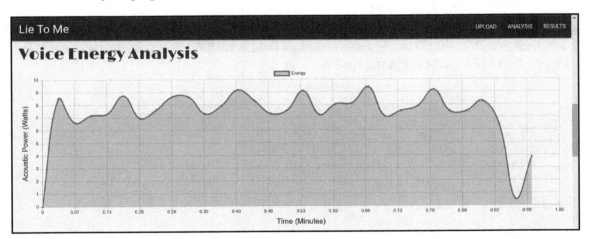

The following screenshot shows the variation happening in the **Voice Pitch Analysis** graph:

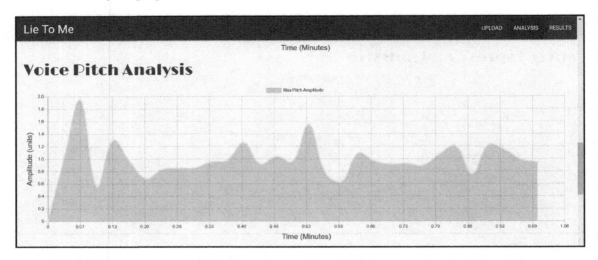

The following screenshot shows the variation happening in the **Voice Pitch Contour Analysis** graph:

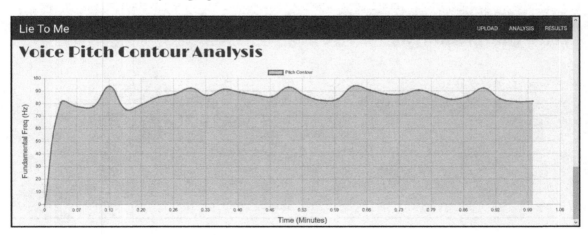

The following screenshot shows the variation happening in the **Vowel Duration Analysis** graph:

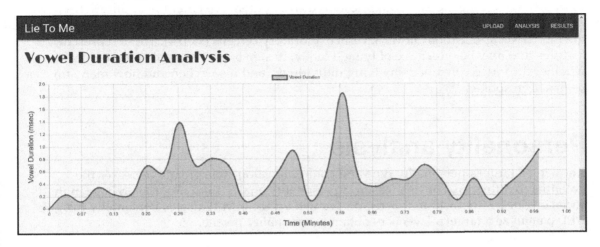

5. Finally, clicking on results shows an analysis of the lies detected in the video:

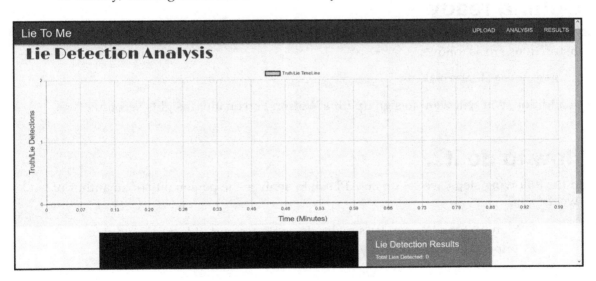

How it works...

In step 1, we run the Lie To Me application using Python. We enter the application's portal and upload a candidate video (steps 2 and 3). Upon completion of the analysis of the video, the Lie To Me application shows several exploratory screens (step 4). These represent features that may be indicative of lying. Finally, in step 5, we see a screen that reveals whether the video contained any lying individuals, and if so, when and how many times a lie has been spoken.

Personality analysis

Knowing a target's personality type and communication style greatly increases the potential to influence. For this reason, a personality analysis is a nice tool to have in the social engineer's toolbelt. In this recipe, we will utilize IBM Watson's Personality Insights API to analyze a target's Tweets to obtain a personality profile.

Getting ready

Preparation for this recipe consists of installing the IBM Watson package in `pip`. The instructions are as follows:

```
pip install ibm-watson
```

In addition, you will want to sign up for a Watson Personality Insights account.

How to do it...

In the following steps, we set up an API call to analyze the personality of an author of tweets:

1. Sign up for a Watson Personality Insights account. It is quick and free.
2. Import the Python library for Watson and record today's date:

   ```
   from ibm_watson import PersonalityInsightsV3
   from datetime import date

   v = str(date.today())
   api_key = "fill me in"
   ```

3. Specify your API key, which you have obtained in step 1, and declare the Personality Insights instance:

```
personality_insights_service = PersonalityInsightsV3(version=v,
iam_apikey=api_key)
```

4. Curate a text file, for example, a collection of tweets:

```
tweets_file = "ElonMuskTweets.txt"
```

5. Call the Personality Insights API on the text file:

```
with open(tweets_file) as input_file:
    profile = personality_insights_service.profile(
        input_file.read(),
        "application/json",
        raw_scores=False,
        consumption_preferences=True,
    ).get_result()
```

6. Finally, print out the personality profile:

```
import json

print(json.dumps(profile, indent=2))
```

```
{ "word_count": 2463, "processed_language": "en", "personality": [
{ "trait_id": "big5_openness", "name": "Openness", "category":
"personality", "percentile": 0.7417085532819794, "significant":
true, "children": [ { "trait_id": "facet_adventurousness", "name":
"Adventurousness", "category": "personality", "percentile":
0.9589655282562557, "significant": true }, { "trait_id":
"facet_artistic_interests", "name": "Artistic interests",
"category": "personality", "percentile": 0.44854779978198406,
"significant": true }, { "trait_id": "facet_emotionality", "name":
"Emotionality", "category": "personality", "percentile":
0.0533351337262023, "significant": true },
 <snip>
 "consumption_preference_id":
"consumption_preferences_books_financial_investing", "name":
"Likely to read financial investment books", "score": 0.0 }, {
"consumption_preference_id":
"consumption_preferences_books_autobiographies", "name": "Likely to
read autobiographical books", "score": 1.0 } ] }, {
"consumption_preference_category_id":
"consumption_preferences_volunteering", "name": "Volunteering
Preferences", "consumption_preferences": [ {
"consumption_preference_id": "consumption_preferences_volunteer",
```

```
"name": "Likely to volunteer for social causes", "score": 0.0 } ] }
], "warnings": [] }
```

How it works...

Start by signing up for a Watson Personality Insights account. There are different tiers for the service, with different limits on API call rates and different prices, but the lowest tier is easy to set up, free, and sufficient enough for this recipe. We save today's date into a variable and import the IBM Watson library (step 2). By specifying the latest date, we are ensuring that we will be employing the latest version of Watson. In the next step, we instantiate IBM Watson personality insights using our API key.

For step 4, we must collate a text dataset produced by the target. It may be helpful to utilize the recipe from the Twitter spear phishing bot to gather a user's Tweets. In step 5, we run the personality insights application on our text set, consisting of Elon Musk's recent tweets. We elected to display the personality profile as a JSON. It is also possible to display in other formats, such as CSV, and details may be found in the personality insights' API documentation. Finally, in step 6, we print a small snippet from the personality profile. As you can see, it even provides actionable insights, such as how likely the target is to agree to volunteer.

Social Mapper

Social Mapper is an OSINT tool that allows you to correlate the multitude of social media profiles of a target using facial recognition. It automatically searches popular social media sites for the target's name and pictures to effortlessly find the user's social media profiles and then outputs the results into a report that you can use to take your investigations further.

The largest benefit of Social Mapper is that by combining name search with image recognition, as opposed to just name search, it can eliminate false positives, saving the social engineer valuable time.

Social Mapper currently supports LinkedIn, Facebook, Twitter, Google Plus, Instagram, VKontakte, Weibo, and Douban.

Getting ready

For this recipe, it is recommended that you prepare a Python 2.7 environment. Social Mapper has been designed to be used on Python 2.7 and may not work with other Python environments. The prerequisites for installation are delineated in `https://github.com/Greenwolf/social_mapper`. Also, you will want to use a Mac or Linux machine for this recipe.

How to do it...

In the following steps, we provide a recipe for using Social Mapper to correlate the social media accounts of an individual:

1. Following the instructions on the GitHub page at `https://github.com/Greenwolf/social_mapper`, install Social Mapper and its prerequisites.

2. Place an image of the face of your target into `Input, Examples/imagefolder/` with the name of the file and the full name of the target:

3. Create throwaway accounts for the social media websites you wish to search your target on. For example, create throwaway Facebook, LinkedIn, and Twitter accounts.

4. Open the `social_mapper.py` file and fill in your throwaway accounts credentials. For instance, you may only be interested in Twitter:

```
global linkedin_username
global linkedin_password
linkedin_username = ""
```

```
linkedin_password = ""
global facebook_username
global facebook_password
facebook_username = ""
facebook_password = ""
global twitter_username
global twitter_password
twitter_username = "FILL ME IN"
twitter_password = "FILL ME IN"
global instagram_username
global instagram_password
instagram_username = ""
instagram_password = ""
global google_username
global google_password
google_username = ""
google_password = ""
global vk_username
global vk_password
```

5. In Terminal, run the command to search for the target's social media profiles:

   Python social_mapper.py -f imagefolder -I ./Input-Examples/imagefolder -m fast -tw

6. Examine the output in the `social_mapper/results-social-mapper.html` file:

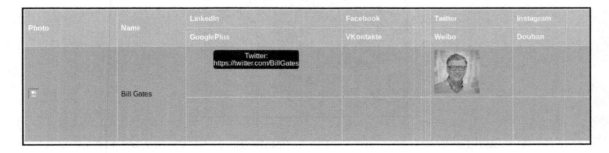

With each target individual, an additional row is added having that individual's social network data.

How it works...

Start by preparing Social Mapper in your environment (step 1). Place an image of your target in the inputs directory (step 2). The image must be named after the target's full name; otherwise, the application will not be able to find the target's accounts. Next, in step 3, create throwaway accounts for the social media websites you wish to search your target on and fill these into the appropriate place in social_mapper.py (step 4). Note that the more different accounts you have, the more data you can gather on the target via Social Mapper. You are ready now to perform the search on the target. In Terminal, run the command to search for the target's social media profiles (step 5). There are many variations on the arguments and options you may wish to use. For instance, we have specified Twitter using the -tw argument. However, you may wish to add in additional social media sites, such as LinkedIn (-li) or Instagram (-ig). Finally, in step 6, observe that Social Mapper was able to find Bill Gates's Twitter account.

Fake review generator

An important part of social engineering is impersonation. A social engineer may want to pretend to represent a company or business that doesn't currently exist. By creating a profile and populating it with convincing reviews, the social engineer can add credibility to the fake business. In this recipe, we show how to train an RNN so that it can generate new reviews, similar to the ones in the training dataset.

Training a fake review generator

Our first step is to train the model. Later, we will utilize it to produce new reviews.

Getting ready

Preparation for this recipe consists of installing keras and tensorflow in pip. The instructions are as follows:

```
pip install keras tensorflow
```

How to do it...

In the following steps, we provide a recipe for training a Recurrent Neural Network (RNN) using a corpus of reviews:

1. Collect the types of reviews you wish to imitate. For more on this, see the discussion in the *How it works...* section:

```
with open("airport_reviews_short.csv", encoding="utf-8") as fp:
    reviews_text = fp.read()
```

2. Create a dictionary to vectorize the characters of the text:

```
chars_list = sorted(list(set(reviews_text)))
char_to_index_dict = {
    character: chars_list.index(character) for character in
chars_list
}
```

The dictionary might look like so, depending on which characters your corpus contains:

```
{' ': 0, '!': 1, '"': 2, '(': 3, ')': 4, ',': 5, '-': 6, '.': 7,
'/': 8, '2': 9, '5': 10, '<': 11, '>': 12, 'A': 13, 'B': 14, 'C':
15, 'D': 16, 'E': 17, 'F': 18, 'G': 19, 'H': 20, 'I': 21, 'J': 22,
'L': 23, 'M': 24, 'O': 25, 'R': 26, 'S': 27, 'T': 28, 'U': 29, 'W':
30, 'a': 31, 'b': 32, 'c': 33, 'd': 34, 'e': 35, 'f': 36, 'g': 37,
'h': 38, 'i': 39, 'j': 40, 'k': 41, 'l': 42, 'm': 43, 'n': 44, 'o':
45, 'p': 46, 'r': 47, 's': 48, 't': 49, 'u': 50, 'v': 51, 'w': 52,
'x': 53, 'y': 54}
```

3. Construct an RNN to learn and predict the sequence of characters:

```
import keras
from keras import layers

max_length = 40
rnn = keras.models.Sequential()
rnn.add(
    layers.LSTM(1024, input_shape=(max_length, len(chars_list)),
return_sequences=True)
)
rnn.add(layers.LSTM(1024, input_shape=(max_length,
len(chars_list))))
rnn.add(layers.Dense(len(chars_list), activation="softmax"))
```

4. Select an optimizer and compile the model:

```
optimizer = keras.optimizers.SGD(lr=0.01, decay=1e-6,
nesterov=True)
rnn.compile(loss="categorical_crossentropy", optimizer=optimizer)
```

5. Define a convenience function to vectorize text:

```
import numpy as np

def text_to_vector(input_txt, max_length):
    """Reads in the text and vectorizes it.
    X will consist of consecutive sequences of characters.
    Y will consist of the next character.
    """
    sentences = []
    next_characters = []
    for i in range(0, len(input_txt) - max_length):
        sentences.append(input_txt[i : i + max_length])
        next_characters.append(input_txt[i + max_length])
    X = np.zeros((len(sentences), max_length, len(chars_list)))
    y = np.zeros((len(sentences), len(chars_list)))
    for i, sentence in enumerate(sentences):
        for t, char in enumerate(sentence):
            X[i, t, char_to_index_dict[char]] = 1
            y[i, char_to_index_dict[next_characters[i]]] = 1
    return [X, y]
```

6. Vectorize our sample input text and train the model in batches:

```
X, y = text_to_vector(reviews_text, max_length)
rnn.fit(X, y, batch_size=256, epochs=1)
```

7. Finally, save the model's weights for future use.

```
rnn.save_weights("weights.hdf5")
```

How it works...

Start by collecting a dataset of reviews you'd like to imitate (step 1). A practical example would require a large corpus of reviews. There are many such datasets available, such as the Yelp reviews dataset. Proceeding to step 2, we create a mapping between characters and numbers. This will allow us to vectorize the text. Depending on your application, you may want to use the standard ASCII code. However, if you are using only a small number of characters, then this will unnecessarily slow down your model. We go on to declare the architecture of an RNN to learn and predict the sequence of characters (step 3). We used a relatively simple architecture. As will be shown in the next section, it nonetheless provides convincing results. The motivated reader is free to experiment with other architectures. Next, we declare a (standard) optimizer (step 4), define a function to take in text, and then vectorize it so we can feed it into our neural network (step 5). In step 5, note the shape of the vectors is as follows:

- **X**: (number of reviews, `maxlen`, **number of characters**)
- **Y**: (number of reviews, number of characters)

In particular, we set `max_length=40` to simplify computation by indicating that we will only be considering the first 40 characters of a review. Having made all the needed preparations, we now pass in our text to be vectorized and then train our model on it (step 6). Specifically, our `text_to_vector` function takes the text and converts it into vectorized sentences, as well as a vectorized label, which is the following character. Finally, we save our model's weights so that we do not have to retrain it in the future (step 7).

Generating fake reviews

Having trained a network, our next step is to utilize it to generate new fake reviews.

Getting ready

Preparation for this recipe consists of installing `keras` and `tensorflow` in `pip`. The instructions are as follows:

```
pip install keras tensorflow
```

How to do it...

In the following steps, we provide a recipe for using a previously trained RNN to generate reviews:

1. We will start by importing `keras`:

```
import keras
from keras import layers
```

2. Create a dictionary of indices for the characters or load up the one from the previous recipe:

```
char_indices = dict((char, chars.index(char)) for char in chars)
```

3. Read in a seed text and declare `max_length` of a sentence taken in by the neural network:

```
text = open("seed_text.txt").read()
max_length = 40
```

4. Construct an RNN model and load in your pre-trained weights:

```
rnn = keras.models.Sequential()
rnn.add(
    layers.LSTM(1024, input_shape=(max_length, len(chars_list)),
return_sequences=True)
)
rnn.add(layers.LSTM(1024, input_shape=(max_length,
len(chars_list))))
rnn.add(layers.Dense(len(chars_list), activation="softmax"))
rnn.load_weights("weights.hdf5")
optimizer = keras.optimizers.SGD(lr=0.01, decay=1e-6,
nesterov=True)
rnn.compile(loss="categorical_crossentropy", optimizer=optimizer)
```

5. Define a function for sampling from a probability vector:

```
import numpy as np

def sample_next_char(preds):
    """Samples the subsequent character based on a probability
distribution."""
    return np.random.choice(chars_list, p=preds)
```

6. Generate random reviews from the initial seed text:

```
import sys

start_index = np.random.randint(0, len(text) - max_length - 1)
generated_text = text[start_index : start_index + max_length]
sys.stdout.write(generated_text)
sentence_length = 1000
for i in range(sentence_length):
    vec_so_far = np.zeros((1, max_length, len(chars_list)))
for t, char in enumerate(generated_text):
    vec_so_far[0, t, char_to_index_dict[char]] = 1.0
preds = rnn.predict(vec_so_far)[0]
next_char = sample_next_char(preds)
generated_text += next_char
generated_text = generated_text[1:]
sys.stdout.write(next_char)
sys.stdout.flush()
print(generated_text)
```

Here is the review output from a run of the code:

```
"<SOR>Very nice atmosphere. I had the burger which was delicious. Also, the chicken curry was the b
est in town.<EOR>"
"<SOR>Amazing! My favorite place to go when your in Vegas! And the breakfast and wine are a definit
e place to eat!<EOR>"
"<SOR>Best pizza in town, crispy and crispy and not crazy about the chocolate level of taste. The b
est part is the location too. Their crepes are amazing!  A must try, best service . We will be retu
rning several times for wonton soups.<EOR>"
"<SOR>The food was fresh and tasty. I was so impressed by the kids and I loved the fresh chsty. I w
as so impressed by the kids and I loved the fresh ch
```

How it works...

Our initial steps (steps 1, 2, and 4) are operations we have performed during the training phase, which we reproduce here to allow the recipe to be self-contained. In step 3, we read in a seed text to initialize our RNN. The seed text can be any text consisting of the listed characters, as long as it is longer than `max_length`. Now, we must be able to create interesting text using our pre-trained, pre loaded, and initialized-on-a-seed-text neural network. To this end, we define a convenience function to sample the consequent character that the neural network will generate (step 5). Sampling from the probability vector ensures that the RNN does not simply select the most likely subsequent character, leading to repetitive generated text. There are more clever ways to sample, employing a temperature parameter and exponential weighing, but this one addresses the basics. Finally, in step 6, we go ahead and generate text using our neural network. We specify 1,000 as the number of characters to generate. Varying this parameter will alter the number of reviews in the output.

Fake news

Fake news is a type of disinformation or propaganda that is spread via traditional news media or online social media. Like any disinformation campaign, its effects can be devastating. In this recipe, you will load a dataset of real and fake news, and utilize ML to determine when a news story is fake.

Getting ready

Preparation for this recipe consists of installing `pandas` and scikit-learn in `pip`. The instructions are as follows:

```
pip install pandas sklearn
```

Also, extract `fake_news_dataset.7z`.

How to do it...

In the following steps, you will read in the fake news dataset, preprocess it, and then train a
Random Forest classifier to detect fake news:

1. Import `pandas` and read in the CSV file, `fake_news_dataset.csv`:

    ```
    import pandas as pd

    columns = [
        "text",
        "language",
        "thread_title",
        "spam_score",
        "replies_count",
        "participants_count",
        "likes",
        "comments",
        "shares",
        "type",
    ]
    df = pd.read_csv("fake_news_dataset.csv", usecols=columns)
    ```

2. Preprocess the dataset by focusing on articles in English and dropping rows with
    missing values:

    ```
    df = df[df["language"] == "english"]
    df = df.dropna()
    df = df.drop("language", axis=1)
    ```

3. Define a convenience function to convert categorical features into numerical:

    ```
    features = 0
    feature_map = {}

    def add_feature(name):
        """Adds a feature to the dictionary of features."""
        if name not in feature_map:
            global features
            feature_map[name] = features
            features += 1
    ```

4. Convert the `"fake"` and `"real"` features into numerical:

    ```
    add_feature("fake")
    add_feature("real")
    ```

5. Define a function that will convert all labels into `real` or `fake`:

```
def article_type(row):
    """Binarizes target into fake or real."""
    if row["type"] == "fake":
        return feature_map["fake"]
    else:
        return feature_map["real"]
```

6. Apply the function to the DataFrame to convert the labels into 0s and 1s:

```
df["type"] = df.apply(article_type, axis=1)
```

7. Create a train-test split on the DataFrame:

```
from sklearn.model_selection import train_test_split

df_train, df_test = train_test_split(df)
```

8. Instantiate two Tf-Idf vectorizers, one for the text of the article and one for its headline:

```
from sklearn.feature_extraction.text import TfidfVectorizer

vectorizer_text = TfidfVectorizer()
vectorizer_title = TfidfVectorizer()
```

9. Fit and transform the text and headline data using the Tf-Idf vectorizers:

```
vectorized_text =
vectorizer_text.fit_transform(df_train.pop("text").values)
vectorized_title =
vectorizer_title.fit_transform(df_train.pop("thread_title").values
```

10. Convert the remaining numerical fields of the DataFrame into matrices:

```
from scipy import sparse

spam_score_train =
sparse.csr_matrix(df_train["spam_score"].values).transpose()
replies_count_train =
sparse.csr_matrix(df_train["replies_count"].values).transpose()
participants_count_train = sparse.csr_matrix(
    df_train["participants_count"].values
).transpose()
likes_train =
sparse.csr_matrix(df_train["likes"].values).transpose()
comments_train =
```

```
sparse.csr_matrix(df_train["comments"].values).transpose()
shares_train =
sparse.csr_matrix(df_train["shares"].values).transpose()
```

11. Merge all of the matrices into one feature matrix and create a set of labels:

```
from scipy.sparse import hstack

X_train = hstack(
    [
        vectorized_text,
        vectorized_title,
        spam_score_train,
        replies_count_train,
        participants_count_train,
        likes_train,
        comments_train,
        shares_train,
    ]
)
y_train = df_train.pop("type").values
```

12. Instantiate a Random Forest classifier and train it on the training data:

```
from sklearn.ensemble import RandomForestClassifier

clf = RandomForestClassifier()
clf.fit(X_train, y_train)
```

13. Transform the text and headlines of the testing data into numerical form using the previously trained Tf-Idf vectorizers:

```
vectorized_text_test =
vectorizer_text.transform(df_test.pop("text").values)
vectorized_title_test =
vectorizer_title.transform(df_test.pop("thread_title").values)
```

14. As before, combine all numerical features into one feature matrix:

```
spam_score_test =
sparse.csr_matrix(df_test["spam_score"].values).transpose()
replies_count_test =
sparse.csr_matrix(df_test["replies_count"].values).transpose()
participants_count_test = sparse.csr_matrix(
    df_test["participants_count"].values
).transpose()
likes_test = sparse.csr_matrix(df_test["likes"].values).transpose()
comments_test =
```

```
sparse.csr_matrix(df_test["comments"].values).transpose()
shares_test =
sparse.csr_matrix(df_test["shares"].values).transpose()
X_test = hstack(
    [
        vectorized_text_test,
        vectorized_title_test,
        spam_score_test,
        replies_count_test,
        participants_count_test,
        likes_test,
        comments_test,
        shares_test,
    ]
)
y_test = df_test.pop("type").values
```

15. Test the Random Forest classifier:

```
clf.score(X_test, y_test)
```

The following is the output:

```
0.9977324263038548
```

How it works...

Our initial steps are to import our dataset of fake news and perform basic data munging (steps 1-6), such as converting the target into a numeric type. Next, in step 7, we train-test split our dataset in preparation for constructing a classifier. Since we are dealing with textual data, we must featurize these. To that end, in steps 8 and 9, we instantiate Tf-Idf vectorizers for NLP on the text and fit these. Other NLP approaches may be fruitful here. Continuing to featurize, we extract the numerical features of our DataFrame (steps 10 and 11). Having finished featurizing the dataset, we can now instantiate a basic classifier and fit it on the dataset (step 12). In steps 13-15, we repeat the process on the testing set and measure our performance. Observe the remarkable performance. Even now, possible steps for increasing the performance of the classifier include accounting for the source of the article, including images, and performing more sophisticated correlations with other events.

5
Penetration Testing Using Machine Learning

A penetration test, aka a pen test, is an authorized simulated cyberattack on an information system, designed to elicit security vulnerabilities. In this chapter, we will be covering a wide selection of machine learning-technologies for penetration testing and security countermeasures. We'll begin by cracking a simple CAPTCHA system. We'll cover the automatic discovery of software vulnerabilities using deep learning, using fuzzing and code gadgets. We'll demonstrate enhancements to Metasploit, as well as covering how to assess the robustness of machine learning systems to adversarial attacks. Finally, we'll cover more specialized topics, such as deanonymizing Tor traffic, recognizing unauthorized access via keystroke dynamics, and detecting malicious URLs.

This chapter covers the following recipes:

- CAPTCHA breaker
- Neural network-assisted fuzzing
- DeepExploit
- Web server vulnerability scanner using machine learning (GyoiThon)
- Deanonymizing Tor using machine learning
- **Internet of Things (IoT)** device type identification using machine learning
- Keystroke dynamics
- Malicious URL detector
- Deep-pwning
- Deep learning-based system for the automatic detection of software vulnerabilities (VulDeePecker)

Technical requirements

In this chapter, we will be using the following:

- TensorFlow
- Keras
- OpenCV
- Google API Client
- Censys
- NetworkX
- Tldextract
- dpkt
- NumPy
- SciPy
- Xlib
- Gensim

The code and datasets can be found at https://github.com/PacktPublishing/Machine-Learning-for-Cybersecurity-Cookbook/tree/master/Chapter05.

CAPTCHA breaker

A **CAPTCHA** is a system intended to prevent automated access or scraping. It does so by asking questions that are meant to recognize when the user is a human and when the user is a program. You have probably seen countless variations of the following screenshot:

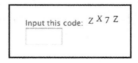

Sometimes, the request is to insert a code, sometimes it is to select some objects, for example, storefronts or traffic lights in a series of images, and sometimes the CAPTCHA is a math question. In this chapter, we are going to break a simple CAPTCHA system, called **Really Simple CAPTCHA**:

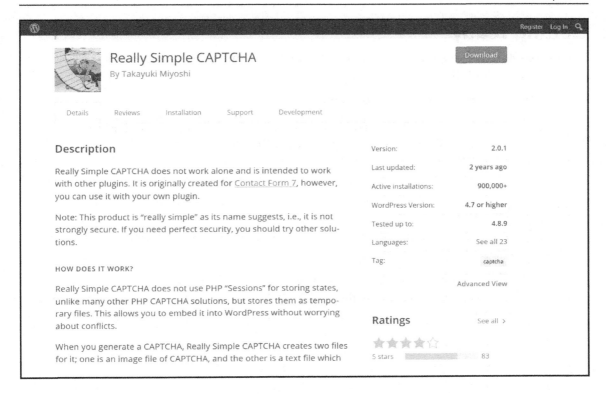

Despite its simplicity, **Really Simple CAPTCHA** is still widely used. Most importantly, it will illustrate how to approach breaking other, more complicated, CAPTCHA systems. The first step will be to process the CAPTCHA dataset so that it is convenient for machine learning. The most naive approach to the problem is likely to fail. Namely, constructing a supervised classifier that takes a four-character CAPTCHA and classifies it into one of the $(26+10)^4 = 1,679,616$ possible classes (26 letters and 10 digits, taken to the fourth power due to the number of possible combinations of four in such a sequence) would require a huge amount of data and computation. Instead, we train a classifier on individual characters, cut the CAPTCHA into individual characters, and then perform classification four times. Here, again, there is a catch, and that is that it is not that easy to precisely crop the characters. Using OpenCV functionality and additional considerations, this recipe will solve this challenge.

Processing a CAPTCHA dataset

In this recipe, we'll perform the first part of creating a CAPTCHA breaker, in which we process a CAPTCHA dataset to make it amenable to training a machine learning model.

Getting ready

The preparation for this recipe consists of installing a number of packages in `pip`. The instructions are as follows:

```
pip install opencv-python imutils
```

In addition, a collection of CAPTCHAs has been included for your convenience in `captcha_images.7z`. To use these, simply extract the archive into a `captcha_images` folder.

How to do it...

In the following steps, we'll process a CAPTCHA dataset to make it amenable to training a machine learning model:

1. Collect a large corpus of CAPTCHAs.
2. Our next goal is to process the CAPTCHAs, specify where the CAPTCHA images are stored and then enumerate all CAPTCHAs in the specified folder:

```
import os

captcha_images_folder = "captcha_images"
captchas = [
    os.path.join(captcha_images_folder, f) for f in
os.listdir(captcha_images_folder)
]
```

3. Define a function that will take the image of a CAPTCHA and produce a grayscale version, as well as a thresholded (that is, black and white) version of the CAPTCHA's image:

```
import cv2

def preprocess_CAPTCHA(img):
    """Takes a CAPTCHA image and thresholds it."""
    gray = cv2.cvtColor(img, cv2.COLOR_BGR2GRAY)
    gray_with_border = cv2.copyMakeBorder(gray, 8, 8, 8, 8,
cv2.BORDER_REPLICATE)
    preprocessed = cv2.threshold(
        gray_with_border, 0, 255, cv2.THRESH_BINARY_INV |
cv2.THRESH_OTSU
    )[1]
    return gray_with_border, preprocessed
```

4. Define a function that will take the path of a CAPTCHA and use it to store the text label of that CAPTCHA:

```
def get_CAPTCHA_label(path_to_file):
    """Get the CAPTCHA text from the file name."""
    filename = os.path.basename(path_to_file)
    label = filename.split(".")[0]
    return label
```

5. Define a function that will take the contours of the CAPTCHA, which we will compute, and then determine their bounding rectangles, in preparation for cropping the CAPTCHA into individual characters:

```
def find_bounding_rectangles_of_contours(contours):
    """Determines the bounding rectangles of the contours of the
cropped letters."""
    letter_bounding_rectangles = []
    for contour in contours:
        (x, y, w, h) = cv2.boundingRect(contour)
        if w / h > 1.25:
            half_width = int(w / 2)
            letter_bounding_rectangles.append((x, y, half_width,
h))
            letter_bounding_rectangles.append((x + half_width, y,
half_width, h))
        else:
            letter_bounding_rectangles.append((x, y, w, h))
    return letter_bounding_rectangles
```

6. Define a function that will take the path of a CAPTCHA, read it in as an image, and then preprocess it using the functions we have defined:

```
def
CAPTCHA_to_gray_scale_and_bounding_rectangles(captcha_image_file):
    """Take a CAPTCHA and output a grayscale version as well as the
bounding rectangles of its cropped letters."""
    image = cv2.imread(captcha_image_file)
    gray, preprocessed = preprocess_CAPTCHA(image)
    contours = cv2.findContours(
        preprocessed.copy(), cv2.RETR_EXTERNAL,
cv2.CHAIN_APPROX_SIMPLE
    )
    contours = contours[0]
    letter_bounding_rectangles =
find_bounding_rectangles_of_contours(contours)
    letter_bounding_rectangles = sorted(letter_bounding_rectangles,
key=lambda x: x[0])
    return gray, letter_bounding_rectangles
```

7. Define another helper function to take the bounding rectangles of contours of letters and produce character images from these:

```
def bounding_rectangle_to_letter_image(letter_bounding_box,
grayscaled):
    """Obtains the letter defined by a bounding box."""
    x, y, w, h = letter_bounding_box
    letter_image = grayscaled[y - 2 : y + h + 2, x - 2 : x + w + 2]
    return letter_image
```

8. Define one last helper function to perform the cropping of a CAPTCHA and then save each cropped character:

```
captcha_processing_output_folder = "extracted_letter_images"
character_counts = {}

def crop_bounding_rectangles_and_save_to_file(
    letter_bounding_rectangles, gray, captcha_label
):
    """Saves the individual letters of a CAPTCHA."""
    for letter_bounding_rectangle, current_letter in zip(
        letter_bounding_rectangles, captcha_label
    ):
        letter_image = bounding_rectangle_to_letter_image(
            letter_bounding_rectangle, gray
        )

        save_path = os.path.join(captcha_processing_output_folder,
current_letter)
        if not os.path.exists(save_path):
            os.makedirs(save_path)

        character_count = character_counts.get(current_letter, 1)

        p = os.path.join(save_path, str(character_count) + ".png")
        cv2.imwrite(p, letter_image)

        character_counts[current_letter] = character_count + 1
```

9. Loop through all of the CAPTCHAs, preprocess them, find the character contours, and then save the corresponding characters:

```
import imutils
import numpy as np

for captcha_image_file in captchas:
    captcha_label = get_CAPTCHA_label(captcha_image_file)
    gray, letter_bounding_rectangles =
CAPTCHA_to_gray_scale_and_bounding_rectangles(
        captcha_image_file
    )
    if len(letter_bounding_rectangles) != 4:
        continue
    crop_bounding_rectangles_and_save_to_file(
        letter_bounding_rectangles, gray, captcha_label
    )
```

How it works...

Our starting point is to collect a large corpus of CAPTCHAs (*step 1*). You can find these in `captcha_images.7z`. Alternatively, since Really Simple CAPTCHA's code is available online, you can modify it to generate a large number of CAPTCHAs. Additional ideas include utilizing bots to scrape CAPTCHAs. Next, in *step 2*, we specify where the CAPTCHA images are stored and then enumerate all CAPTCHAs in the specified folder. Our goal is to begin processing these. In *step 3*, we define a function to threshold and grayscale the CAPTCHA images. This allows us to reduce the computation, as well as making it easier to determine where one character starts and where the next one ends. We then define a function to obtain the label of a CAPTCHA (*step 4*). Continuing, to prepare for processing, we define a utility function that takes the contours of the CAPTCHA and uses them to determine each character's bounding rectangles. Once a bounding rectangle is found, it is easy to crop the character in order to isolate it (*step 5*). Next, in *step 6*, we combine the functions we have defined thus far into one convenient function. We also define an additional function, to actually crop the characters. Putting the above together, in *step 8*, we write a function that will perform the preceding steps, and then save the resulting isolated character, as well as keeping count of how many of each character has been saved. This is helpful for naming, as well as accounting. We are now in a position to perform the cropping, so, in *step 9*, we iterate through all the CAPTCHAs and, using our utility functions, crop individual characters. Note that the `if` statement is meant to skip any incorrectly cropped CAPTCHAs.

At the conclusion of the recipe, your output folder, `extracted_letter_images`, should have a folder for most letters and digits, as shown in the following screenshot:

```
Directory of C:\Users\ETsukerman\Desktop\Machine Learning for Cybersecurity Cookbook Code\Chapter05\extracted_letter_images

04/23/2019  06:17 PM    <DIR>          .
04/23/2019  06:17 PM    <DIR>          ..
04/23/2019  06:19 PM    <DIR>          2
04/23/2019  06:19 PM    <DIR>          3
04/23/2019  06:19 PM    <DIR>          4
04/23/2019  06:19 PM    <DIR>          5
04/23/2019  06:19 PM    <DIR>          6
04/23/2019  06:19 PM    <DIR>          7
04/23/2019  06:19 PM    <DIR>          8
04/23/2019  06:19 PM    <DIR>          9
04/23/2019  06:19 PM    <DIR>          A
04/23/2019  06:19 PM    <DIR>          B
04/23/2019  06:19 PM    <DIR>          C
04/23/2019  06:19 PM    <DIR>          D
04/23/2019  06:19 PM    <DIR>          E
04/23/2019  06:19 PM    <DIR>          F
04/23/2019  06:19 PM    <DIR>          G
04/23/2019  06:19 PM    <DIR>          H
04/23/2019  06:19 PM    <DIR>          J
04/23/2019  06:19 PM    <DIR>          K
04/23/2019  06:19 PM    <DIR>          L
04/23/2019  06:19 PM    <DIR>          M
04/23/2019  06:19 PM    <DIR>          N
04/23/2019  06:19 PM    <DIR>          P
04/23/2019  06:19 PM    <DIR>          Q
04/23/2019  06:19 PM    <DIR>          R
04/23/2019  06:19 PM    <DIR>          S
04/23/2019  06:19 PM    <DIR>          T
04/23/2019  06:19 PM    <DIR>          U
04/23/2019  06:19 PM    <DIR>          V
04/23/2019  06:19 PM    <DIR>          W
04/23/2019  06:19 PM    <DIR>          X
04/23/2019  06:19 PM    <DIR>          Y
04/23/2019  06:19 PM    <DIR>          Z
               0 File(s)              0 bytes
              34 Dir(s)  79,015,010,304 bytes free
```

The reason not all characters and digits are represented is that the CAPTCHAs do not contain the digit 1 and letter I, as the two are easily confused. Similarly for 0 and O. Inside each folder, you will have a large collection of instances of that letter or digit, cropped and processed from the initial CAPTCHAs:

This concludes the preprocessing step.

Training a CAPTCHA solver neural network

Now that our data is nicely processed, we can train a neural network to perform CAPTCHA prediction.

Getting ready

Preparation for this recipe consists of installing a number of packages in pip. The instructions are as follows:

```
pip install opencv-python imutils sklearn keras tensorflow
```

How to do it...

In the following steps, we'll train a neural network to solve Really Simple CAPTCHA's CAPTCHAs:

1. Specify the folder where the extracted letter images are located:

```
captcha_processing_output_folder = "extracted_letter_images"
```

2. Import OpenCV and imutils for image manipulation:

```
import cv2
import imutils
```

3. Define a helper function to resize an image to a given size:

```
def resize_image_to_dimensions(image, desired_width,
desired_height):
    """Resizes an image to the desired dimensions."""
    (h, w) = image.shape[:2]
    if w > h:
        image = imutils.resize(image, width=desired_width)
    else:
        image = imutils.resize(image, height=desired_height)
    pad_width = int((desired_width - image.shape[1]) / 2.0)
    pad_height = int((desired_height - image.shape[0]) / 2.0)
    image_with_border = cv2.copyMakeBorder(
        image, pad_height, pad_height, pad_width, pad_width,
cv2.BORDER_REPLICATE
    )
    image_with_border_resized = cv2.resize(
        image_with_border, (desired_width, desired_height)
    )
    return image_with_border_resized
```

4. Prepare to read in the images:

```
def read_image(image_file_path):
    """Read in an image file."""
    img = cv2.imread(image_file_path)
    img = cv2.cvtColor(img, cv2.COLOR_BGR2GRAY)
    img = resize_image_to_dimensions(img, 20, 20)
    img = np.expand_dims(img, axis=2)
    return img
```

5. Read in each letter image and record its label:

```
import numpy as np
import os
from imutils import paths

images = []
labels = []

for image_file_path in
imutils.paths.list_images(captcha_processing_output_folder):
    image_file = read_image(image_file_path)
    label = image_file_path.split(os.path.sep)[-2]
    images.append(image_file)
    labels.append(label)
```

6. Normalize all images, that is, rescale the pixel values to 0-1 and convert labels to a NumPy array:

```
images = np.array(images, dtype="float") / 255.0
labels = np.array(labels)
```

7. Create a train-test split:

```
from sklearn.model_selection import train_test_split

(X_train, X_test, y_train, y_test) = train_test_split(
    images, labels, test_size=0.3, random_state=11
)
```

8. Import `LabelBinarizer` in order to encode the labels:

```
from sklearn.preprocessing import LabelBinarizer

label_binarizer = LabelBinarizer().fit(y_train)
y_train = label_binarizer.transform(y_train)
y_test = label_binarizer.transform(y_test)
```

9. Define a neural network architecture:

```
from keras.models import Sequential
from keras.layers.convolutional import Conv2D, MaxPooling2D
from keras.layers.core import Flatten, Dense

num_classes = 32
NN_model = Sequential()
NN_model.add(
    Conv2D(20, (5, 5), padding="same", input_shape=(20, 20, 1),
activation="relu")
)
NN_model.add(MaxPooling2D(pool_size=(2, 2), strides=(2, 2)))
NN_model.add(Conv2D(50, (5, 5), padding="same", activation="relu"))
NN_model.add(MaxPooling2D(pool_size=(2, 2), strides=(2, 2)))
NN_model.add(Flatten())
NN_model.add(Dense(512, activation="relu"))
NN_model.add(Dense(num_classes, activation="softmax"))
NN_model.compile(
    loss="categorical_crossentropy", optimizer="adam",
metrics=["accuracy"]
)
NN_model.summary()
```

10. Fit the neural network to the training data:

```
NN_model.fit(
    X_train,
    y_train,
    validation_data=(X_test, y_test),
    batch_size=16,
    epochs=5,
    verbose=1,
)
```

11. Select a CAPTCHA instance you would like to break:

```
CAPTCHA = "captcha_images\\NZH2.png"
```

12. We'll import all of the functions we used to process images in the previous recipe, namely, `find_bounding_rectangles_of_contours`, `preprocess_CAPTCHA`, `get_CAPTCHA_label`, and `CAPTCHA_to_grayscale_and_bounding_rectangles`.

13. Process the CAPTCHA image as we did in the previous recipe:

```
captcha_label = get_CAPTCHA_label(CAPTCHA)
gray, letter_bounding_rectangles =
CAPTCHA_to_gray_scale_and_bounding_rectangles(
    CAPTCHA
)
predictions = []
```

14. Read in each cropped letter and use the neural network to predict the label:

```
for letter_bounding_rectangle in letter_bounding_rectangles:
    x, y, w, h = letter_bounding_rectangle
    letter_image = gray[y - 2 : y + h + 2, x - 2 : x + w + 2]
    letter_image = resize_image_to_dimensions(letter_image, 20, 20)
    letter_image = np.expand_dims(letter_image, axis=2)
    letter_image = np.expand_dims(letter_image, axis=0)
    prediction = NN_model.predict(letter_image)
    letter = label_binarizer.inverse_transform(prediction)[0]
    predictions.append(letter)
```

15. Print out the prediction:

```
predicted_captcha_text = "".join(predictions)
print("Predicted CAPTCHA text is:
{}".format(predicted_captcha_text))
print("CAPTCHA text is:
{}".format(CAPTCHA.split("\\")[-1].split(".")[0]))

Predicted CAPTCHA text is: NZH2
CAPTCHA text is: NZH2
```

How it works...

Having completed our preprocessing of CAPTCHAs in the previous recipe, we are now ready to utilize these to train a CAPTCHA breaker. We start by setting a variable to the path of all of our individual characters extracted from CAPTCHAs. We import the image manipulation libraries we will be using (*step 2*) and then define a function to resize an image in *step 3*. This is a relatively standard method for character recognition, which allows training to proceed faster, and memory utilization to be reduced. In *step 4*, we define a convenience function to read in files as NumPy arrays, for training purposes, and then, in *step 5*, we iterate through all the letters and record their labels. Next, we normalize all of the images (*step 6*), another standard computer vision trick. We now create a train-test split in preparation for fitting our classifier (*step 7*) and then utilize label binarizers to encode our labels (*step 8*). This is necessary since the labels are the characters, which may not be numerical. In *step 9*, we define the architecture of our neural network. The architecture stated is relatively common, and offers both precision and speed. We fit our neural network to the training set in *step 10*. Other parameters can enhance the performance of the network. The hard work is now finished. We now proceed to demonstrate how the CAPTCHA breaker works. In *step 11*, we choose a singleton instance to demonstrate the efficacy of our CAPTCHA breaker. In steps 12-14, we pass this image through our pipeline and produce predicted text for this CAPTCHA. Finally, we verify that the prediction is correct (*step 15*).

Neural network-assisted fuzzing

Fuzzing is a software vulnerability detection method wherein a large number of random inputs are fed into a program in search of ones that will cause a crash, unwanted information leak, or other unintended behavior. In automated fuzzing, a program generates these inputs. Generally, automated fuzzers suffer from the shortcoming that they tend to get stuck trying redundant inputs. For this reason, AI-based fuzzers have recently been developed. In this recipe, we'll employ NEUZZ, a neural network-based fuzzer by She et al. (see `https://arxiv.org/abs/1807.05620`), to find unknown vulnerabilities in software.

Getting ready

The following recipe requires an Ubuntu 16.04 or 18.04 virtual or physical machine. On this device, run the following:

```
pip install keras
```

Extract `neuzz-modified.7z` to a folder of your choosing.

How to do it...

In the following steps, we provide a recipe for using NEUZZ to find crash-causing inputs to the readelf Unix tool:

1. Build neuzz using the following:

```
gcc -O3 -funroll-loops ./neuzz.c -o neuzz
```

If you receive warnings, that's okay.

2. Install the libraries needed for 32-bit binaries:

```
sudo dpkg --add-architecture i386
sudo apt-get update
sudo apt-get install libc6:i386 libncurses5:i386 libstdc++6:i386
lib32z1
```

3. As root, set the CPU scaling algorithm and core dump notification:

```
cd /sys/devices/system/cpu
echo performance | tee cpu*/cpufreq/scaling_governor
echo core >/proc/sys/kernel/core_pattern
```

4. Copy neuzz, nn.py, and afl-showmap to programs/readelf:

```
cp /path_to_neuzz/neuzz /path_to_neuzz/programs/readelf
cp /path_to_neuzz/nn.py /path_to_neuzz/programs/readelf
cp /path_to_neuzz/afl-showmap /path_to_neuzz/programs/readelf
```

5. Provide all files with executable permission:

```
chmod +x /path_to_neuzz/programs/readelf/neuzz
chmod +x /path_to_neuzz/programs/readelf/nn.py
chmod +x /path_to_neuzz/programs/readelf/afl-showmap
chmod +x /path_to_neuzz/programs/readelf/readelf
```

6. Open a Terminal to start the neural network module:

```
cd /path_to_neuzz/programs/readelf
python nn.py ./readelf -a
```

7. Open another Terminal and start NEUZZ:

```
./neuzz -i neuzz_in -o seeds -l 7507 ./readelf -a @@
```

Here is a snippet from running the commands:

8. Test the crashes that NEUZZ has collected by running the following:

```
./readelf -a crash/file_name
```

How it works...

Most popular fuzzers, while effective in some limited situations, often get stuck in a loop. Gradient-based methods, such as the one discussed here, are promising but do not clearly apply to the problem, because real-world program behaviors are not necessarily smooth functions (for example, they can be discontinuous). The idea behind NEUZZ is to approximate the program's behavior as a smooth function using neural networks. Then, it is possible to apply gradient methods to improve fuzzing efficiency. We start our recipe by compiling NEUZZ (*step 1*). The `funroll-loops` flag causes the compiler to unroll loops whose number of iterations can be determined at compile time or upon entry to the loop. As a result, the code is larger, and may run faster, although not necessarily. Continuing to setup NEUZZ, we add in 32-bit support (*step 2*). We set the CPU scaling algorithm and core dump notification (*step 3*); the CPU frequency scaling is a setting that enables the OS to save power by scaling the CPU frequency up or down. In the next two steps, we simply place the files in a convenient location and allow permissions to execute them. We are done setting up NEUZZ. We can now use it to find inputs that cause programs to crash. In *step 6* and *step 7*, we begin the search for crashes using our neural network. After waiting a sufficient amount of time for *step 6* and *step 7* to gather enough inputs to cause the readelf tool to crash, we execute one of these inputs (*step 8*) to see the result. Indeed, we see that the input resulted in readelf crashing.

DeepExploit

DeepExploit is a penetration testing tool that elevates Metasploit to a whole new level by leveraging AI. Its key features are as follows:

- **Deep penetration**: If DeepExploit successfully exploits the target, it will automatically execute the exploit to other internal servers as well.
- **Learning**: DeepExploit is a reinforcement learning system, akin to AlphaGo.

Using DeepExploit to pentest your security systems will take you a long way toward keeping your systems secure. In this recipe, we will set up and run DeepExploit.

Getting ready

You will now be guided through the steps required to install `DeepExploit`:

1. Download and set up Kali Linux. You can find VM images online at `https://www.offensive-security.com/kali-linux-vm-vmware-virtualbox-image-download/`. The following steps all take place in your Kali Linux box.

2. Install Git by running the following in a Terminal:

   ```
   sudo apt install git
   ```

3. Install Python by running the following:

   ```
   sudo apt install python3-pip
   ```

4. Clone the `git` repository. In a Terminal, run the following:

   ```
   git clone
   https://github.com/emmanueltsukerman/machine_learning_security.git
   ```

5. Open the `DeepExploit` directory:

   In a Terminal, run the following:

   ```
   cd machine_learning_security/DeepExploit
   ```

6. Install the prerequisite packages for `DeepExploit`.

   In a Terminal, run the following:

   ```
   pip3 install -r requirements.txt
   ```

How to do it...

In this recipe, you will use `DeepExploit` to compromise a victim virtual machine.

1. Download a `Metasploitable2` VM image.

Details can be found at `https://metasploit.help.rapid7.com/docs/metasploitable-2`.

2. Run a `Metasploitable2` instance on a VM.

3. Obtain the IP address of your `Metasploitable2`.

4. The next step is to set up DeepExploit's configurations.

5. In a Terminal, run `ifconfig` to obtain your Kali Linux's IP. Edit `config.ini` (for example, using `vim`) by setting `server_host` under `[common]` to your Kali Linux IP.

6. Set the values of `proxy_host` and `proxy_port` in `config.ini` to those in `proxychains.conf`.

7. In the Terminal, run `cat /etc/proxychains.conf` and find the value next to `socks4`:

```
...snip...
[ProxyList]
...snip...
socks4   127.0.0.1 9050
```

8. Then, set the values of `proxy_host` and `proxy_port` in `config.ini` equal to these values:

```
vim config.ini
...snip...
proxy_host       : 127.0.0.1
proxy_port       : 9050
```

9. Launch Metasploit in the Terminal by running `msfconsole`.

10. Launch an RPC server on Metasploit. Where indicated, type in your Kali Linux's IP:

```
msf> load msgrpc ServerHost="kali linux ip" ServerPort=55553
User=test Pass=test1234.
```

You should see the following:

```
[*] MSGRPC Service: "kali linux ip":55553
[*] MSGRPC Username: test
[*] MSGRPC Password: test1234
[*] Successfully loaded plugin: msgrpc
```

11. In a Terminal of your Kali Linux machine, run `python3 DeepExploit.py -t "Metasploitable2 ip" -m train` to train `DeepExploit`. The beginning of the training should look as follows:

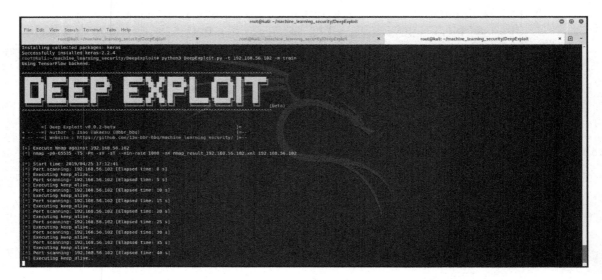

Whenever `DeepExploit` finds a vulnerability, you will see a `BINGO!!!` notification, as in the following screenshot:

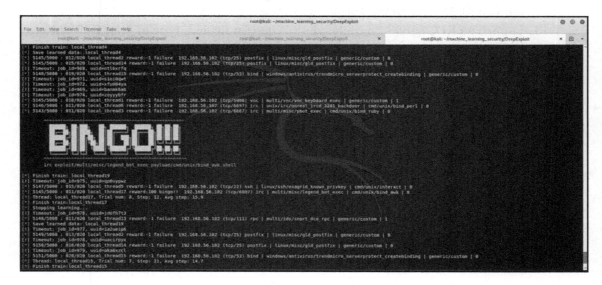

Upon conclusion of the training, the learning is saved. You can see the completion screen here:

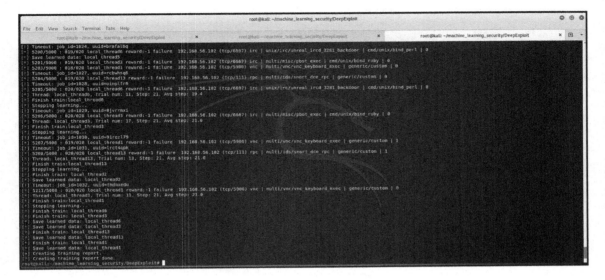

12. Test `Metasploitable2` for vulnerabilities using `DeepExploit`. In a Terminal, run `python DeepExploit.py -t "Metasploitable2 ip" -m test`.

13. Check the report of the pen test as shown:

```
firefox report/DeepExploit_test_report.html
```

We'll get the following as the output:

Index	Item	Value
	Deep Exploit scan Report	
1	IP address	192.168.56.102
	Port number	21
	Source IP address	192.168.56.101
	Product name	vsftpd
	Vuln name	VSFTPD v2.3.4 Backdoor Command Execution
	Type	shell
	Description	This module exploits a malicious backdoor that was added to the VSFTPD download archive. This backdoor was introduced into the vsftpd-2.3.4.tar.gz archive between June 30th 2011 and July 1st 2011 according to the most recent information available. This backdoor was removed on July 3rd 2011.
	Exploit module	exploit/unix/ftp/vsftpd_234_backdoor
	Target	0
	Payload	payload/cmd/unix/interact
	Reference	[OSVDB] 73573 [URL] http://pastebin.com/AetT9sS5 [URL] http://scarybeastsecurity.blogspot.com/2011/07/alert-vsftpd-download-backdoored.html
2	IP address	192.168.56.102
	Port number	25
	Source IP address	192.168.56.101
	Product name	postfix
	Vuln name	GLD (Greylisting Daemon) Postfix Buffer Overflow
	Type	shell
	Description	This module exploits a stack buffer overflow in the Salim Gasmi GLD <= 1.4 greylisting daemon for Postfix. By sending an overly long string the stack can be overwritten.
	Exploit module	exploit/linux/misc/gld_postfix
	Target	0
	Payload	payload/generic/shell_bind_tcp
	Reference	[CVE] 2005-1099 [OSVDB] 15492 [BID] 13129 [EDB] 934

How it works...

This recipe requires a large amount of preparation and configuration. The initial steps are to set up a victim virtual machine (*steps 1 and 2*). In *step 3*, we determine the IP address of the victim VM. Note that the credentials of `Metasploitable2` are `msfadmin/msfadmin`. You can use the credentials to log in and then use `ifconfig` to obtain your `Metasploitable2` IP. If you are using a Kali Linux VM and a `Metasploitable2` VM on the same host, make sure that the two can communicate. For instance, put both VMs on a Host-Only Adapter and ping from your Kali Linux machine to the Metasploitable2 machine. Proceeding, we now configure `DeepExploit` so we can target the victim VM (*steps 4-8*). In *steps 9* and *10*, we open up Metasploit, which is used as a submodule by `DeepExploit`. Metasploit is a major penetration testing framework. Having finished all the preparation, we can now start to train our model. In *step 11*, we train `DeepExploit` on the `Metasploitable2` VM. The model utilizes the **Asynchronous Actor-Critic Agents** (`A3C`) algorithm, released by Google's DeepMind group a few years back, famous for outperforming the `deep Q-network` (`DQN`) approach. Next, we test our model (*step 12*) and print out the results of its analysis in a report (*step 13*). As you can see from the long report, a large number of vulnerabilities were found by `DeepExploit`. Speaking from a high level, the application of reinforcement learning to penetration testing suggests that extremely efficient automated penetration testing is on the horizon.

Web server vulnerability scanner using machine learning (GyoiThon)

GyoiThon is an intelligence-gathering tool for web servers. It executes remote access to a target web server and identifies products operated on the server, such as the **Content Management System** (**CMS**), web server software, framework, and programming language. In addition, it can execute exploit modules for the identified products using Metasploit.

Some of the main features of GyoiThon are as follows:

- **Remote access/Fully automatic**: GyoiThon can automatically gather information on a target web server using only remote access. You only execute GyoiThon once for your operation.
- **Non-destructive test**: GyoiThon can gather information on the target web server using only normal access. A feature permits GyoiThon to access abnormally, such as by sending exploit modules.

- **Gathering varied information**: GyoiThon has a number of intelligence gathering engines such as a web crawler, the Google Custom Search API, Censys, an explorer of default contents, and the examination of cloud services. By analyzing gathered information using string pattern matching and machine learning, GyoiThon can identify a product/version/CVE number operated on the target web server, HTML comments/debug messages, login pages, and other information.
- **Examination of real vulnerabilities**: GyoiThon can execute exploit modules on identified products using Metasploit. As a result, it can determine the real vulnerabilities of the target web server.

Getting ready

You will now be guided through the steps for installing and running GyoiThon:

1. Download and set up Kali Linux. You can find VM images online at `https://www.offensive-security.com/kali-linux-vm-vmware-virtualbox-image-download/`. The following steps all take place in your Kali Linux box.

2. Install `git` in the Terminal by running the following:

   ```
   sudo apt install git
   ```

3. Install `python` in the Terminal by running the following command:

   ```
   sudo apt install python3-pip
   ```

4. Clone the Git repository into your Linux box in the Terminal by running the following command:

   ```
   git clone https://github.com/gyoisamurai/GyoiThon.git
   ```

5. Open the `GyoiThon` directory in the Terminal by running the following command:

   ```
   cd GyoiThon
   ```

6. Install the prerequisites for DeepExploit in the Terminal by running the following:

   ```
   pip3 install -r requirements.txt
   ```

7. (Optional.) Substitute the `Gyoi_CveExplorerNVD` file in modules with the one available in the repository for this book. In some cases, the original code has malfunctioned and the modified code available in the repository for this book may address this problem.

How to do it...

In this recipe, you will use DeepExploit to compromise a victim virtual machine:

1. Download a `Metasploitable2` VM image.
2. Run a `Metasploitable2` instance on a VM.
3. Obtain the IP address of your `Metasploitable2`.
4. In your Kali Linux machine, you should be able to see your `Metasploitable2's` website instance by typing `Metasploitable2's ip address:80` into a web browser:

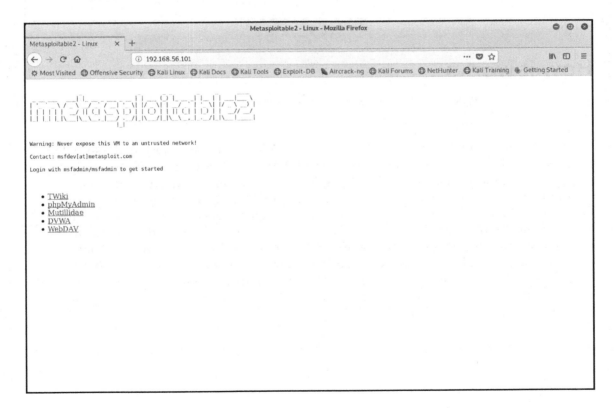

5. In a Terminal, run `ifconfig` to obtain your Kali Linux's IP. Edit `config.ini` (for example, using `vim`) by setting `proxy` to `empty`, `server host` to your `Kali Linux IP`, `LHOST` to your `Metasploitable2 IP`, and `LPORT` to 80.

6. Open the host file and add the `Metasploitable2` web server address by typing in `http:Metasploitable2 ip:80/`.

7. In a Terminal of your Kali Linux machine, run `python3 Gyoithon.py` to begin the attack.

8. Upon the conclusion of the attack, check the report of the pen test in the folder report:

ip_addr	port	cloud_type	method	vendor_name	prod_name	prod_version	prod_trigger	prod_type	prod_vuln	server_header
192.168.56.101	80	Unknown	Crawling	-	-	-	-	-	-	Server: Apache/2.2.8 (Ubuntu) DAV/2
192.168.56.101	80	Unknown	Crawling	php	php	5.2.4	PHP/5.2.4	Language	CVE-2015-8994 CVE-2016-7478 CVE-2008-0599	Server: Apache/2.2.8 (Ubuntu) DAV/2
192.168.56.101	80	Unknown	Crawling	ubuntu	ubuntu_linux	*	(Ubuntu)	OS	CVE-2005-0109 CVE-2004-0882 CVE-2004-0888	Server: Apache/2.2.8 (Ubuntu) DAV/2
192.168.56.101	80	Unknown	Crawling	apache	http_server	2.2.8	Apache/2.2.8	Web	CVE-2016-4975 CVE-2010-0425 CVE-2011-3192	Server: Apache/2.2.8 (Ubuntu) DAV/2

How it works...

Steps 1-3 are no different than in the recipe for DeepExploit, where we prepared a victim VM. The credentials of `Metasploitable2` are `msfadmin/msfadmin`. You can use the credentials to log in and then use `ifconfig` to obtain your `Metasploitable2` IP. If you are using a Kali Linux VM and `Metasploitable2` VM on the same host, make sure that the two can communicate. For instance, put both VMs on a **Host-only Adapter** and ping from your Kali Linux machine to the Metasploitable2 machine. Next, we verify that the environment has been properly set up by checking that we are able to access the victim VM's web page in *step 4*. In *step 5* and *step 6*, we configure GyoiThon in preparation for our pen test. Having finished setting up our environments, we are now ready to perform the pen test. In *step 7*, we utilize GyoiThon to search for vulnerabilities. We then output a full report of the vulnerabilities detected (*step 8*). Looking at the report, we can see that GyoiThon was able to find a large number of vulnerabilities. Having now determined the vulnerabilities of the victim box, we can go ahead and exploit these, using, for example, Metasploit, to hack the victim box.

Deanonymizing Tor using machine learning

Tor is a free, open source software for enabling anonymous communication. In addition, websites accessible only when using the Tor browser exist, and are part of the **dark web** ecosystem – the name given to the part of the internet that is hidden from the average user. In this recipe, we will deanonymize Tor traffic by collecting enough features and information from individual sessions to be able to identify the activity of anonymized users. This recipe utilizes the **conmarap/website-fingerprinting** repository.

Getting ready

You will now be guided through the steps needed to set up Tor and the Lynx web browser:

1. Set up an Ubuntu VM.
2. Install `git` in the Terminal by running the following command:

   ```
   sudo apt install git
   ```

3. Clone the code repository in the Terminal by running the following command:

   ```
   git clone https://github.com/conmarap/website-fingerprinting
   ```

4. Install `tor` and `lynx` in the Terminal by running the following command:

   ```
   sudo apt install tor lynx
   ```

How to do it...

This recipe consists of three parts. The first part consists of the data collection of Tor traffic. The second consists of training a classifier on this data. And the final part consists of using the classifier to predict the type of traffic being observed.

Collecting data

The following steps need to be followed for data collection:

1. List the classes of traffic you wish to classify in `config.json`:

```
et@et-VirtualBox:~/Desktop/website-fingerprinting$ cat config.json
{
  "pcaps": [
    "duckduckgo.com",
    "github.com",
    "jjay.cuny.edu",
    "telegram.org",
    "reddit.com",
    "torproject.org",
    "perdu.com"
  ]
}
```

2. Collect an additional data point for one of the classes, say duckduckgo.com, in a Terminal, from the website-fingerprinting directory by running the following command:

   ```
   ./pcaps/capture.sh duckduckgo.com
   ```

3. Open another Terminal, and run the following command:

   ```
   torsocks lynx https://duckduckgo.com
   ```

   Your two Terminals should look as follows, at this point:

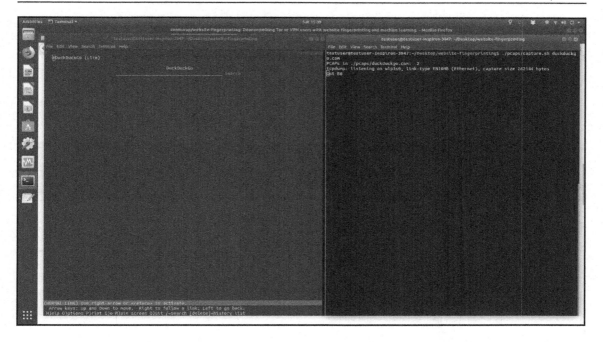

4. Once you have finished the browsing session, end the capture by pressing *Q* twice.

When a sufficient amount of training data has been gathered, we are ready to train a classifier.

Training

To train a classifier on the data, run the following script using Python:

```
python gather_and_train.py
```

The result is a file classifier: nb.dmp.

Predicting

Let's use the classifier to predict the type of traffic being observed:

1. To predict a new instance of traffic, collect the `pcap` file.
2. Using Python, run the `predict.py` script with the `pcap` file as an argument:

```
* Parsing configuration
Loading the classifier...
/home/et/.local/lib/python2.7/site-packages/sklearn/base.py:253: UserWarning: Trying to unpickle estimator KNeighborsClassifier from version 0.20.2 when usi
ng version 0.20.3. This might lead to breaking code or invalid results. Use at your own risk.
  UserWarning)
OUT: 124, IN: 107, TOTAL: 231, SIZE: 25782, RATIO: 0.862903225806
[[1. 0. 0. 0. 0. 0. 0.]]
[1] Prediction: duckduckgo.com
```

The clustering by the author looks like this:

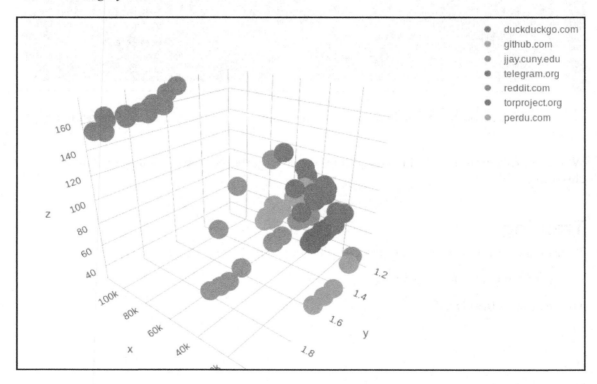

The preceding diagram shows that the features do indeed differentiate between the type of traffic, despite it being anonymous.

How it works...

We start constructing our classifier by creating a catalog of all of the websites we wish to profile (*step 1*). The more there are, the more likely the target is to visit one of these. On the other hand, the fewer there are, the smaller the training dataset will have to be. In *steps 2-4*, we perform the steps required to collect a data point for our classifier. Specifically, we do so by visiting one of the websites defined in *step 1* and then capture the packets for that visit. By repeating these steps for different browsing sessions, we are able to construct a robust dataset. In *step 5*, we train a classifier on our data, which we have collected up until now. We are now ready to test out our classifier. In *step 6*, we visit a website and collect its `pcap`, just as we did when collecting our training data. We then employ the classifier to classify this visit (*step 7*). We see that it did, indeed, correctly determine which web page the user visited, despite the user using Tor.

In summary, in this recipe, scikit-learn was used to write a k-nearest neighbors classifier that would classify Tor `pcap` files. In practice, traffic is never as *clean*, so accuracy is likely to decrease on a real dataset of the same size. However, an entity with large amounts of resources can create a very accurate classifier. This means that it is entirely possible to use a method like this to accurately compromise anonymized users.

IoT device type identification using machine learning

With the advent of IoT, the attack surfaces on any given target have increased exponentially. With new technology comes new risks, and, in the case of IoT, one such risk to an organization is the addition of a malicious IoT device connected to the organization's network. It is essential to be able to tell when such a device has been added to a network and to understand its nature. In this recipe, we'll build a machine learning model to classify network IoT devices by type.

Getting ready

The preparation for this recipe consists of installing the `sklearn`, `pandas`, and `xgboost` packages in `pip`. The instructions are as follows:

```
pip install pandas sklearn xgboost
```

A dataset has been provided for you in the `iot_train.csv` and `iot_test.csv` files.

How to do it...

In the following steps, we'll train and test a classifier on IoT network information:

1. Import `pandas` and `os` and read in the training and testing data:

```
import pandas as pd
import os

training_data = pd.read_csv("iot_devices_train.csv")
testing_data = pd.read_csv("iot_devices_test.csv")
```

The data contains 298 features, as shown in the following screenshot:

	ack	ack_A	ack_B	bytes	bytes_A	bytes_A_B_ratio	bytes_B	ds_field_A	ds_field_B	duration	...	suffix_is_co.il	suffix_is_com	suffix_is_com.sg	suffix_is_
0	9	5	5	1213	743	0.713924	668	0	0	1.5756	...	0	0	0	
1	9	5	5	1213	743	1.806874	668	0	0	0.6890	...	0	0	0	
2	9	5	5	1213	743	0.103124	668	0	0	0.9852	...	0	0	0	
3	9	5	5	1213	743	1.806874	668	0	0	1.5756	...	0	0	0	
4	9	5	5	1213	743	1.806874	668	0	0	1.5756	...	0	0	0	

5 rows × 298 columns

2. Create a training and testing dataset, where the target is the device category:

```
X_train, y_train = (
    training_data.loc[:, training_data.columns !=
"device_category"].values,
    training_data["device_category"],
)
X_test, y_test = (
    testing_data.loc[:, testing_data.columns !=
"device_category"].values,
    testing_data["device_category"],
)
```

The device categories are security camera, TV, smoke detector, thermostat, water sensor, watch, baby monitor, motion sensor, lights, and socket.

3. Encode the class categories into numerical form:

```
from sklearn import preprocessing

le = preprocessing.LabelEncoder()
le.fit(training_data["device_category"].unique())
y_train_encoded = le.transform(y_train)
y_test_encoded = le.transform(y_test)
```

4. Instantiate an `xgboost` classifier:

```
from xgboost import XGBClassifier

model = XGBClassifier()
```

5. Train and test the `xgboost` classifier:

```
model.fit(X_train, y_train_encoded)
model.score(X_test, y_test_encoded)
```

The output is as follows:

```
0.6622222222222223
```

How it works...

An important motivation for this recipe is that we can't rely on the IP address as an identifier of the device, since this value can be spoofed. Consequently, we would like to analyze the traffic's high-level data, that is, the metadata and traffic statistics, rather than content, to determine whether the device belongs to the network. We begin by reading in the training and testing datasets. We go on to featurize these and perform a quick data exploration step by observing the classification labels (*step 2*). To feed these into our classifier, we convert these categorical labels into numerical ones to be used to train our machine learning classifier (*step 3*). Having featurized the data in *step 4* and *step 5*, we instantiate, train and test an `xgboost` classifier, obtaining a score of 0.66 on the testing set. There are 10 categories of IoT devices in the associated data. The baseline of randomly guessing between the 10 would yield an accuracy of 0.1. The XGBoost classifier trained here attains an accuracy of 0.66, suggesting that it is indeed a promising approach to classify IoT devices successfully based on high-level traffic data.

Keystroke dynamics

Keystroke dynamics, aka typing biometrics, is the study of recognizing a person by the way they type. One important use case is recognizing which user is logging in using a given credential, for example, who is logging in as root? Another use case is recognizing when a different user has typed a sequence of keystrokes. In this recipe, we'll show how to use a machine learning-based keystroke dynamics algorithm.

Getting ready

This recipe will require a Linux virtual or real machine. In preparation, do the following:

1. Install `git` on your device.

   In a Terminal, run the following command:

   ```
   sudo apt install git
   ```

2. Clone the `git` repository containing the code for the keystroke dynamics algorithm:

   ```
   git clone
   https://github.com/emmanueltsukerman/keystroke_dynamics.git
   ```

How to do it...

In the following steps, we'll train the model on two users' typing patterns and then use the model to recognize one of the user's typing patterns. The recipe should be run on a Linux virtual or real machine:

1. Run `example.py`:

   ```
   python example.py
   ```

2. Train on the keystrokes of user 1 by selecting option 1 and then typing in the text:

```
et@et-VirtualBox:~/Desktop/keystroke_dynamics-master 2$ python example.py
Choose an option:
  1) create new fingerprint
  2) match text to a existing fingerprint
1


what's your name? Emmanuel
Please write the following text. When you're finished, press Ctrl-C
------------------
Wikipedia is a free-access, free content Internet encyclopedia, supported and hosted by the non-
profit Wikimedia Foundation. Those who can access the site and follow its rules can edit most of
 its articles. Wikipedia is ranked among the ten most popular websites and constitutes the Inter
net's largest and most popular general reference work.
Wikipedia is a free-access, free content Internet encyclopedia, supported and hosted by the non-
profit Wikimedia Foundation. Those who can access the site and follow its rules can edit most of
 its articles. Wikipedia is ranked among the ten most popular websites and constitutes the Inter
net's largest and most popular general reference work.
^C

Finished creating fingerprint!
```

3. Run `example.py` and train on the keystrokes of user 2 by selecting option 1 and then having user 2 type in the text:

```
et@et-VirtualBox:~/Desktop/keystroke_dynamics-master 2$ python example.py
Choose an option:
  1) create new fingerprint
  2) match text to a existing fingerprint
1


what's your name? Bob
Please write the following text. When you're finished, press Ctrl-C
-----------------
Wikipedia is a free-access, free content Internet encyclopedia, supported and hosted by the non-
profit Wikimedia Foundation. Those who can access the site and follow its rules can edit most of
 its articles. Wikipedia is ranked among the ten most popular websites and constitutes the Inter
net's largest and most popular general reference work.
Wikipedia is a free-access, free content Internet encyclopedia, supported and hosted by the non-
profit Wikimedia Foundation. Those who can access the site and follow its rules can edit most of
 its articles. Wikipedia is ranked among the ten most popular websites and consitutes the Intern
et's largest and most popular general reference work.^C

Finished creating fingerprint!
```

4. Run `example.py` and, this time, select option 2.
5. Have one of the users type the text again. The algorithm will match the keyboard dynamics to the most similar typist from the training data:

```
et@et-VirtualBox:~/Desktop/keystroke_dynamics-master 2$ python example.py
Choose an option:
  1) create new fingerprint
  2) match text to a existing fingerprint
2


Please write the following text. When you're finished, press Ctrl-C
-----------------
Wikipedia is a free-access, free content Internet encyclopedia, supported and hosted by the non-
profit Wikimedia Foundation. Those who can access the site and follow its rules can edit most of
 its articles. Wikipedia is ranked among the ten most popular websites and constitutes the Inter
net's largest and most popular general reference work.
Wikipedia is a free-access, free content Internet encyclopedia, supported and hosted by the non-
profit Wikimedia Foundation. Those who can access the site and follow its rules can edit most of
 its articles. Wikiepdia is ranked among the ten most popular websites and constitutes the Inter
net's largest and most popular general reference work.^C

computing similarity for fingerprints:    Fingerprint(Bob)      Fingerprint(NoName)
computing similarity for fingerprints:    Fingerprint(Emmanuel)    Fingerprint(NoName)
Score for Bob: 5.32711338919e-37
Score for Emmanuel: 2.09209471999e-08
Best match:  Emmanuel
```

How it works...

Analyzing keystroke dynamics utilizes the rhythm and pace at which a user types on a keyboard to verify that individual's identity. We begin by setting up some baselines. In *step 1* and *step 2*, we set up the keystroke dynamics system to learn the typing pattern of the first user. We then do the same for the second user (*step 3*). This establishes our *normal* users, as well as their typing patterns. In *step 4* and *step 5*, we utilize our trained model (trained in *steps 1-3*), to determine who the current user is. As you can see, the classifier outputs a similarity score and a prediction of who the current user is from its catalog of saved users. This allows us to detect unauthorized users, as well as to simply keep track of system usage.

Malicious URL detector

Malicious URLs cause billions of dollars of damage every year by hosting spam, malware, and exploits, as well as stealing information. Traditionally, defenses against these have relied on blacklists and whitelists – lists of URLs that are considered malicious, and lists of URLs that are considered safe. However, blacklists suffer from a lack of generality and an inability to defend against previously unseen malicious URLs. To remedy the situation, machine learning techniques have been developed. In this recipe, we'll run a malicious URL detector using character-level recurrent neural networks with Keras. The code is based on `https://github.com/chen0040/keras-malicious-url-detector`.

Getting ready

The preparation for this recipe consists of installing a number of packages in `pip`. The instructions are as follows:

```
pip install keras tensorflow sklearn pandas matplotlib
```

In addition, clone the following `git` repository:

```
git clone
https://github.com/emmanueltsukerman/keras-malicious-url-detector.git
```

How to do it...

1. Train the bidirectional LSTM model:

    ```
    python bidirectional_lstm_train.py
    ```

    The training screen should look something like this:

2. Test the classifier:

    ```
    python bidirectional_lstm_predict.py
    ```

The testing screen should look like the following:

```
C:\Users\ETsukerman\Desktop\Malicious URL Detector\keras-malicious-url-detector>python bidirectional_lstm_predict.py
Using TensorFlow backend.
WARNING:tensorflow:From C:\Users\ETsukerman\AppData\Local\Programs\Python\Python37\lib\site-packages\tensorflow\python\framework\op_def_library.py:263: colocate_with (from tensorflow.python.framework.ops) is
recated and will be removed in a future version.
Instructions for updating:
Colocations handled automatically by placer.
WARNING:tensorflow:From C:\Users\ETsukerman\AppData\Local\Programs\Python\Python37\lib\site-packages\keras\backend\tensorflow_backend.py:3445: calling dropout (from tensorflow.python.ops.nn_ops) with keep_prob
s deprecated and will be removed in a future version.
Instructions for updating:
Please use `rate` instead of `keep_prob`. Rate should be set to `rate = 1 - keep_prob`
2019-04-30 08:42:08.509978: I tensorflow/core/platform/cpu_feature_guard.cc:141] Your CPU supports instructions that this TensorFlow binary was not compiled to use: AVX2
http://naver.com. predicted: 0 actual: 0
http://google.com.hk. predicted: 0 actual: 0
http://reddit.com. predicted: 0 actual: 0
http://newyorkrealestate.eu. predicted: 1 actual: 1
http://siteadvisor.com. predicted: 1 actual: 0
http://google.co.ve. predicted: 0 actual: 0
http://best cv templates.com. predicted: 1 actual: 1
http://ladamejeanne.fr. predicted: 1 actual: 1
http://vube.com. predicted: 0 actual: 0
http://www.docentesentrerrianos.com/coldwellbanker.com/googledoc/index.htm. predicted: 1 actual: 1
http://archive.org. predicted: 1 actual: 0
http://speedtest.net. predicted: 0 actual: 0
http://ikea.com. predicted: 0 actual: 0
http://axebet.com. predicted: 0 actual: 1
http://clickpage.net. predicted: 1 actual: 1
http://clkmon.com. predicted: 0 actual: 0
http://beeg.com. predicted: 0 actual: 0
http://vai.le. predicted: 1 actual: 1
http://google.com. predicted: 0 actual: 0
http://plus.lapvoi.tk. predicted: 1 actual: 1
http://bbc.co.uk. predicted: 0 actual: 0
```

Finally, you can see the results under the `reports` folder:

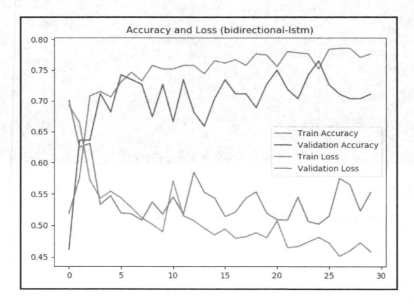

How it works...

This is a relatively simple recipe but serves as a good starting point for a more high-powered malicious URL detector. The dataset consists of URLs with the labels 0 and 1, depending on whether they are malicious or benign:

```
http://google.com, 0
http://facebook.com, 0
http://youtube.com, 0
http://yahoo.com, 0
http://baidu.com, 0
http://wikipedia.org, 0
http://qq.com, 0
http://linkedin.com, 0
http://live.com, 0
http://twitter.com, 0
http://amazon.com, 0
http://taobao.com, 0
http://blogspot.com, 0

<snip>
http://360.cn, 0
http://go.com, 0
http://bbc.co.uk, 0
http://xhamster.com, 0
```

In *step 1*, we train a bidirectional LSTM model. By digging deeper into the code, you can adjust the network to your needs. Having trained our model, it is important to assess its performance and perform some sanity checks. We do so in *step 2*, the testing step, consisting of displaying the results of the classifier on a random selection of 20 URLs. In general, a bidirectional LSTM is a recurrent neural network architecture that shows great promise, due to its ability to remember information and analyze data from both beginning to end, and end to beginning.

Deep-pwning

Deep-pwning is a framework for evaluating the robustness of machine learning tools against adversarial attacks. It has become widely known in the data science community that naive machine learning models, such as deep neural networks trained with the sole aim of classifying images, are very easily fooled.

The following diagram shows Explaining and Harnessing Adversarial Examples, I. J. Goodfellow et al:

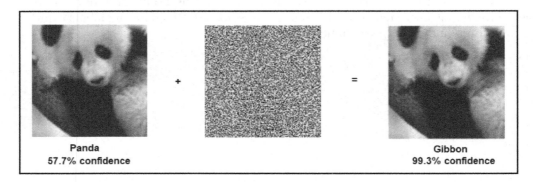

Cybersecurity being an adversarial field of battle, a machine learning model used to secure from attackers ought to be robust against adversaries. As a consequence, it is important to not only report the usual performance metrics, such as accuracy, precision, and recall, but also to have some measure of the adversarial robustness of the model. The deep-pwning framework is a simple toolkit for doing so.

Getting ready

In preparation for this recipe, follow these steps:

1. Install `git` on your device.

2. Download or clone the repository using Git by using the following:

```
git clone https://github.com/emmanueltsukerman/deep-pwning.git
```

3. Install the requirements for the repo.

   In a Terminal, go to the root directory of your repository and run the following command:

```
pip install -r requirements.txt
```

How to do it...

In the following steps, you will utilize deep-pwning to attack LeNet5 on the MNIST digits dataset:

1. From the directory down, run the MNIST driver using the following command:

```
python mnist_driver.py –restore_checkpoint
```

The result should appear like this:

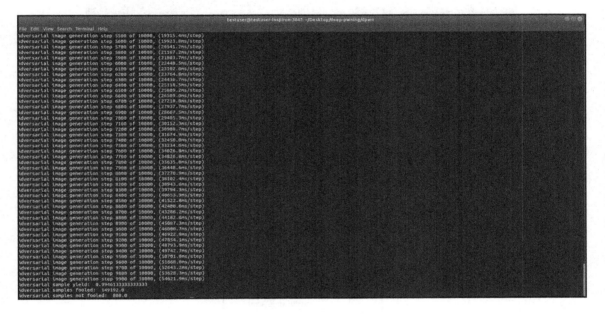

How it works...

In *step 1*, we create a large dataset of adversarial samples; namely, 150,000 adversarial samples are created, almost all of which are able to fool LeNet5 on digits. To examine these adversarial samples, unpickle the pickle in the output directory, like so:

```
File Edit View Search Terminal Help
testuser@testuser-Inspiron-3847:~/Desktop/deep-pwning/dpwn/output/mnist/pickle$ python3
Python 3.6.7 (default, Oct 22 2018, 11:32:17)
[GCC 8.2.0] on linux
Type "help", "copyright", "credits" or "license" for more information.
>>> import pickle
>>> advImagesUnpickle = pickle.load(open("generated-adv-images.pkl","rb"))
>>> advImagesUnpickle.shape
(150000, 11)
>>> advImagesUnpickle.iloc[0]
Adversarial Image              [[[[-0.49], [-0.51], [-0.51], [-0.49], [-0.51]...
Gradient                       [[[[[ 0.0571566 ]\n [-0.21229117]\n [-0.128913...
Gradient Norm                  [[[0.057156596], [0.21229117], [0.12891318], [...
Gradient Step                                                              0.01
Idx                                                                           0
Image                          [[[-0.5], [-0.5], [-0.5], [-0.5], [-0.5], [-0....
Predicted Label                                                               8
Predicted Label Adversarial                                                   8
Predicted Prob                 [[0.023965867, 0.20235294, 0.0024297407, 0.002...
Predicted Prob Adversarial     [[0.019035637, 0.17733964, 0.0020470265, 0.002...
True Label                                                                    7
Name: 0, dtype: object
>>> []
```

Under `utils`, a file named `mnist_read_pickle.py` takes as an argument the `pickle` file. Running it displays one of the adversarial samples. The following image tricks LeNet5 into thinking that it is seeing the number 1:

The deep-pwning framework is designed to be modular, so a user plugs in and modifies pieces to suit their needs. For instance, replacing the MNIST dataset and the LeNet5 architecture.

Deep learning-based system for the automatic detection of software vulnerabilities

Experts in information security can usually identify potentially exploitable pieces of code. Yet, the work is intensive and costly, and may not be sufficient to make a program secure. One of the great advantages of deep learning over traditional machine learning is that features can be automatically discovered. This allows us to alleviate the need for a human expert on vulnerabilities, as well as to produce more effective systems. In this recipe, we'll utilize a modified version of *VulDeePecker : A Deep Learning-Based System for Vulnerability Detection* (https://arxiv.org/pdf/1801.01681.pdf), to automatically detect buffer error vulnerabilities and resource management errors in C/C++ software.

Getting ready

The preparation for this recipe consists of installing the pandas, gensim, keras, tensorflow, and sklearn packages in pip. The instructions are as follows:

```
pip install pandas gensim keras tensorflow sklearn
```

In addition, for this recipe, clone the repository for VulDeePecker:

1. Install git and then, in a Terminal, run the following command:

```
git clone
https://github.com/emmanueltsukerman/Deep-Learning-Based-System-for
-Automatic-Detection-of-Software-Vulnerabilities.git
```

Two datasets are available in the datasets folder, cwe119_cgd.7z and cwe399_cgd.7z. If you wish to use them for this recipe, extract them.

How to do it...

1. Collect a training dataset of gadgets and place it under `datasets`. Two datasets are available in the `datasets` folder, and they are of this form:

```
cwe119_cgd - Notepad                                                    —   □   ×
File  Edit  Format  View  Help
1 CVE-2010-1444/vlc_media_player_1.1.0_CVE-2010-1444_zipstream.c cfunc 449
ZIP_FILENAME_LEN, NULL, 0, NULL, 0 )
char *psz_fileName = calloc( ZIP_FILENAME_LEN, 1 );
if( unzGetCurrentFileInfo( file, p_fileInfo, psz_fileName,
vlc_array_append( p_filenames, strdup( psz_fileName ) );
free( psz_fileName );
0
----------------------------------
2 CVE-2010-1444/vlc_media_player_1.1.0_CVE-2010-1444_zipstream.c cppfunc 449
char *psz_fileName = calloc( ZIP_FILENAME_LEN, 1 );
ZIP_FILENAME_LEN, NULL, 0, NULL, 0 )
if( unzGetCurrentFileInfo( file, p_fileInfo, psz_fileName,
vlc_array_append( p_filenames, strdup( psz_fileName ) );
free( psz_fileName );
0
----------------------------------
3 CVE-2011-2896/cups_1.4.2_CVE-2011-2896_image-gif.c inputfunc 100
fread(buf, 13, 1, fp);
img->xsize = (buf[7] << 8) | buf[6];
img->ysize = (buf[9] << 8) | buf[8];
ncolors    = 2 << (buf[10] & 0x07);
if (buf[10] & GIF_COLORMAP)
if (gif_read_cmap(fp, ncolors, cmap, &gray))
switch (getc(fp))
fclose(fp);
buf[0] = getc(fp);
if (buf[0] == 0xf9)
gif_get_block(fp, buf);
fread(buf, 9, 1, fp);
if (buf[8] & GIF_COLORMAP)
ncolors = 2 << (buf[8] & 0x07);
if (gif_read_cmap(fp, ncolors, cmap, &gray))
img->xsize = (buf[5] << 8) | buf[4];
img->ysize = (buf[7] << 8) | buf[6];
if (img->xsize == 0 || img->ysize == 0)
img->xsize, img->ysize);
fprintf(stderr, "DEBUG: Bad GIF image dimensions: %dx%d\n",
fclose(fp);
i = gif_read_image(fp, img, cmap, buf[8] & GIF_INTERLACE);
int interlace);
i = gif_read_image(fp, img, cmap, buf[8] & GIF_INTERLACE);
static int     gif_read_cmap(FILE *fp, int ncolors, gif_cmap_t cmap,
fclose(fp);
```

2. Train and test the deep learning model on your dataset.

This is accomplished by running the following command:

```
python vuldeepecker_train.py "path to dataset"
```

The output is displayed in the following screenshot:

3. Collect the dataset you would like to predict on and place it under `datasets`:

```
some_gadgets - Notepad
File  Edit  Format  View  Help
4 CVE-2013-1706/Firefox_22.0b6_CVE_2013_1706_toolkit_components_maintenanceservice_workmonitor.cpp cppfunc 111
WCHAR installDir[MAX_PATH + 1] = {L'\0'};
if (!GetInstallationDir(argc, argv, installDir)) {
GetInstallationDir(int argcTmp, LPWSTR *argvTmp, WCHAR aResultDir[MAX_PATH + 1])
wcsncpy(aResultDir, argvTmp[2], MAX_PATH);
WCHAR* backSlash = wcsrchr(aResultDir, L'\\');
0
--------------------------------
5 CVE-2013-1732/Firefox_20.0.1_CVE_2013_1732_layout_generic_nsBlockFrame.cpp cfunc 196
DumpStyleGeneaology(nsIFrame* aFrame, const char* gap)
nsFrame::ListTag(stdout, aFrame);
nsStyleContext* sc = aFrame->GetStyleContext();
printf("%p ", sc);
psc = sc->GetParent();
sc = psc;
printf("%p ", sc);
0
--------------------------------
```

4. Use your trained model to predict whether these are vulnerable pieces of code by running the following command:

```
python vuldeepecker_predict.py "path to data" "path to model"
```

C:\Users\ETsukerman\Desktop\Machine Learning for Cybersecurity Cookbook Code\Chapter05\Deep Learning-Based System for Automatic Detection of Software Vulnerabilities>python vuldeepecker_predict.py datasets\some_gadgets.txt cwe119_cpd_model.h5
Using TensorFlow backend.
Found 0 forward slices and 2 backward slices

Training model...
Processing gadgets... 2
WARNING:tensorflow:From C:\Users\ETsukerman\AppData\Local\Programs\Python\Python37\lib\site-packages\tensorflow\python\framework\op_def_library.py:263: colocate_with (from tensorflow.python.framework.ops) is deprecated and will be removed in a future version.
Instructions for updating:
Colocations handled automatically by placer.
WARNING:tensorflow:From C:\Users\ETsukerman\AppData\Local\Programs\Python\Python37\lib\site-packages\keras\backend\tensorflow_backend.py:3445: calling dropout (from tensorflow.python.ops.nn_ops) with keep_prob is deprecated and will be removed in a future version.
Instructions for updating:
Please use `rate` instead of `keep_prob`. Rate should be set to `rate = 1 - keep_prob`.
2019-05-09 12:21:57.663411: I tensorflow/core/platform/cpu_feature_guard.cc:141] Your CPU supports instructions that this TensorFlow binary was not compiled to use: AVX2
[[1. 0.]
 [1. 0.]]

How it works...

For machine learning to work for vulnerability detection, you need to find representations of the software programs that are amenable to learning. For this purpose, we use code gadgets, which are transformed into vectors. A code gadget is a selection of lines of code that are semantically related to each other. In *step 1*, we collect such code gadgets for training. You can see an image of three code gadgets, along with labels. Here, a label of 1 indicates a vulnerability, while a label of 0 indicates no vulnerability. To extract gadgets from the desired program, it is advised to use the commercial product Checkmarx to extract program slices, and then assemble them into code gadgets. Another dataset is available. That dataset, `cwe-119`, corresponds to buffer error vulnerabilities. Next, we train a deep learning model on our vulnerability dataset (*step 2*). The deep learning model used is a **Bidirectional Long Short-Term Memory (BLSTM)**, whose architecture is given as follows:

```
Bidirectional(LSTM(300), input_shape=(50, 50))
Dense(300)
LeakyReLU()
Dropout(0.5)
Dense(300)
LeakyReLU()
Dropout(0.5)
Dense(2, activation='softmax')
Adamax(lr=0.002)
'categorical_crossentropy'
```

Note that the training phase automatically saves the model as `[base-name-of-training-dataset]_model.h5`. We are now ready to look for new vulnerabilities. So, we place a testing set in `datasets` (*step 3*) and then put our neural network to use by predicting vulnerabilities in this new set (*step 4*).

Automatic Intrusion Detection **6**

An intrusion detection system monitors a network or a collection of systems for malicious activity or policy violations. Any malicious activity or violation caught is stopped or reported. In this chapter, we will design and implement several intrusion detection systems using machine learning. We will begin with the classical problem of detecting spam email. We will then move on to classifying malicious URLs. We will take a brief detour to explain how to capture network traffic, so that we may tackle more challenging network problems, such as botnet and DDoS detection. We will construct a classifier for insider threats. Finally, we will address the example-dependent, cost-sensitive, radically imbalanced, and challenging problem of credit card fraud.

This chapter contains the following recipes:

- Spam filtering using machine learning
- Phishing URL detection
- Capturing network traffic
- Network behavior anomaly detection
- Botnet traffic detection
- Feature engineering for insider threat detection
- Employing anomaly detection for insider threats
- Detecting DDoS
- Credit card fraud detection
- Counterfeit bank note detection
- Ad blocking using machine learning
- Wireless indoor localization

Technical requirements

The following are the technical prerequisites for this chapter:

- Wireshark
- PyShark
- costcla
- scikit-learn
- pandas
- NumPy

Code and datasets may be found at `https://github.com/PacktPublishing/Machine-Learning-for-Cybersecurity-Cookbook/tree/master/Chapter06`.

Spam filtering using machine learning

Spam mails (unwanted mails) constitute around 60% of global email traffic. Aside from the fact that spam detection software has progressed since the first spam message in 1978, anyone with an email account knows that spam continues to be a time-consuming and expensive problem. Here, we provide a recipe for spam-ham (non-spam) classification using machine learning.

Getting ready

Preparation for this recipe involves installing the `scikit-learn` package in `pip`. The command is as follows:

```
pip install sklearn
```

In addition, extract `spamassassin-public-corpus.7z` into a folder named `spamassassin-public-corpus`.

How to do it...

In the following steps, we build a classifier for wanted and unwanted email:

1. Unzip the `spamassassin-public-corpus.7z` dataset.

2. Specify the path of your `spam` and `ham` directories:

```
import os

spam_emails_path = os.path.join("spamassassin-public-corpus",
"spam")
ham_emails_path = os.path.join("spamassassin-public-corpus", "ham")
labeled_file_directories = [(spam_emails_path, 0),
(ham_emails_path, 1)]
```

3. Create labels for the two classes and read the emails into a corpus:

```
email_corpus = []
labels = []

for class_files, label in labeled_file_directories:
    files = os.listdir(class_files)
    for file in files:
        file_path = os.path.join(class_files, file)
        try:
            with open(file_path, "r") as currentFile:
                email_content = currentFile.read().replace("\n",
"")
                email_content = str(email_content)
                email_corpus.append(email_content)
                labels.append(label)
        except:
            pass
```

4. Train-test split the dataset:

```
from sklearn.model_selection import train_test_split

X_train, X_test, y_train, y_test = train_test_split(
    email_corpus, labels, test_size=0.2, random_state=11
)
```

5. Train an NLP pipeline on the training data:

```
from sklearn.pipeline import Pipeline
from sklearn.feature_extraction.text import HashingVectorizer,
TfidfTransformer
from sklearn import tree

nlp_followed_by_dt = Pipeline(
    [
        ("vect", HashingVectorizer(input="content", ngram_range=(1,
3))),
```

```
        ("tfidf", TfidfTransformer(use_idf=True,)),
        ("dt",
 tree.DecisionTreeClassifier(class_weight="balanced")),
     ]
 )
 nlp_followed_by_dt.fit(X_train, y_train)
```

6. Evaluate the classifier on the testing data:

```
from sklearn.metrics import accuracy_score, confusion_matrix

y_test_pred = nlp_followed_by_dt.predict(X_test)
print(accuracy_score(y_test, y_test_pred))
print(confusion_matrix(y_test, y_test_pred))
```

The following is the output:

```
0.9761620977353993
[[291  7]
 [ 13 528]]
```

How it works...

We start by preparing a dataset consisting of raw emails (*Step 1*), which the reader can examine by looking at the dataset. In *Step 2*, we specify the paths of the spam and ham emails, as well as assign labels to their directories. We proceed to read all of the emails into an array, and create a labels array in *Step 3*. Next, we train-test split our dataset (*Step 4*), and then fit an NLP pipeline on it in *Step 5*. Finally, in *Step 6*, we test our pipeline. We see that accuracy is pretty high. Since the dataset is relatively balanced, there is no need to use special metrics to evaluate success.

Phishing URL detection

A phishing website is a website that tries to obtain your account password or other personal information by making you think that you are on a legitimate website. Some phishing URLs differ from the intended URL in a single character specially chosen to increase the odds of a typo, while others utilize other channels to generate traffic.

Here is an example of a phishing website attempting to obtain a user's email address by pressuring a user into believing that their email will be shut down:

Since phishing is one of the most successful modes of attack, it is crucial to be able to identify when a URL is not legitimate. In this recipe, we will build a machine learning model to detect phishing URLs.

Getting ready

Preparation for this recipe involves installing `scikit-learn` and `pandas` in `pip`. The command is as follows:

```
pip install sklearn pandas
```

In addition, extract the archive named `phishing-dataset.7z`.

How to do it...

In the following steps, we will read in a featurized dataset of URLs and train a classifier on it.

1. Download the phishing dataset from this chapter's directory.
2. Read in the training and testing data using `pandas`:

```
import pandas as pd
import os

train_CSV = os.path.join("phishing-dataset", "train.csv")
test_CSV = os.path.join("phishing-dataset", "test.csv")
train_df = pd.read_csv(train_CSV)
test_df = pd.read_csv(test_CSV)
```

3. Prepare the labels of the phishing web pages:

```
y_train = train_df.pop("target").values
y_test = test_df.pop("target").values
```

4. Prepare the features:

```
X_train = train_df.values
X_test = test_df.values
```

5. Train, test, and assess a classifier:

```
from sklearn.ensemble import RandomForestClassifier
from sklearn.metrics import accuracy_score, confusion_matrix

clf = RandomForestClassifier()
clf.fit(X_train, y_train)
y_test_pred = clf.predict(X_test)
print(accuracy_score(y_test, y_test_pred))
print(confusion_matrix(y_test, y_test_pred))
```

The following is the output:

```
0.9820846905537459
[[343 4]
 [  7 260]]
```

How it works...

We begin by downloading the dataset, and then reading it into data frames (*Steps 1* and *2*) for convenient examination and manipulation. Moving on, we place the dataset into arrays in preparation for machine learning (*Steps 3* and *4*). The dataset consists of several thousand feature vectors for phishing URLs. There are 30 features, whose names and values are tabulated here:

Attributes	Values	Column name
Having an IP address	{ 1,0 }	has_ip
Having a long URL	{ 1,0,-1 }	long_url
Uses Shortening Service	{ 0,1 }	short_service
Having the '@' symbol	{ 0,1 }	has_at
Double slash redirecting	{ 0,1 }	double_slash_redirect
Having a prefix and suffix	{ -1,0,1 }	pref_suf
Having a subdomain	{ -1,0,1 }	has_sub_domain
SSLfinal state	{ -1,1,0 }	ssl_state
Domain registration length	{ 0,1,-1 }	long_domain
Favicon	{ 0,1 }	favicon
Is a standard port	{ 0,1 }	port
Uses HTTPS tokens	{ 0,1 }	https_token
Request_URL	{ 1,-1 }	req_url
Abnormal URL anchor	{ -1,0,1 }	url_of_anchor
Links_in_tags	{ 1,-1,0 }	tag_links
SFH	{ -1,1 }	SFH
Submitting to email	{ 1,0 }	submit_to_email
Abnormal URL	{ 1,0 }	abnormal_url
Redirect	{ 0,1 }	redirect
On mouseover	{ 0,1 }	mouseover
Right-click	{ 0,1 }	right_click
Pop-up window	{ 0,1 }	popup
Iframe	{ 0,1 }	iframe
Age of domain	{ -1,0,1 }	domain_age
DNS record	{ 1,0 }	dns_record
Web traffic	{ -1,0,1 }	traffic
Page rank	{ -1,0,1 }	page_rank
Google index	{ 0,1 }	google_index
Links pointing to page	{ 1,0,-1 }	links_to_page
Statistical report	{ 1,0 }	stats_report
Result	{ 1,-1 }	target

In *Step 5*, we train and test a random forest classifier. The accuracy is pretty high, but depending on how balanced the dataset is, it might be necessary to consider an FP constraint. There are many ways to expand upon such a detector, such as by adding other features and growing the dataset. Given that most websites contain some images, an image classifier is just one way in which the model may improve its results.

Capturing network traffic

Capturing network traffic is important for troubleshooting, analysis, and software and communications protocol development. For the security-minded individual, monitoring network traffic is crucial for detecting malicious activity or policy violation. In this recipe, we will demonstrate how to capture and inspect network traffic.

Getting ready

In preparation for this recipe, observe the following steps:

1. Install `pyshark`:

    ```
    pip install pyshark
    ```

2. Install `wireshark`. The latest version can be found at https://www.wireshark.org/download.html.

How to do it...

In the following steps, we utilize a Python library named PyShark, along with Wireshark, to capture and examine network traffic.

1. You must add `tshark` to PyShark's configuration path. Tshark is a command-line variant of Wireshark. To do this, run the following command:

    ```
    pip show pyshark
    ```

    Note the location of the package. In the `pyshark` directory in this location, find the file, `config.ini`. Edit `tshark_path` to the location of `tshark` inside your `wireshark` installation folder. Similarly, edit `dumpcap_path` to the location of `dumpcap` inside your `wireshark` installation folder.

Steps 2 and *4* should be executed in a Python environment. Note that, as of the current version, `pyshark` may have some bugs when run in a Jupyter notebook.

2. Import `pyshark` and specify the duration of the capture:

```
import pyshark

capture_time = 20
```

3. Specify the name of the file to output the capture, `to`:

```
import datetime
start = datetime.datetime.now()
end = start+datetime.timedelta(seconds=capture_time)
file_name = "networkTrafficCatpureFrom"+str(start).replace(" ",
"T")+"to"+str(end).replace(" ","T")+".pcap"
```

4. Capture network traffic:

```
cap = pyshark.LiveCapture(output_file=file_name)
cap.sniff(timeout=capture_time)
```

5. To examine the capture, open the `pcap` file in Wireshark:

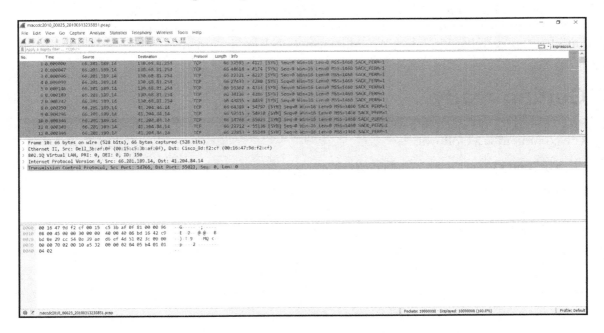

How it works...

We start this recipe by configuring `tshark`, the command-line variant of Wireshark. Once we are finished configuring `tshark`, it is now accessible through `pyshark`. We import `pyshark` and specify the duration of the network capture (*Step 2*). Captured network traffic data can be overwhelming in size, so it is important to control the duration. Next, we specify the name of the output capture in a way that makes it unique and easily understandable (*Step 3*), and then, in *Step 4*, we proceed to capture traffic. Finally, in *Step 6*, we employ Wireshark for its GUI to examine the captured network traffic. In able hands, such network traffic facilitates the detection of insecure IoT devices, misconfigurations, anomalous events, hacking attempts, and even data exfiltration.

Network behavior anomaly detection

Network behavior anomaly detection (**NBAD**) is the continuous monitoring of a network for unusual events or trends. Ideally, an NBAD program tracks critical network characteristics in real time and generates an alarm if a strange event or trend is detected that indicates a threat. In this recipe, we will build an NBAD using machine learning.

The dataset used is a modified subset from a famous dataset known as the KDD dataset, and is a standard set for testing and constructing IDS systems. This dataset contains a wide variety of intrusions simulated in a military network environment.

Getting ready

Preparation for this recipe involves installing `scikit-learn`, `pandas`, and `matplotlib`. The command is as follows:

```
pip install sklearn pandas matplotlib
```

In addition, extract the archive, `kddcup_dataset.7z`.

How to do it...

In the following steps, we will utilize isolation forest to detect anomalies in the KDD dataset:

1. Import `pandas` and read the dataset into a data frame:

    ```
    import pandas as pd

    kdd_df = pd.read_csv("kddcup_dataset.csv", index_col=None)
    ```

2. Examine the proportion of types of traffic:

    ```
    y = kdd_df["label"].values
    from collections import Counter

    Counter(y).most_common()
    ```

    The following output will be observed:

    ```
    [('normal', 39247),
     ('back', 1098),
     ('apache2', 794),
     ('neptune', 93),
     ('phf', 2),
     ('portsweep', 2),
     ('saint', 1)]
    ```

3. Convert all non-normal observations into a single class:

    ```
    def label_anomalous(text):
        """Binarize target labels into normal or anomalous."""
        if text == "normal":
            return 0
        else:
            return 1

    kdd_df["label"] = kdd_df["label"].apply(label_anomalous)
    ```

4. Obtain the ratio of anomalies to normal observations. This is the contamination parameter that will be used in our isolation forest:

    ```
    y = kdd_df["label"].values
    counts = Counter(y).most_common()
    contamination_parameter = counts[1][1] / (counts[0][1] +
    counts[1][1])
    ```

5. Convert all categorical features into numerical form:

```
from sklearn.preprocessing import LabelEncoder

encodings_dictionary = dict()
for c in kdd_df.columns:
    if kdd_df[c].dtype == "object":
        encodings_dictionary[c] = LabelEncoder()
        kdd_df[c] =
encodings_dictionary[c].fit_transform(kdd_df[c])
```

6. Split the dataset into normal and abnormal observations:

```
kdd_df_normal = kdd_df[kdd_df["label"] == 0]
kdd_df_abnormal = kdd_df[kdd_df["label"] == 1]
y_normal = kdd_df_normal.pop("label").values
X_normal = kdd_df_normal.values
y_anomaly = kdd_df_abnormal.pop("label").values
X_anomaly = kdd_df_abnormal.values
```

7. Train-test split the dataset:

```
from sklearn.model_selection import train_test_split

X_normal_train, X_normal_test, y_normal_train, y_normal_test =
train_test_split(
    X_normal, y_normal, test_size=0.3, random_state=11
)
X_anomaly_train, X_anomaly_test, y_anomaly_train, y_anomaly_test =
train_test_split(
    X_anomaly, y_anomaly, test_size=0.3, random_state=11
)

import numpy as np

X_train = np.concatenate((X_normal_train, X_anomaly_train))
y_train = np.concatenate((y_normal_train, y_anomaly_train))
X_test = np.concatenate((X_normal_test, X_anomaly_test))
y_test = np.concatenate((y_normal_test, y_anomaly_test))
```

8. Instantiate and train an isolation forest classifier:

```
from sklearn.ensemble import IsolationForest

IF = IsolationForest(contamination=contamination_parameter)
IF.fit(X_train
```

9. Score the classifier on normal and anomalous observations:

```
decisionScores_train_normal = IF.decision_function(X_normal_train)
decisionScores_train_anomaly =
IF.decision_function(X_anomaly_train)
```

10. Plot the scores for the normal set:

```
import matplotlib.pyplot as plt

%matplotlib inline
plt.figure(figsize=(20, 10))
_ = plt.hist(decisionScores_train_normal, bins=50)
```

The following graph provides the output:

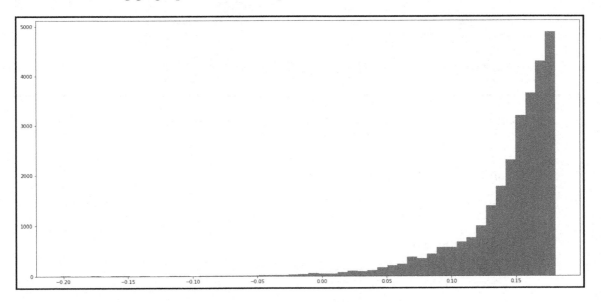

11. Similarly, plot the scores on the anomalous observations for a visual examination:

```
plt.figure(figsize=(20, 10))
_ = plt.hist(decisionScores_train_anomaly, bins=50)
```

The following graph provides the output:

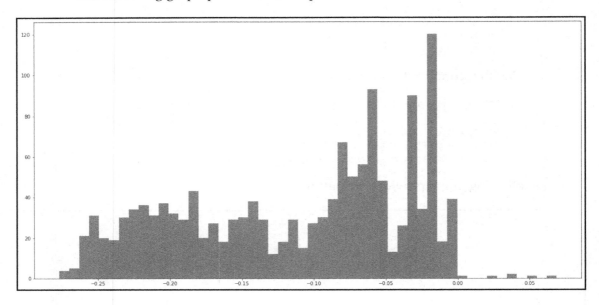

12. Select a cut-off so as to separate out the anomalies from the normal observations:

    ```
    cutoff = 0
    ```

13. Examine this cut-off on the test set:

    ```
    print(Counter(y_test))
    print(Counter(y_test[cutoff > IF.decision_function(X_test)]))
    ```

The following is the output:

    ```
    Counter({0: 11775, 1: 597})
    Counter({1: 595, 0: 85})
    ```

How it works...

We start by reading the `KDD cup` dataset into a data frame. Next, in *Step 2*, we examine our data, to see that a majority of the traffic is normal, as expected, but a small amount is abnormal. Evidently, the problem is highly imbalanced. Consequently, this problem is a promising candidate for an anomaly detection approach. In *Steps 3 and 5*, we transform all non-normal traffic into a single class, namely, **anomalous**.

We also make sure to compute the ratio of anomalies to normal observations (*Step 4*), known as the contamination parameter. This is one of the parameters that facilitates setting of the sensitivity of isolation forest. This is optional, but is likely to improve performance. We split our dataset into normal and anomalous observations in *Step 6*, as well as split our dataset into training and testing versions of the normal and anomalous data (*Step 7*). We instantiate an isolation forest classifier, and set its contamination parameter (*Step 8*). The default parameters, `n_estimators` and `max_samples`, are recommended in the paper *Isolation Forest* by Liu et al. In *Steps 9 and 10*, we use the decision function of isolation forest to provide a score to the normal training set, and then examine the results in a plot. In *Step 11*, we similarly provide a score to the anomalous training set.

Knowing that the decision function is a measure of how simple a point is to describe, we would like to separate out simple points from complicated points by picking a numerical cut-off that gives clear separation. A visual examination suggests the value chosen in *Step 12*.

Finally, we can use our model to make predictions and provide an assessment of its performance. In *Step 13*, we see that the model was able to pick up on a large number of anomalies without triggering too many false positives (instances of normal traffic), speaking proportion-wise.

Botnet traffic detection

A botnet is a network of internet-connected compromised devices. Botnets can be used to perform a distributed **denial-of-service attack** (**DDoS attack**), steal data, send spam, among many other creative malicious uses. Botnets can cause absurd amounts of damage. For example, a quick search for the word botnet on Google shows that 3 days before the time of writing, the Electrum Botnet Stole $4.6 Million in cryptocurrencies. In this recipe, we build a classifier to detect botnet traffic.

The dataset used is a processed subset of a dataset called **CTU-13**, and consists of botnet traffic captured in Czechia, at the CTU University in 2011. The dataset is a large capture of real botnet traffic mixed with normal and background traffic.

Getting ready

Preparation for this recipe involves installing scikit-learn in pip. The command is as follows:

```
pip install sklearn
```

In addition, extract CTU13Scenario1flowData.7z. To unpickle the CTU13Scenario1flowData.pickle file, you will need to use Python 2:

How to do it...

1. Begin by reading in the pickled data:

```
import pickle

file = open('CTU13Scenario1flowData.pickle', 'rb')
botnet_dataset = pickle.load(file)
```

2. The data is already split into train-test sets, and you only need assign these to their respective variables:

```
X_train, y_train, X_test, y_test = (
    botnet_dataset[0],
    botnet_dataset[1],
    botnet_dataset[2],
    botnet_dataset[3],
)
```

3. Instantiate a decision tree classifier with default parameters:

```
from sklearn.tree import *

clf = DecisionTreeClassifier()
```

4. Fit the classifier to the training data:

```
clf.fit(X_train, y_train)
```

5. Test it on the test set:

```
clf.score(X_test, y_test)
```

The following is the output:

```
0.9991001799640072
```

How it works...

We begin *Step 1* by loading the data by unpickling it. The dataset has been pre-engineered to be balanced, so we do not need to worry about imbalanced data challenges. In practice, the detection of botnets may require satisfying a constraint on false positives. Moving on, we utilize the already predefined train-test split to split our data (*Step 2*). We can now instantiate a classifier, fit it to the data, and then test it (*Steps 3* and *5*). Looking at the accuracy, we see that it is quite high. Since the dataset is already balanced, we need not worry that our metric is misleading. In general, detecting botnets can be challenging. The difficulty in detecting botnets is illustrated by the GameOver Zeus botnet malware package. Originally discovered in 2007, it operated for over three years, eventually resulting in an estimated $70 million in stolen funds that led to the arrest of over a hundred individuals by the FBI in 2010. It wasn't until March 2012 that Microsoft announced that it was able to shut down the majority of the botnet's command and control (C&C) servers.

Insider threat detection

Insider threat is a complex and growing challenge for employers. It is generally defined as any actions taken by an employee that are potentially harmful to the organization. These can include actions such as unsanctioned data transfer or the sabotaging of resources. Insider threats may manifest in various and novel forms motivated by differing goals, ranging from a disgruntled employee subverting the prestige of an employer, to **advanced persistent threats** (**APT**).

The insider risk database of the CERT Program of the Carnegie Mellon University Software Engineering Institute contains the largest public archive of red team scenarios. The simulation is built by combining real-world insider risk case studies with actual neutral clients secretly obtained from a defense corporation. The dataset represents months of traffic in a single engineering company from internet, phone, logon, folder, and system access (dtaa.com). The mock company employs several thousand people who each perform an average of 1,000 logged activities per day. There are several threat scenarios depicted, such as a leaker, thief, and saboteur. A notable feature of the issue is its very low signal-to-noise, whether this is expressed in total malicious users, frequent tallies, or overall usage.

The analysis we perform is on the CERT insider threat scenario (v.4.2), specifically because it represents a dense needle dataset, meaning that it has a high incidence of attacks.

The basic plan of attack is, first, to hand-engineer new features, such as whether an email has been sent to an outsider or a login has occurred outside of business hours. Next, the idea is to extract a multivariate time series per user. This time series will consist of a sequence of vectors—each vector constitutes a count of the number of times our hand-engineered features took place in a day. Hence, the shape of our input dataset will be as follows:

(# of users, total # of features examined per day, # of days in the time series).

We will then flatten the time series of each user, and utilize isolation forest to detect anomalies.

Feature engineering for insider threat detection

Generally, whenever a machine learning solution does not rely on end-to-end deep learning, performance can be improved by creating insightful and informative features. In this recipe, we will construct several promising new features for insider threat detection.

Getting ready

Preparation for this recipe involves installing pandas in pip. The command is as follows:

```
pip install pandas
```

In addition, download the CERT insider threat dataset from the following link: ftp://ftp.sei.cmu.edu/pub/cert-data/r4.2.tar.bz2. More information about the dataset, as well as answers, can be found at https://resources.sei.cmu.edu/library/asset-view.cfm?assetid=508099.

How to do it...

In the following steps, you will construct new features for the CERT insider threat dataset:

1. Import `numpy` and `pandas`, and point to where the downloaded data is located:

```
import numpy as np
import pandas as pd
path_to_dataset = "./r42short/"
```

2. Specify the `.csv` files and which of their columns to read:

```
log_types = ["device", "email", "file", "logon", "http"]
log_fields_list = [
    ["date", "user", "activity"],
    ["date", "user", "to", "cc", "bcc"],
    ["date", "user", "filename"],
    ["date", "user", "activity"],
    ["date", "user", "url"],
]
```

3. We will hand-engineer a number of features and encode them, thereby creating a dictionary to track these.

```
features = 0
feature_map = {}


def add_feature(name):
    """Add a feature to a dictionary to be encoded."""
    if name not in feature_map:
        global features
        feature_map[name] = features
        features += 1
```

4. Add the features we will be using to our dictionary:

```
add_feature("Weekday_Logon_Normal")
add_feature("Weekday_Logon_After")
add_feature("Weekend_Logon")
add_feature("Logoff")

add_feature("Connect_Normal")
add_feature("Connect_After")
add_feature("Connect_Weekend")
add_feature("Disconnect")

add_feature("Email_In")
```

```
add_feature("Email_Out")

add_feature("File_exe")
add_feature("File_jpg")
add_feature("File_zip")
add_feature("File_txt")
add_feature("File_doc")
add_feature("File_pdf")
add_feature("File_other")

add_feature("url")
```

5. Define a function to note the file type that was copied to removable media:

```
def file_features(row):
    """Creates a feature recording the file extension of the file
used."""
    if row["filename"].endswith(".exe"):
        return feature_map["File_exe"]
    if row["filename"].endswith(".jpg"):
        return feature_map["File_jpg"]
    if row["filename"].endswith(".zip"):
        return feature_map["File_zip"]
    if row["filename"].endswith(".txt"):
        return feature_map["File_txt"]
    if row["filename"].endswith(".doc"):
        return feature_map["File_doc"]
    if row["filename"].endswith(".pdf"):
        return feature_map["File_pdf"]
    else:
        return feature_map["File_other"]
```

6. Define a function to identify whether an employee has sent an email to a non-company email:

```
def email_features(row):
    """Creates a feature recording whether an email has been sent
externally."""
    outsider = False
    if not pd.isnull(row["to"]):
        for address in row["to"].split(";"):
            if not address.endswith("dtaa.com"):
                outsider = True

    if not pd.isnull(row["cc"]):
        for address in row["cc"].split(";"):
            if not address.endswith("dtaa.com"):
                outsider = True
```

```
    if not pd.isnull(row["bcc"]):
        for address in row["bcc"].split(";"):
            if not address.endswith("dtaa.com"):
                outsider = True
    if outsider:
        return feature_map["Email_Out"]
    else:
        return feature_map["Email_In"]
```

7. Define a function to note whether the employee used removable media outside of business hours:

```
def device_features(row):
    """Creates a feature for whether the user has connected during
normal hours or otherwise."""
    if row["activity"] == "Connect":
        if row["date"].weekday() < 5:
            if row["date"].hour >= 8 and row["date"].hour < 17:
                return feature_map["Connect_Normal"]
            else:
                return feature_map["Connect_After"]
        else:
            return feature_map["Connect_Weekend"]
    else:
        return feature_map["Disconnect"]
```

8. Define a function to note whether an employee has logged onto a machine outside of business hours:

```
def logon_features(row):
    """Creates a feature for whether the user logged in during
normal hours or otherwise."""
    if row["activity"] == "Logon":
        if row["date"].weekday() < 5:
            if row["date"].hour >= 8 and row["date"].hour < 17:
                return feature_map["Weekday_Logon_Normal"]
            else:
                return feature_map["Weekday_Logon_After"]
        else:
            return feature_map["Weekend_Logon"]
    else:
        return feature_map["Logoff"]
```

9. We will not take advantage of the information contained in URLs visited by an employee:

```
def http_features(row):
    """Encodes the URL visited."""
    return feature_map["url"]
```

10. We preserve only the day when an event has occurred, rather than the full timestamp:

```
def date_to_day(row):
    """Converts a full datetime to date only."""
    day_only = row["date"].date()
    return day_only
```

11. We loop over the .csv files containing the logs and read them into pandas data frames:

```
log_feature_functions = [
    device_features,
    email_features,
    file_features,
    logon_features,
    http_features,
]
dfs = []
for i in range(len(log_types)):
    log_type = log_types[i]
    log_fields = log_fields_list[i]
    log_feature_function = log_feature_functions[i]
    df = pd.read_csv(
        path_to_dataset + log_type + ".csv", usecols=log_fields,
index_col=None
    )
```

12. Convert the date data to a pandas timestamp:

```
date_format = "%m/%d/%Y %H:%M:%S"
df["date"] = pd.to_datetime(df["date"], format=date_format)
```

13. Create the new features defined above and then drop all features except the date, user, and our new feature:

```
new_feature = df.apply(log_feature_function, axis=1)
df["feature"] = new_feature

cols_to_keep = ["date", "user", "feature"]
df = df[cols_to_keep]
```

14. Convert the date to just a day:

```
df["date"] = df.apply(date_to_day, axis=1)

dfs.append(df)
```

15. Concatenate all the data frames into one and sort by `date`:

```
joint = pd.concat(dfs)
joint = joint.sort_values(by="date")
```

How it works...

Start by importing `pandas` and `numpy` and creating a variable pointing to the dataset (*Step 1*). There are several datasets available from CERT. Version 4.2 is distinguished in being a dense needle dataset, meaning that it has a higher incidence of insider threats than the other datasets. Since the dataset is so massive, it is convenient to filter and downsample it, at the very least during the experimentation phases, so we do so in *Step 2*. In the following steps, we will hand-engineer features that we believe will help our classifier catch insider threats. In *Step 3*, we create a convenient function to encode features, so that a dictionary can track these. We provide the names of the features we will be adding in *Step 4*. In *Step 5*, we create a feature that will track the file type of a file copied to removable media. Presumably, this is indicative of criminal data leaking. In *Step 6*, we create a feature that tracks whether the employee has emailed an external entity. We create another feature to track whether an employee has used a removable media device outside of business hours (*Step 7*).

An additional feature tracks whether an employee has logged into a device outside of business hours (*Step 8*). For simplicity, we do not utilize the URLs visited by employees (*Step 9*), though these may be indicative of malicious behavior.

Next, we simplify our data by using only the date (*Step 10*), rather than the full timestamp in our featurized data. In *Step 11*, we read our data into a pandas data frame. We then edit the current date format to fit pandas (*Step 12*), and then gather up all of the new features, while dropping the old ones (*Step 13*). In *Step 14*, we transform the data into a time series whose delta are single days. Finally, in *Step 15*, we aggregate all of the data into one large sorted data frame. We have now completed the first iteration of the feature-engineering phase. There are many directions you can pursue in order to improve performance and add features. These include observing email text for negative sentiment and analyzing personality using psychometrics.

Employing anomaly detection for insider threats

Having engineered promising new features, our next steps are to train-test split, process the data into a convenient time series form, and then classify. Our training and testing sets will be two temporal halves of the dataset. This way, we can easily ensure that the shape of the input for training is the same as the shape of the input for testing, without cheating in our evaluation.

Getting ready

Preparation for this recipe involves installing scikit-learn, pandas, and matplotlib in pip. The command is as follows:

```
pip install sklearn pandas matplotlib
```

In preparation for this recipe, you will want to load in the data frame from the previous recipe (or just continue from where the previous recipe ended).

How to do it...

In the following steps, you will convert the featurized data into a collection of time series and detect crime using isolation forest:

1. List all threat actors in preparation for creating labels:

```
threat_actors = [
    "AAM0658",
    "AJR0932",
    "BDV0168",
    <snip>
    "MSO0222",
]
```

2. We then index the dates:

```
start_date = joint["date"].iloc[0]
end_date = joint["date"].iloc[-1]
time_horizon = (end_date - start_date).days + 1


def date_to_index(date):
    """Indexes dates by counting the number of days since the
starting date of the dataset."""
    return (date - start_date).days
```

3. Define a function to extract the time series information of a given user:

```
def extract_time_series_by_user(user_name, df):
    """Filters the dataframe down to a specific user."""
    return df[df["user"] == user_name]
```

4. Define a function to vectorize the time series information of a user:

```
def vectorize_user_time_series(user_name, df):
    """Convert the sequence of features of a user to a vector-
valued time series."""
    user_time_series = extract_time_series_by_user(user_name, df)
    x = np.zeros((len(feature_map), time_horizon))
    event_date_indices =
user_time_series["date"].apply(date_to_index).to_numpy()
    event_features = user_time_series["feature"].to_numpy()
    for i in range(len(event_date_indices)):
        x[event_features[i], event_date_indices[i]] += 1
    return x
```

5. Define a function to vectorize a time series of all users' features:

```
def vectorize_dataset(df):
    """Takes the dataset and featurizes it."""
    users = set(df["user"].values)
    X = np.zeros((len(users), len(feature_map), time_horizon))
    y = np.zeros((len(users)))
    for index, user in enumerate(users):
        x = vectorize_user_time_series(user, df)
        X[index, :, :] = x
        y[index] = int(user in threat_actors)
    return X, y
```

6. Vectorize the dataset:

```
X, y = vectorize_dataset(joint)
```

7. Train-test split the vectorized data:

```
from sklearn.model_selection import train_test_split

X_train, X_test, y_train, y_test = train_test_split(X, y,
stratify=y)
```

8. Reshape the vectorized data:

```
X_train_reshaped = X_train.reshape(
    [X_train.shape[0], X_train.shape[1] * X_train.shape[2]]
)
X_test_reshaped = X_test.reshape([X_test.shape[0], X_test.shape[1]
* X_test.shape[2]])
```

9. Split the training and testing datasets into threat and non-threat subsets:

```
X_train_normal = X_train_reshaped[y_train == 0, :]
X_train_threat = X_train_reshaped[y_train == 1, :]
X_test_normal = X_test_reshaped[y_test == 0, :]
X_test_threat = X_test_reshaped[y_test == 1, :]
```

10. Define and instantiate an isolation forest classifier:

```
from sklearn.ensemble import IsolationForest

contamination_parameter = 0.035
IF = IsolationForest(
    n_estimators=100, max_samples=256,
contamination=contamination_parameter
)
```

11. Fit the isolation forest classifier to the training data:

```
IF.fit(X_train_reshaped)
```

12. Plot the decision scores of the normal subset of the training data:

```
normal_scores = IF.decision_function(X_train_normal)
import matplotlib.mlab as mlab
import matplotlib.pyplot as plt

fig = plt.figure(figsize=(8, 4), dpi=600, facecolor="w",
edgecolor="k")

normal = plt.hist(normal_scores, 50, density=True)

plt.xlim((-0.2, 0.2))
plt.xlabel("Anomaly score")
plt.ylabel("Percentage")
plt.title("Distribution of anomaly score for non threats")
```

Take a look at the following screenshot:

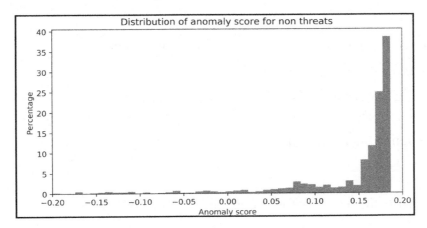

13. Do the same for the threat actors in the training data:

```
anomaly_scores = IF.decision_function(X_train_threat)
fig = plt.figure(figsize=(8, 4), dpi=600, facecolor="w",
edgecolor="k")

anomaly = plt.hist(anomaly_scores, 50, density=True)

plt.xlim((-0.2, 0.2))
plt.xlabel("Anomaly score")
plt.ylabel("Percentage")
plt.title("Distribution of anomaly score for threats")
```

Take a look at the following screenshot:

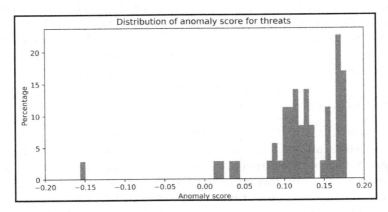

14. Select a cut-off score:

```
cutoff = 0.12
```

15. Observe the results of the cut-off on the training data:

```
from collections import Counter

s = IF.decision_function(X_train_reshaped)
print(Counter(y_train[cutoff > s]))
```

The following is the output:

```
Counter({0.0: 155, 1.0: 23})
```

16. Measure the results of the cut-off choice on the testing set:

```
s = IF.decision_function(X_test_reshaped)
print(Counter(y_test[cutoff > s]))
```

The following is the output:

```
Counter({0.0: 46, 1.0: 8})
```

How it works...

Having completed the feature-engineering phase in the previous recipe, we went ahead and created a model. In *Step 1*, we listed all threat actors in preparation for the next steps. In *Step 2*, we created an indexing for the dates, so that 0 corresponded to the starting date, 1 to the next day, and so on. In the subsequent *Steps 3* and *5*, we defined functions to read in the whole dataset time series, filter it down to individual users, and then vectorize the time series for each user. We went ahead and vectorized the dataset (*Step 6*) and then train-test split it (*Step 7*). We reshaped the data in *Step 8* in order to be able to feed it into the isolation forest classifier. We split the data further into benign and threat subsets (*Step 9*) to allow us to tune our parameters. We instantiated an isolation forest classifier in *Step 10* and then fit it on the data in *Step 11*. For our contamination parameter, we used a value corresponding to the proportion of threats-to-benign actors.

In the next three steps (*Steps 12-14*), we examined the decision scores of isolation forest on benign and threat actors, and concluded, via inspection, that the cut-off value of 0.12 detects a large proportion of the threat actors without flagging too many of the benign actors. Finally, assessing our performance in *Steps 15* and *16*, we saw that there were some false positives, but also a significant number of insider threats detected. Since the ratio was not too high, the classifier can be of great help in informing analysts about plausible threats.

Detecting DDoS

DDoS, or **Distributed Denial of Service**, is an attack in which traffic from different sources floods a victim, resulting in service interruption. There are many types of DDoS attacks, falling under three general categories: application-level, protocol, and volumetric attacks. Much of the DDoS defense today is manual. Certain IP addresses or domains are identified and then blocked. As DDoS bots become more sophisticated, such approaches are becoming outdated. Machine learning offers a promising automated solution.

The dataset we will be working with is a subsampling of the CSE-CIC-IDS2018, CICIDS2017, and CIC DoS datasets (2017). It consists of 80% benign and 20% DDoS traffic, in order to represent a more realistic ratio of normal-to-DDoS traffic.

Getting ready

Preparation for this recipe involves installing a couple of packages in `pip`, namely, `scikit-learn` and `pandas`. The command is as follows:

```
pip install sklearn pandas
```

In preparation for this recipe, extract the archive, `ddos_dataset.7z`.

How to do it...

In the following steps, we will train a random forest classifier to detect DDoS traffic:

1. Import `pandas` and specify the data types for the columns you will be reading in the code:

    ```
    import pandas as pd

    features = [
        "Fwd Seg Size Min",
        "Init Bwd Win Byts",
        "Init Fwd Win Byts",
        "Fwd Seg Size Min",
        "Fwd Pkt Len Mean",
        "Fwd Seg Size Avg",
        "Label",
        "Timestamp",
    ]
    dtypes = {
    ```

```
        "Fwd Pkt Len Mean": "float",
        "Fwd Seg Size Avg": "float",
        "Init Fwd Win Byts": "int",
        "Init Bwd Win Byts": "int",
        "Fwd Seg Size Min": "int",
        "Label": "str",
    }
    date_columns = ["Timestamp"]
```

2. Read in the `.csv` file containing the dataset:

```
df = pd.read_csv("ddos_dataset.csv", usecols=features,
dtype=dtypes, parse_dates=date_columns, index_col=None)
```

3. Sort the data by date:

```
df2 = df.sort_values("Timestamp")
```

4. Drop the date column, as it is no longer needed:

```
df3 = df2.drop(columns=["Timestamp"])
```

5. Split the data into training and testing subsets, consisting of the first 80% and last 20% of the data:

```
l = len(df3.index)
train_df = df3.head(int(l * 0.8))
test_df = df3.tail(int(l * 0.2))
```

6. Prepare the labels:

```
y_train = train_df.pop("Label").values
y_test = test_df.pop("Label").values
```

7. Prepare the feature vectors:

```
X_train = train_df.values
X_test = test_df.values
```

8. Import and instantiate a random forest classifier:

```
from sklearn.ensemble import RandomForestClassifier

clf = RandomForestClassifier(n_estimators=50)
```

9. Fit random forest to the training data and score it on the testing data:

```
clf.fit(X_train, y_train)
clf.score(X_test, y_test)
```

The following is the output:

```
0.83262
```

How it works...

Since the dataset is large, even importing all of it is computationally intensive. For this reason, we begin *Step 1* by specifying a subset of features from our dataset, the ones we consider most promising, as well as recording their data type so that we don't have to convert them later. We then proceed to read the data into a data frame in *Step 2*. In *Steps 3* and *4*, we sort the data by date, since the problem requires being able to predict events in the future, and then drop the date column since we will not be employing it further. In the next two steps, we perform a train-test split, keeping in mind temporal progression. We then instantiate, fit, and test a random forest classifier in *Steps 8* and *9*. Depending on the application, the accuracy achieved is a good starting point. A promising direction to improve performance is to account for the source and destination IPs. The reasoning is that, intuitively, where a connection is coming from should have a significant bearing on whether it is part of a DDoS.

Credit card fraud detection

Credit card companies must monitor for fraudulent transactions in order to keep their customers from being charged for items they have not purchased. Such data is unique in being extremely imbalanced, with the particular dataset we will be working on in this chapter having fraud constituting 0.172% of the total transactions. It contains only numeric input variables, which are the result of a PCA transformation, and the features *Time* and *Amount*. The *Time* feature contains the seconds elapsed between each transaction and the first transaction in the dataset. The *Amount* feature is the amount transaction, a feature that we will use, for instance, in cost-sensitive learning. The *Class* feature is the response parameter and, in case of fraud, it takes the value 1, and 0 otherwise.

So what is example-dependent, cost-sensitive learning? Consider the costs associated with each type of classification. If the program does not identify a fraudulent transaction, the money will be wasted and the card holder must be reimbursed for the entire amount of the transaction. If a payment is considered fraudulent by the program, the transaction will be stopped. In that situation, administrative costs arise due to the need to contact the card holder and the card needs to be replaced (if the transaction was correctly labeled fraudulent) or reactivated (if the transaction was actually legitimate). Let's assume, for simplicity's sake, that administrative costs are always the same. If the system finds the transaction valid, then the transaction will automatically be accepted and there will be no charge. This results in the following costs associated with each prediction scenario:

	Fraud $y = 1$	Benign $y = 0$
Predicted fraud $y\_pred = 1$	TP cost = administrative	FP cost = administrative
Predicted benign $y\_pred = 0$	FN cost = transaction amount	TN cost = \$0

Unlike most scenarios, our interest is to minimize the total cost, derived from the above considerations, rather than accuracy, precision, or recall.

Getting ready

Preparation for this recipe involves installing `scikit-learn`, `pandas`, and `matplotlib` in `pip`, as well as a new package called `costcla`. The command is as follows:

```
pip install sklearn pandas matplotlib costcla
```

In preparation for this recipe, download the credit card transactions dataset from `https://www.kaggle.com/mlg-ulb/creditcardfraud/downloads/creditcardfraud.zip/3` (open database license).

How to do it...

In the following steps, we will build an example-dependent, cost-sensitive classifier using the `costcla` library on credit card transaction data:

1. Import `pandas` and read the data pertaining to transactions into a data frame:

```
import pandas as pd

fraud_df = pd.read_csv("FinancialFraudDB.csv", index_col=None)
```

2. Set a cost to `false` positives and `false` negatives:

```
card_replacement_cost = 5
customer_freeze_cost = 3
```

3. Define a cost matrix corresponding to the figure:

```
import numpy as np

cost_matrix = np.zeros((len(fraud_df.index), 4))
cost_matrix[:, 0] = customer_freeze_cost *
np.ones(len(fraud_df.index))
cost_matrix[:, 1] = fraud_df["Amount"].values
cost_matrix[:, 2] = card_replacement_cost *
np.ones(len(fraud_df.index))
```

4. Create labels and feature matrices:

```
y = fraud_df.pop("Class").values
X = fraud_df.values
```

5. Create a train-test split:

```
from sklearn.model_selection import train_test_split

sets = train_test_split(X, y, cost_matrix, test_size=0.25,
random_state=11)
X_train, X_test, y_train, y_test, cost_matrix_train,
cost_matrix_test = sets
```

6. Import the decision tree, fit it to the training data, and then predict on the testing set:

```
from sklearn import tree

y_pred_test_dt = tree.DecisionTreeClassifier().fit(X_train,
y_train).predict(X_test)
```

7. Import the cost-sensitive decision tree, fit it to the training data, and then predict on the testing set:

```
from costcla.models import CostSensitiveDecisionTreeClassifier

y_pred_test_csdt =
CostSensitiveDecisionTreeClassifier().fit(X_train, y_train,
cost_matrix_train).predict(X_test)
```

8. Calculate the savings score of the two models:

```
from costcla.metrics import savings_score

print(savings_score(y_test, y_pred_test_dt, cost_matrix_test))
print(savings_score(y_test, y_pred_test_csdt, cost_matrix_test))
```

The following is the output:

```
0.5231523713991505
0.5994028394464614
```

How it works...

The first step is simply to load the data. In *Step 2*, we set an administrative cost based on the expected cost of replacing a credit card. In addition, we estimate the business cost of freezing a customer's banking operations until all transactions are verified. In practice, you should obtain an accurate figure that is appropriate to the credit card company or business use case in question. Using the parameters we have defined, we define a cost matrix in *Step 3* that takes into account the administrative cost of replacing a credit card, business interruption from freezing a customer, and so on. In *Steps 4* and *5*, we train-test split our data. Next, we would like to see how the example-dependent, cost-sensitive classifier performs as compared with a vanilla classifier. To that end, we instantiate a simple classifier, train it, and then use it to predict on the testing set in *Step 6*, and then utilize the cost-sensitive random forest model from the `costcla` library in *Step 7* to do the same. Finally, in *Step 8*, we utilize the `savings_score` function from `costcla` to calculate the savings cost of using `y_pred` on `y_true` with a cost matrix. The higher the number, the larger the cost savings. Consequently, we see that the cost-sensitive random forest model outperformed the vanilla model.

Counterfeit bank note detection

Counterfeit money is a currency created without the state or government's legal sanction, usually in a deliberate attempt to imitate the currency and to deceive its user. In this recipe, you will train a machine learning classifier to distinguish between genuine and fake bank notes.

Getting ready

Preparation for this recipe involves installing `scikit-learn` and `pandas` in `pip`. The command is as follows:

```
pip install sklearn pandas
```

In preparation for this recipe, download the banknote authentication dataset from UCI's machine learning repository: `https://archive.ics.uci.edu/ml/datasets/banknote+authentication`.

How to do it...

In the following steps, you will download a labeled dataset of counterfeit and legitimate bank notes and construct a classifier to detect counterfeit currency:

1. Obtain a labeled dataset of authentic and counterfeit bank notes.
2. Read in the bank note dataset using `pandas`:

   ```
   import pandas as pd

   df = pd.read_csv("data_banknote_authentication.txt", header=None)
   df.columns = ["0", "1", "2", "3", "label"]
   ```

   The following is the output:

   ```
   feature 1 feature 2 feature 3 feature 4 label
   0 3.62160 8.6661 -2.8073 -0.44699 0
   1 4.54590 8.1674 -2.4586 -1.46210 0
   2 3.86600 -2.6383 1.9242 0.10645 0
   3 3.45660 9.5228 -4.0112 -3.59440 0
   4 0.32924 -4.4552 4.5718 -0.98880 0
   ```

3. Create a train-test split:

   ```
   from sklearn.model_selection import train_test_split

   df_train, df_test = train_test_split(df)
   ```

4. Collect the features and labels into arrays:

   ```
   y_train = df_train.pop("label").values
   X_train = df_train.values
   y_test = df_test.pop("label").values
   X_test = df_test.values
   ```

5. Instantiate a random forest classifier:

```
from sklearn.ensemble import RandomForestClassifier

clf = RandomForestClassifier()
```

6. Train and test the classifier:

```
clf.fit(X_train, y_train)
print(clf.score(X_test, y_test))
```

The following is the output:

```
0.9825072886297376
```

How it works...

The greatest potential for a counterfeiting solution lies in obtaining a large dataset of images and using deep learning technology. In a regime where the dataset is relatively small, as is the case here, however, feature-engineering is mandatory. We begin attacking our problem by loading and then reading in a dataset into pandas (*Steps 1* and *2*). In the case of this dataset, a wavelet transform tool was used to extract features from the images. Next, in *Steps 3* and *4*, we train-test split the data and gather it into arrays. Finally, we fit and test a basic classifier on the dataset in *Steps 5* and *6*. The high score (98%) suggests that the features extracted for this dataset are indeed able to distinguish between authentic and counterfeit notes.

Ad blocking using machine learning

Ad blocking is the operation of removing or altering online advertising in a web browser or an application. In this recipe, you will utilize machine learning to detect ads so that they can be blocked and you can browse hassle-free!

Getting ready

Preparation for this recipe involves installing scikit-learn and pandas in pip. The command is as follows:

```
pip install sklearn pandas
```

In preparation for this recipe, download the internet advertisements dataset from UCI's machine learning repository: `https://archive.ics.uci.edu/ml/datasets/ internet+advertisements`.

How to do it...

The following steps show how ad blocking is implemented using machine learning:

1. Collect a dataset of internet advertisements.
2. Import the data into a data frame using `pandas`:

```
import pandas as pd

df = pd.read_csv("ad.data", header=None)
df.rename(columns={1558: "label"}, inplace=True)
```

3. The data is dirty in the sense of having missing values. Let's find all the rows that have a missing value:

```
improper_rows = []
for index, row in df.iterrows():
    for col in df.columns:
        val = str(row[col]).strip()
        if val == "?":
            improper_rows.append(index)
```

4. In the case at hand, it makes sense to drop the rows with missing values, as seen in the following code:

```
df = df.drop(df.index[list(set(improper_rows))])
```

5. Convert the label into numerical form:

```
def label_to_numeric(row):
    """Binarize the label."""
    if row["label"] == "ad.":
        return 1
    else:
        return 0

df["label"] = df.apply(label_to_numeric, axis=1)
```

6. Split the data into training and testing data:

```
from sklearn.model_selection import train_test_split

df_train, df_test = train_test_split(df)
```

7. Distribute the data into feature arrays and label arrays:

```
y_train = df_train.pop("label").values
y_test = df_test.pop("label").values
X_train = df_train.values
X_test = df_test.values
```

8. Instantiate a random forest classifier and train it:

```
from sklearn.ensemble import RandomForestClassifier

clf = RandomForestClassifier()
clf.fit(X_train, y_train)
```

9. Score the classifier on the testing data:

```
clf.score(X_test, y_test)
```

The following is the output:

0.9847457627118644

How it works...

We begin our recipe for blocking unwanted ads by importing the dataset. The data we have used in this recipe has been feature-engineered for us. In *Step 2*, we import the data into a data frame. Looking at the data, we see that it consists of 1,558 numerical features and an ad or non-ad label:

```
In [104]: df.head()

Out[104]:
```

	0	1	2	3	4	5	6	7	8	9	...	1549	1550	1551	1552	1553	1554	1555	1556	1557	label
0	125	125	1.0	1	0	0	0	0	0	0	...	0	0	0	0	0	0	0	0	0	ad.
1	57	468	8.2105	1	0	0	0	0	0	0	...	0	0	0	0	0	0	0	0	0	ad.
2	33	230	6.9696	1	0	0	0	0	0	0	...	0	0	0	0	0	0	0	0	0	ad.
3	60	468	7.8	1	0	0	0	0	0	0	...	0	0	0	0	0	0	0	0	0	ad.
4	60	468	7.8	1	0	0	0	0	0	0	...	0	0	0	0	0	0	0	0	0	ad.

5 rows × 1559 columns

The features encode the geometry of the image, sentences in the URL, the URL of the image, alt text, anchor text, and words near the anchor text. Our goal is to predict whether an image is an advertisement (ad) or not (non-ad). We proceed to clean our data by dropping rows with missing values in *Steps*3 and *4*. Generally, it may make sense to use other techniques to impute missing values, such as using an average or most common value. Proceeding to *Step 5*, we convert our target to numerical form. Then, we train-test split our data in preparation for learning in *Steps 6* and *7*. Finally, in *Steps 8* and *9*, we fit and test a basic classifier on the data. The results suggest that the features do provide high discrimination power.

Recent approaches have utilized deep learning on screen images to tackle ads. The approach is very promising, but so far has been unsuccessful due to deep learning's adversarial sensitivity. With robustness to adversarial attacks improving in the field, deep learning-based ad blockers may become commonplace.

Wireless indoor localization

Tales of a hacker parked outside a home, and hacking into their network for malice, are legendary. Though these tales may exaggerate the ease and motivation of this scenario, there are many situations where it is best to only permit users inside the home, or, in the case of an enterprise environment, in a designated area, to have specified network privileges. In this recipe, you will utilize machine learning to localize an entity based on the Wi-Fi signal. The dataset we will be working with was collected in an indoor space by observing signal strengths of seven Wi-Fi signals visible on a smartphone. One of the four rooms is the decision factor.

Getting ready

Preparation for this recipe involves installing `scikit-learn` and `pandas`. In your Python environment, run the following command:

```
pip install sklearn pandas
```

In preparation for this recipe, download the wireless indoor localization dataset from UCI's machine learning repository: `https://archive.ics.uci.edu/ml/datasets/Wireless+Indoor+Localization`.

How to do it...

To localize an entity based on the Wi-Fi signal using machine learning, observe the following steps:

1. Collect a dataset of Wi-Fi signal strengths from different locations in the area of interest.

2. Load the data into a data frame using `pandas`:

```
import pandas as pd

df = pd.read_csv("wifi_localization.txt", sep="\t", header=None)
df = df.rename(columns={7: "room"})
```

3. Train-test split the data frame:

```
from sklearn.model_selection import train_test_split

df_train, df_test = train_test_split(df)
```

4. Distribute the features and labels into an array:

```
y_train = df_train.pop("room").values
y_test = df_test.pop("room").values
X_train = df_train.values
X_test = df_test.values
```

5. Instantiate a random forest classifier:

```
from sklearn.ensemble import RandomForestClassifier

clf = RandomForestClassifier()
```

6. Fit the classifier to the training data:

```
clf.fit(X_train, y_train)
```

7. Predict on the testing dataset and print out the confusion matrix:

```
y_pred = clf.predict(X_test)
from sklearn.metrics import confusion_matrix

print(confusion_matrix(y_test, y_pred))
```

The following output shows us the confusion matrix:

```
[[124   0   0   0]
 [  0 124   4   0]
 [  0   2 134   0]
 [  1   0   0 111]]
```

How it works...

Step 1 consists of assembling a dataset of Wi-Fi signal strengths from different locations in the area of interest. This is something that can be done relatively easily, simply by walking through a room with a GPS-enabled phone, and running a script to record the strength of the Wi-Fi. In *Step 2*, we read the data into a data frame, and then rename the target column to room so we know what it refers to. Moving on, in *Step 3*, we train-test split our data in preparation for learning. We divide up the features and labels into arrays (*Step 4*). Finally, in *Steps 5* and 6, we train and test a basic classifier. Observe that the performance of the model is very high. This suggests that it is not a difficult task to localize a device based on the strength of the Wi-Fi signals that it is able to pick up, provided the region has been learned previously.

Securing and Attacking Data with Machine Learning

7

In this chapter, we will learn how to employ **machine learning** (**ML**) to secure and attack data. We will cover how to assess the strength of a password using ML, and conversely, how to crack passwords using deep learning. Similarly, we will cover how to hide messages in plain sight using steganography, as well as how to detect steganography using ML. In addition, we will apply ML with hardware security to attack **physically unclonable functions** (**PUFs**) using AI.

In this chapter, we will cover the following recipes:

- Assessing password security using ML
- Deep learning for password cracking
- Deep steganography
- ML-based steganalysis
- ML attacks on PUFs
- Encryption using deep learning
- HIPAA data breaches – data exploration and visualization

Technical requirements

In this chapter, we will be using the following technologies:

- PyTorch
- TensorBoardX
- XGBoost
- scikit-learn
- pandas

- TensorFlow
- Keras
- Octave

The code and datasets for this chapter can be found at `https://github.com/`
`PacktPublishing/Machine-Learning-for-Cybersecurity-Cookbook/tree/master/`
`Chapter07.`

Assessing password security using ML

Password cracking is the systematic endeavor of discovering the password of a secure system. Cracking can involve using common passwords, cleverly generated candidate passwords (for example, replacing the letter O with the number 0 or writing a word backward), or just using a plain bruteforce exhaustive search. To make it more difficult to crack a password, a strong password must be chosen.

Getting ready

To prepare for this recipe, we need to install `pandas`, `sklearn`, and `xgboost` in `pip`. Use the following code to do so:

```
pip install pandas sklearn xgboost
```

In addition, extract the archived dataset, that is, `PasswordDataset.7z`.

How to do it...

In the following steps, we will read in a dataset of passwords, along with labels for their strength, and build a classifier to assess password strength. Let's get started:

1. Import `pandas` and read in the passwords into a dataframe:

```
import pandas as pd

df = pd.read_csv(
    "passwordDataset.csv", dtype={"password": "str", "strength":
"int"}, index_col=None
)
```

2. Shuffle the data at random:

```
df = df.sample(frac=1)
```

3. Split the dataframe into two separate dataframes, one for training and one for testing:

```
l = len(df.index)
train_df = df.head(int(l * 0.8))
test_df = df.tail(int(l * 0.2))
```

4. Create the required labels and featured data:

```
y_train = train_df.pop("strength").values
y_test = test_df.pop("strength").values
X_train = train_df.values.flatten()
X_test = test_df.values.flatten()
```

5. Define a function that splits a string into its characters:

```
def character_tokens(input_string):
    """Break string into characters."""
    return [x for x in input_string]
```

6. Create a pipeline to perform TF-IDF on the characters of the passwords, followed by gradient boosting:

```
from sklearn.pipeline import Pipeline
from sklearn.feature_extraction.text import TfidfVectorizer
from xgboost import XGBClassifier

password_clf = Pipeline(
    [("vect", TfidfVectorizer(tokenizer=character_tokens)), ("clf",
XGBClassifier()),]
)
```

7. Train and test the pipeline:

```
password_clf.fit(X_train, y_train)
password_clf.score(X_test, y_test)
```

The following is the output:

```
0.9137365878426307
```

8. Set one variable as a commonly used password and one as a computer-generated, high-entropy password:

```
common_password = "qwerty"
strong_computer_generated_password = "c9lCwLBFmdLbG6iWla4H"
```

9. Check what the classifier predicts for the strength of the two passwords:

```
password_clf.predict([common_password,
strong_computer_generated_password])
```

The following is the output:

```
array([0, 2])
```

How it works...

We start by importing `pandas` and then reading our data into a dataframe (*step 1*). There are two fields in this data: password and password strength. Password strength consists of three levels of difficulty. We shuffle the data to create more robust training in *step 2*. In *step 3*, we split the dataframe via an 80-20 split, and then distribute the features and labels into arrays (*step 4*). In *step 5*, we define a function that splits the password strings into characters in order to tokenize passwords into characters, rather than into words. This will allow the classifier to learn fine-grained information about the password dataset. In *step 6*, we define a pipeline to perform NLP on the characters of a password, followed by using an XGBoost classifier. Next, we train and test our classifier (*step 7*). For a somewhat subjective task such as this, the performance of a classifier will not necessarily be reflected in a high or low score.

Having finished the training, we perform a sanity check/demonstration of the efficacy of the classifier. We choose one of the most common passwords and one that was generated using a password management system in *step 8*. In *step 9*, we can see that the classifier indeed classified the common password as weak (strength 0) and the strong password as strong (strength 2). Success.

Deep learning for password cracking

Modern password cracking tools, such as **John the Ripper**, allow a hacker to test billions of potential passwords in a matter of seconds. Not only do such tools allow a hacker to try out every password in a dictionary of common passwords, but they can also automatically transform these passwords by using concatenation (for example, `password1234`), leetspeak (`p4s5w0rd`), and other promising techniques. Though these techniques are promising, finding additional promising transformations is a difficult task. The ML system known as PassGAN uses a **generative adversarial network** (**GAN**) to automatically learn such rules by observing large datasets of real passwords (gathered from a corpus of actual password leaks) and to generate high-probability password candidates. In this recipe, you will train PassGAN on a corpus of leaked passwords and use it to generate password guesses.

This project will require a machine with a GPU.

Getting ready

In preparation for this recipe, perform the following steps:

1. Clone the `PassGAN` repository using the following command:

   ```
   git clone https://github.com/emmanueltsukerman/PassGAN.git
   ```

2. Place a dataset under the `data` folder. For example, you may download the famous `rockyou` password dataset using the following command:

   ```
   curl -L -o data/train.txt
   https://github.com/brannondorsey/PassGAN/releases/download/data/roc
   kyou-train.txt
   ```

You should see something like the following when running the password dataset:

```
emmanueltsukerman@instance-2:~/PassGAN$ curl -L -o data/train.txt https://github.com/brannondorsey/PassGAN/releases
/download/data/rockyou-train.txt
  % Total    % Received % Xferd  Average Speed   Time    Time     Time  Current
                                 Dload  Upload   Total   Spent    Left  Speed
100   608    0   608    0     0   1601      0 --:--:-- --:--:-- --:--:--  1600
100  164M  100  164M    0     0  3761k      0  0:00:44  0:00:44 --:--:-- 5602k
```

In addition, this recipe requires CUDA 8 to be preinstalled. The required `pip` packages can be installed by running the following command:

```
pip install -r requirements.txt
```

How to do it...

In the following steps, we will train PassGAN on a corpus of leaked passwords and then use it to generate new password guesses. Let's get started:

1. Train your neural network on the dataset by running the following command:

    ```
    python train.py --output-dir output --training-data data/train.txt
    ```

2. Generate a list of (100,000) password guesses by running the following command:

    ```
    python sample.py \
    --input-dir pretrained \
    --checkpoint pretrained/checkpoints/195000.ckpt \
    --output gen_passwords.txt \
    --batch-size 1024 \
    --num-samples 100000
    ```

Your Terminal should look something like the following:

How it works...

We hit the ground running in this recipe by training our neural network straight away in *step 1*. Several additional flags are available to customize training, depending on our needs. Now that we've trained our model, we need to output a list of 100,000 passwords, all of which have been generated by the model (*step 2*). These serve as intelligent guesses of likely passwords. By examining the output of *step 2*, we can see that the passwords appear as follows:

```
emmanueltsukerman@instance-2:~/PassGAN$ head -10 gen_passwords.txt
149032
9101ja
namalo
harrien
teugaj
0122060
notch
yudla1
0105263
mariosa
```

Now, we can use these as candidates for cracking passwords.

There's more

The original paper describing PassGAN can be found at `https://arxiv.org/abs/1709.00440`.

Deep steganography

Steganography is the practice of hiding a message (that is, the secret) within another medium, such as a file, text, image, or video (that is, the cover). When the secret is embedded into the cover, the result is called the **container**. In this recipe, we will use deep neural networks to create the hiding and revealing processes. Unlike common steganographic methods, which encode the secret in the LSB of the cover, deep learning distributes the secret across all bits.

Getting ready

In this recipe, you will need access to a GPU.

How to do it...

1. Clone the repository using the following command:

```
git clone
https://github.com/emmanueltsukerman/PyTorch-Deep-Image-Steganograp
hy.git
```

2. Prepare a pretrained model:

```
cat ./checkPoint/netH.tar.gz* | tar -xzv -C ./checkPoint/
```

3. Prepare a secret image and a cover image in the example_pics folder:

As you can see, we are using the following image as the cover image:

We are using the following image as the secret image:

4. Execute the pretrained model to produce a container image and a reconstructed secret:

```
CUDA_VISIBLE_DEVICES=0 python main.py –test=./example_pics
```

The first part of the output is displayed in the following screenshot:

```
emmanueltauserganginstance-2:~/PyTorch-Deep-Image-Steganography$ CUDA_VISIBLE_DEVICES=0 python3 main.py --test=./example_pics
Namespace(Hnet='', Rnet='', batchsize=32, beta=0.75, beta1=0.5, cuda=True, dataset='train', debug=False, decay_round=10, hostname='instance-2', imageSize=256, logFrequency=10, lr=0.001, ngpu=1, ni
ter=100, outckpts='./training/instance-2_2019-05-11-14_25_31/checkpoints', outcodes='./training/instance-2_2019-05-11-14_25_31/codes', outlogs='./training/instance-2_2019-05-11-14_25_31/trainingLo
gs', remark='', resultPicFrequency=100, test='./example_pics', testPics='./training/instance-2_2019-05-11-14_25_31/testPics', trainpics='./training/instance-2_2019-05-11-14_25_31/trainPics', valid
ationpics='./training/instance-2_2018-05-11-14_25_31/validationPics', workers=8)
)netGenerator(
  (model): UnetSkipConnectionBlock(
    (model): Sequential(
      (0): Conv2d(6, 64, kernel_size=(4, 4), stride=(2, 2), padding=(1, 1), bias=False)
      (1): UnetSkipConnectionBlock(
        (model): Sequential(
          (0): LeakyReLU(negative_slope=0.2, inplace)
          (1): Conv2d(64, 128, kernel_size=(4, 4), stride=(2, 2), padding=(1, 1), bias=False)
          (2): BatchNorm2d(128, eps=1e-05, momentum=0.1, affine=True, track_running_stats=True)
          (3): UnetSkipConnectionBlock(
            (model): Sequential(
              (0): LeakyReLU(negative_slope=0.2, inplace)
              (1): Conv2d(128, 256, kernel_size=(4, 4), stride=(2, 2), padding=(1, 1), bias=False)
              (2): BatchNorm2d(256, eps=1e-05, momentum=0.1, affine=True, track_running_stats=True)
              (3): UnetSkipConnectionBlock(
                (model): Sequential(
                  (0): LeakyReLU(negative_slope=0.2, inplace)
                  (1): Conv2d(256, 512, kernel_size=(4, 4), stride=(2, 2), padding=(1, 1), bias=False)
                  (2): BatchNorm2d(512, eps=1e-05, momentum=0.1, affine=True, track_running_stats=True)
                  (3): UnetSkipConnectionBlock(
                    (model): Sequential(
                      (0): LeakyReLU(negative_slope=0.2, inplace)
                      (1): Conv2d(512, 512, kernel_size=(4, 4), stride=(2, 2), padding=(1, 1), bias=False)
                      (2): BatchNorm2d(512, eps=1e-05, momentum=0.1, affine=True, track_running_stats=True)
                      (3): UnetSkipConnectionBlock(
                        (model): Sequential(
                          (0): LeakyReLU(negative_slope=0.2, inplace)
                          (1): Conv2d(512, 512, kernel_size=(4, 4), stride=(2, 2), padding=(1, 1), bias=False)
                          (2): BatchNorm2d(512, eps=1e-05, momentum=0.1, affine=True, track_running_stats=True)
                          (3): UnetSkipConnectionBlock(
                            (model): Sequential(
                              (0): LeakyReLU(negative_slope=0.2, inplace)
                              (1): Conv2d(512, 512, kernel_size=(4, 4), stride=(2, 2), padding=(1, 1), bias=False)
                              (2): ReLU(inplace)
                              (3): ConvTranspose2d(512, 512, kernel_size=(4, 4), stride=(2, 2), padding=(1, 1), bias=False)
                              (4): BatchNorm2d(512, eps=1e-05, momentum=0.1, affine=True, track_running_stats=True)
                            )
                          )
                          (4): ReLU(inplace)
                          (5): ConvTranspose2d(1024, 512, kernel_size=(4, 4), stride=(2, 2), padding=(1, 1), bias=False)
                          (6): BatchNorm2d(512, eps=1e-05, momentum=0.1, affine=True, track_running_stats=True)
                        )
                      )
```

The second part of the output is displayed in the following screenshot:

```
              )
            )
            (4): ReLU(inplace)
            (5): ConvTranspose2d(1024, 512, kernel_size=(4, 4), stride=(2, 2), padding=(1, 1), bias=False)
            (6): BatchNorm2d(512, eps=1e-05, momentum=0.1, affine=True, track_running_stats=True)
          )
        )
        (4): ReLU(inplace)
        (5): ConvTranspose2d(1024, 256, kernel_size=(4, 4), stride=(2, 2), padding=(1, 1), bias=False)
        (6): BatchNorm2d(256, eps=1e-05, momentum=0.1, affine=True, track_running_stats=True)
      )
    )
    (4): ReLU(inplace)
    (5): ConvTranspose2d(512, 128, kernel_size=(4, 4), stride=(2, 2), padding=(1, 1), bias=False)
    (6): BatchNorm2d(128, eps=1e-05, momentum=0.1, affine=True, track_running_stats=True)
  )
)
    (4): ReLU(inplace)
    (5): ConvTranspose2d(256, 64, kernel_size=(4, 4), stride=(2, 2), padding=(1, 1), bias=False)
    (6): BatchNorm2d(64, eps=1e-05, momentum=0.1, affine=True, track_running_stats=True)
  )
)
    (2): ReLU(inplace)
    (3): ConvTranspose2d(128, 3, kernel_size=(4, 4), stride=(2, 2), padding=(1, 1))
    (4): Sigmoid()
  )
)
)
Total number of parameters: 41832067
RevealNet(
  (main): Sequential(
    (0): Conv2d(3, 64, kernel_size=(3, 3), stride=(1, 1), padding=(1, 1))
    (1): BatchNorm2d(64, eps=1e-05, momentum=0.1, affine=True, track_running_stats=True)
    (2): ReLU(inplace)
    (3): Conv2d(64, 128, kernel_size=(3, 3), stride=(1, 1), padding=(1, 1))
    (4): BatchNorm2d(128, eps=1e-05, momentum=0.1, affine=True, track_running_stats=True)
    (5): ReLU(inplace)
    (6): Conv2d(128, 256, kernel_size=(3, 3), stride=(1, 1), padding=(1, 1))
    (7): BatchNorm2d(256, eps=1e-05, momentum=0.1, affine=True, track_running_stats=True)
    (8): ReLU(inplace)
    (9): Conv2d(256, 128, kernel_size=(3, 3), stride=(1, 1), padding=(1, 1))
    (10): BatchNorm2d(128, eps=1e-05, momentum=0.1, affine=True, track_running_stats=True)
    (11): ReLU(inplace)
    (12): Conv2d(128, 64, kernel_size=(3, 3), stride=(1, 1), padding=(1, 1))
    (13): BatchNorm2d(64, eps=1e-05, momentum=0.1, affine=True, track_running_stats=True)
    (14): ReLU(inplace)
    (15): Conv2d(64, 3, kernel_size=(3, 3), stride=(1, 1), padding=(1, 1))
    (16): Sigmoid()
  )
)
```

The final part of the output is displayed in the following screenshot:

```
Total number of parameters: 742659
############################################### test begin ###############################################
main.py:450: UserWarning: volatile was removed and now has no effect. Use `with torch.no_grad():` instead.
  concat_imgv = Variable(concat_img, volatile=True)  # concat_img as input of Hiding net
main.py:451: UserWarning: volatile was removed and now has no effect. Use `with torch.no_grad():` instead.
  cover_imgv = Variable(cover_img, volatile=True)  # cover_imgv as label of Hiding net
tensor(0.0003, device='cuda:0', grad_fn=<MseLossBackward>)
main.py:461: UserWarning: volatile was removed and now has no effect. Use `with torch.no_grad():` instead.
  secret_imgv = Variable(secret_img, volatile=True)  # secret_imgv as label of R-net
validation[0] val_Hloss = 0.000278      val_Rloss = 0.000178    val_Sumloss = 0.000412  validation time=6.41
############################################### test end ###############################################
####################   test is completed, the result pic is saved in the ./training/yourcompuer+time/testPics/   ####################
```

5. Examine your results under the training folder. You should see the following image:

Row 1: cover. Row 2: container. Row 3: secret. Row 4: reconstructed secret

How it works...

In *step 1*, we simply clone the repository for the deep steganography project. Some background on the theory and implementation of this project can be found in the paper *Hiding Images in Plain Sight: Deep Steganography* (`https://papers.nips.cc/paper/6802-hiding-images-in-plain-sight-deep-steganography`).

The basic idea is that there is a **hiding network (H-net)** and a **reveal network (R-net)**, both of which are trained adversarially. Continuing to *step 2*, we prepare our pretrained model. The model that we used here was trained on 45,000 images from ImageNet, and evaluated on 5,000 images. All of the images were resized to 256 × 256 without normalization and the task took 24 hours of training on a single NVIDIA GTX 1080 Ti. Next, we pick two images of our choosing to serve as a cover and a secret (*step 3*). Feel free to use your own pair of images. In *steps 4* and *5*, we run the model, create a container image (the one containing the hidden secret), and produce an image showing our results. As you can see, the container image and cover image are indistinguishable to the human eye, meaning that no one will be able to tell that you have hidden a secret in the cover image.

ML-based steganalysis

One of the main techniques in steganography is hiding messages in images by altering the **least significant bits (LSB)** of the pixels with those of the message bits. The result is an image with a message hidden in it that the human eye cannot distinguish from the original image. This is because, on changing the LSB in the pixels of an image, the pixel values are only altered by a small amount, resulting in a visually similar image.

There are two prominent methods for LSB:

- The naïve method is called LSB replacement. In this method, the LSB bit remains unchanged if the message bit is the same as the LSB; otherwise, the bit is altered. Hence, the odd pixels are reduced by 1 in intensity, whereas the even pixel values are incremented by 1. However, this causes an imbalance in the image histogram, which can be easily detected by statistical methods for steganalysis.
- The second method of LSB steganography, LSB matching, solves this issue by randomly incrementing or decrementing the pixel values by 1 in the case of an LSB bit mismatch. This avoids the issue of histogram imbalance and makes it difficult to perform steganalysis by using simple statistical methods alone.

The following images showcase an instance of LSB steganography.

The following image will be represented as the cover image:

The following image will be represented as the secret image:

The following image will be represented as the container image:

The following image will be shown as the recovered secret image:

Getting ready

It is recommended that you complete this recipe on a Linux machine. Follow these steps to get everything set up:

1. Install octave, as well as its packages, image and signal:

   sudo apt-get install octave octave-image octave-signal

2. Clone the repository for aletheia, as shown in the following code:

   git clone https://github.com/emmanueltsukerman/aletheia.git

3. Download a BOSS dataset, which you can download via the following link:

   wget http://dde.binghamton.edu/download/ImageDB/BOSSbase_1.01.zip

   This will retrieve a database of grayscale images.

4. Unzip the dataset and rename the BOSSbase folder:

   unzip BOSSbase_1.01.zip

For your convenience, the processed datasets, namely bossbase.7z and bossbase_lsb.7z, can be found in this book's repository.

How to do it...

In this recipe, we will curate an LSB dataset and then train and test an ML model to detect the presence of LSB steganography in an image. Let's get started:

1. Create an LSB database using the following command:

   python aletheia.py lsbm-sim bossbase 0.40 bossbase_lsb

   The result is a new folder named bossbase_lsb, which contains the BOSS images with embeddings. It does this using an LSB matching simulator.

2. Featurize the BOSS dataset, as shown in the following code:

   ./aletheia.py srm bossbase bossbase.fea

3. Featurize the LSB dataset, as shown in the following code:

   ./aletheia.py srm bossbase_lsb bossbase_lsb.fea

The remaining steps can be run in a Python environment for your convenience.

4. Create some variables that point to the path of the extracted features:

```
bossbase_features_path = "bossbase.fea"
bossbase_lsb_features_path = "bossbase_lsb.fea"
features_with_labels = [(bossbase_features_path, 0),
(bossbase_lsb_features_path, 1)]
```

5. Collect the features and labels and put them in arrays:

```
X = []
y = []
for feature_path, label in features_with_labels:
    with open(feature_path, "r") as f:
        for line in f:
            fv = line.split()
            X.append(fv)
            y.append(label)
```

6. Perform a train-test split:

```
from sklearn.model_selection import train_test_split

X_train, X_test, y_train, y_test = train_test_split(
    X, y, test_size=0.2, random_state=11
)
```

7. Instantiate a RandomForestClassifier and train it:

```
from sklearn.ensemble import RandomForestClassifier

clf = RandomForestClassifier()
clf = clf.fit(X_train, y_train)
```

8. Score the classifier on the test set:

```
print(clf.score(X_test, y_test))
```

The following is the output:

```
0.825
```

How it works...

We start this recipe by creating a large dataset of LSB steganography container images using the software known as Aletheia (*step 1*). Aletheia offers a wide array of functionality. Run the following command with no arguments:

```
$ ./aletheia.py
```

The preceding command prints out the following information about `aletheia`:

```
./aletheia.py <command>
COMMANDS:
Attacks to LSB replacement:
- spa: Sample Pairs Analysis.
- rs: RS attack.
ML-based detectors:
- esvm-predict: Predict using eSVM.
- e4s-predict: Predict using EC.
Feature extractors:
- srm: Full Spatial Rich Models.
- hill-maxsrm: Selection-Channel-Aware Spatial Rich Models for HILL.
- srmq1: Spatial Rich Models with fixed quantization q=1c.
- scrmq1: Spatial Color Rich Models with fixed quantization q=1c.
- gfr: JPEG steganalysis with 2D Gabor Filters.
Embedding simulators:
- lsbr-sim: Embedding using LSB replacement simulator.
- lsbm-sim: Embedding using LSB matching simulator.
- hugo-sim: Embedding using HUGO simulator.
- wow-sim: Embedding using WOW simulator.
- s-uniward-sim: Embedding using S-UNIWARD simulator.
- j-uniward-sim: Embedding using J-UNIWARD simulator.
- j-uniward-color-sim: Embedding using J-UNIWARD color simulator.
- hill-sim: Embedding using HILL simulator.
- ebs-sim: Embedding using EBS simulator.
- ebs-color-sim: Embedding using EBS color simulator.
- ued-sim: Embedding using UED simulator.
- ued-color-sim: Embedding using UED color simulator.
- nsf5-sim: Embedding using nsF5 simulator.
- nsf5-color-sim: Embedding using nsF5 color simulator.
Model training:
- esvm: Ensemble of Support Vector Machines.
- e4s: Ensemble Classifiers for Steganalysis.
- xu-net: Convolutional Neural Network for Steganalysis.
Unsupervised attacks:
- ats: Artificial Training Sets.
Naive attacks:
- brute-force: Brute force attack using a list of passwords.
```

```
- hpf: High-pass filter.
- imgdiff: Differences between two images.
- imgdiff-pixels: Differences between two images (show pixel values).
- rm-alpha: Opacity of the alpha channel to 255.
```

In *steps 2* and *3*, we employ the `srm` command of Aletheia to extract features of the plain images and container images. The `srm` command extracts a full and spatially rich feature set. Other alternative feature sets are available as well. Next, we create variables pointing to the paths of our dataset (*step 4*) and then collect our features and our labels into arrays (*step 5*). In *steps 6-8*, we create a train-test split, train a classifier, and then test it. Looking at the performance of 80% on the balanced dataset, we can see that the features do help us to distinguish between plain and container images. In other words, we can conclude that ML can detect steganography.

ML attacks on PUFs

Classical cryptography offers several measures for securing electronic devices. These mainly rely on a secret key and expensive resources due to the device permanently storing a piece of digital information that's unknown to our adversaries. In practice, it is difficult to keep this information confidential. This problem motivated the invention of PUF – physical devices that produce an output that's quick to evaluate yet hard to predict.

To authenticate using a PUF, we need to construct a database of **Challenge-Response Pairs (CRPs)**. A challenge is a binary string (for example, 1100101...01) of length n, and a response is some other binary string of length m. To find out whether an unknown device is the aforementioned PUF, we need to issue it a number of challenges, verifying that it produces the correct responses until we reach the desired probability that it is indeed the same PUF. Note that PUFs themselves are not 100% reliable, and the same challenge may yield different responses due to varying environmental conditions and noise:

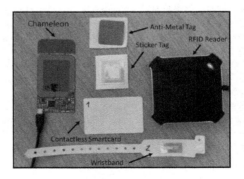

Figure 8: PUF-based commercial RFID tag

In this recipe, we will be attacking a specific PUF using ML. Note that the field is ever-evolving, and other, more secure, PUFs have been proposed, as well as methods to increase the reliability and security of PUFs using ML.

Getting ready

For this recipe, we need to install pandas, sklearn, and xgboost in pip. Use the following code to do so:

```
pip install pandas sklearn xgboost
```

In addition, the CRPDataset.csv dataset has been provided for this recipe.

How to do it...

Let's learn how to crack a PUF with ML:

1. Load a CRP dataset, in this case, CRPDataset.csv:

   ```
   import pandas as pd

   df = pd.read_csv("CRPdataset.csv")
   ```

   The data is made up of pairs (x,y), where x is a binary string that's 64 in length and y is a binary digit. Here, x is a challenge and y is a response.

2. Convert the pandas dataframe into a NumPy array of features and labels:

   ```
   y = df.pop("Label").values
   X = df.values
   ```

3. Perform a train-test split:

   ```
   from sklearn.model_selection import train_test_split

   X_train, X_test, y_train, y_test = train_test_split(
       X, y, test_size=0.25, random_state=11
   )
   ```

4. Instantiate and train an XGBoost classifier:

```
from xgboost import XGBClassifier

clf = XGBClassifier()
clf.fit(X_train, y_train)
print(clf.score(X_train, y_train))
```

The following is the output:

0.6405208333333333

5. Test the classifier, as shown in the following code:

```
clf.score(X_test, y_test)
```

The following is the output:

0.6270833333333333

How it works...

We start by reading a CRP dataset into a dataframe (*step 1*). In *step 2*, we create x and y NumPy arrays to hold the features and labels. Next, we train-test split our data (*step 3*) and then train and test a classifier for CRPs (*steps 4* and *5*). Based on performance, we can see that ML can accurately predict responses to PUF challenges. The implications are that, while using our trained model, we can build a software clone of the PUF and use it to (falsely) authenticate.

There's more

The original unprocessed dataset for this recipe can be found at https://archive.ics.uci. edu/ml/datasets/Physical+Unclonable+Functions. Additional background information can be found in the paper, *A Machine Learning-Based Security Vulnerability Study on XOR PUFs for Resource-Constraint Internet of Things*, by Aseeri, A. O., Zhuang, Y., and Alkatheiri, M. S. (July 2018) in 2018 IEEE International Congress on Internet of Things (ICIOT) (pp. 49-56). IEEE.

Encryption using deep learning

Encryption is the process of converting information into code to prevent unauthorized access. In this recipe, we will utilize a convolutional neural network to encrypt and decrypt data.

Getting ready

For this recipe, you will need to install the click, keras, tensorflow, and tqdm packages in pip. Use the following code to do so:

```
pip install click keras tensorflow tqdm
```

Additionally, clone the repository using the following command:

```
git clone https://github.com/emmanueltsukerman/convcrypt.git
```

How to do it...

The following steps will guide you through how to use ConvCrypt in order to encrypt an image. Let's get started:

1. Run the encrypt.py script against the image or file you would like to encrypt:

```
python encrypt.py --input_file "input file path" --output_file
"encrypted file path" --key_file "key file name"
```

The output of the preceding code is displayed in the following screenshot:

```
:convcrypt etsukerman$ python encrypt.py --input_file 0.jpeg --output_file 0enc.jpeg --key_file key
/anaconda3/lib/python3.6/site-packages/h5py/__init__.py:36: FutureWarning: Conversion of the second argument of issubdtype from 'float' to 'np.floating' is deprecated. In future, it wi
ll be treated as 'np.float64 == np.dtype(float).type'.
  from ._conv import register_converters as _register_converters
Using TensorFlow backend.
 0%|                                                                                                                                            | 0/5 [00:00<?, ?it/s]
2019-05-14 10:44:16.602113: I tensorflow/core/platform/cpu_feature_guard.cc:141] Your CPU supports instructions that this TensorFlow binary was not compiled to use: AVX2 FMA
100%|████████████████████████████████████████████████████████████████████████████████████████████████████████████████████████████████████████| 5/5 [3:05:39<00:00, 2208.89s/it]
Encryption complete.
```

To see that the file has been encrypted, attempt to open it. We will see that it cannot be opened due to it being encrypted:

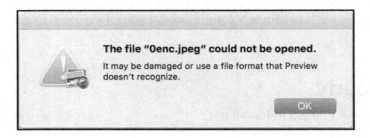

2. To decrypt the file, execute the `decrypt.py` script against the encrypted file and the key file:

```
python decrypt.py --input_file "encrypted file path" --output_file
"reconstructed file path" --key_file "key file name"
```

The result is the original file.

How it works...

We begin this recipe by encrypting our image using ConvCrypt (*step 1*). ConvCrypt is a proof-of-concept experimental encryption algorithm that uses *n*-dimensional convolutional neural networks. Currently, it only supports three-dimensional convolutions. Then, in *step 2*, we reverse the encryption and test it to ensure that the result is the original file. Success!

For those of you who are interested, the first thing the ConvCrypt algorithm does is separate the data into blocks. Then, a key is generated for 3D convolutions; this is a randomly generated cube of bits that are the same size as a data block. Lastly, a convolutional neural network is trained to convolve the key into each data block so that each data block gets its own trained network. The resulting encrypted data is the weights of each of the networks (the values of the kernel tensors).

HIPAA data breaches – data exploration and visualization

Data exploration is the initial step in data analysis, whereby visual exploration is used to understand a dataset and the characteristics of the data. Data visualization helps us understand the data by placing it in an optical context so that our powerful visual processing centers can quickly find patterns and correlations in the data.

In this recipe, you will explore and visualize a public domain dataset regarding breaches of HIPAA confidential information.

Getting ready

For this recipe, you will need to install `pandas` and `sklearn` in `pip`. Use the following code to do so:

```
pip install pandas sklearn
```

In addition, the `HIPAA-breach-report-2009-to-2017.csv` dataset has been provided so that you can use it in this recipe.

How to do it...

In the following steps, you will visualize the HIPAA breaches dataset in pandas and use TF-IDF to extract important keywords from the descriptions of the breaches. Let's get started:

1. Load and clean the HIPAA breaches dataset using `pandas`:

```
import pandas as pd

df = pd.read_csv("HIPAA-breach-report-2009-to-2017.csv")
df = df.dropna()
```

The output of the preceding code is shown in the following screenshot:

```
In [104]: df.head()

Out[104]:
          0    1       2  3 4 5 6 7 8 9 ...  1549 1550 1551 1552 1553 1554 1555 1556 1557 label
     0  125  125    1.0   1 0 0 0 0 0 0 ...     0    0    0    0    0    0    0    0    0   ad.
     1   57  468  8.2105  1 0 0 0 0 0 0 ...     0    0    0    0    0    0    0    0    0   ad.
     2   33  230  6.9696  1 0 0 0 0 0 0 ...     0    0    0    0    0    0    0    0    0   ad.
     3   60  468    7.8   1 0 0 0 0 0 0 ...     0    0    0    0    0    0    0    0    0   ad.
     4   60  468    7.8   1 0 0 0 0 0 0 ...     0    0    0    0    0    0    0    0    0   ad.

5 rows × 1559 columns
```

2. Plot a histogram of the number of individuals who have been affected by a breach against the frequency of such breaches by using the following code:

```
%matplotlib inline
def_fig_size = (15, 6)
df["Individuals Affected"].plot(
kind="hist", figsize=def_fig_size, log=True, title="Breach Size
Distribution"
)
```

The following output shows the **Breach Size Distribution**:

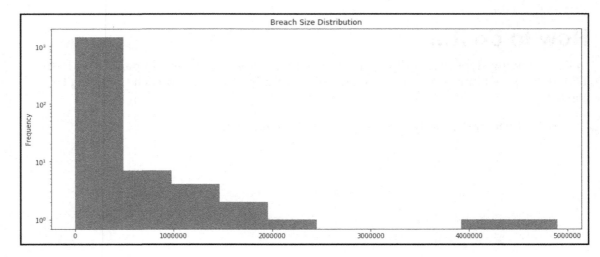

3. Plot the average breach size based on the entity type:

```
df.groupby("Covered Entity Type").mean().plot(
  kind="bar", figsize=def_fig_size, title="Average Breach Size by
Entity Type"
  )
```

The following screenshot shows the output of the **Average Breach Size by Entity Type**:

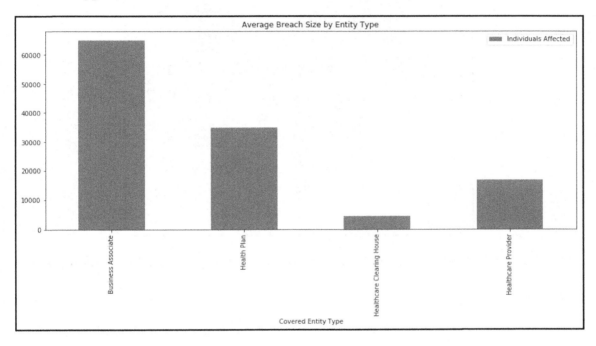

4. Plot a pie chart that shows the number of individuals affected by breaches per state, filtered by the top 20 states:

```
df.groupby("State").sum().nlargest(20, "Individuals
Affected").plot.pie(
  y="Individuals Affected", figsize=def_fig_size, legend=False
  )
```

The following chart shows us those individuals who are affected by breaches per state:

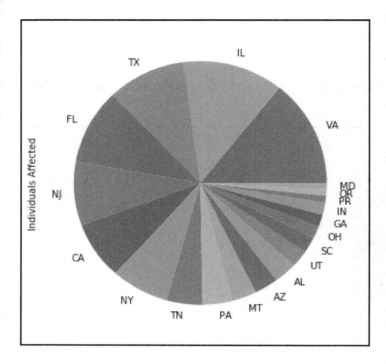

5. Plot the average breach size against the type of breach (theft, loss, hacking, and so on):

```
df.groupby("Type of Breach").mean().plot(
 kind="bar", figsize=def_fig_size, title="Average Breach Size by
Entity Type"
 )
```

The following graph shows the **Type of Breach**:

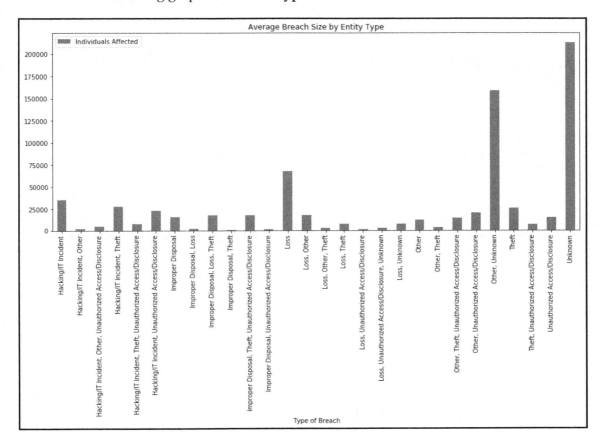

6. Instantiate a TF-IDF vectorizer:

```
from sklearn.feature_extraction.text import TfidfVectorizer

vectorizer = TfidfVectorizer()
```

7. Fit the vectorizer to the breach descriptions and vectorize them:

```
df["Web Description"] = df["Web Description"].str.replace("\r", " ")
X = df["Web Description"].values
X_transformed = vectorizer.fit_transform(X)
```

8. Select the 15 most important features in the breach descriptions based on TF-IDF:

```
import numpy as np

feature_array = np.array(vectorizer.get_feature_names())
tfidf_sorting =
np.argsort(X_transformed.toarray()).flatten()[::-1]
n = 15
top_n = feature_array[tfidf_sorting][:n]
print(top_n)
```

The output is as follows:

```
['this' 'review' '842' 'south' 'ransomware' 'memorial' 'specific'
'birthdates' 'consolidated' 'malware' 'license' 'driver' 'found'
'clinic' 'information']
```

9. Print out a couple of breach descriptions containing the `review` keyword:

```
k = 2
i = 0
for x in df["Web Description"].values:
if "review" in x:
i += 1
print(x)
print()
if i == k:
break
```

The following are some of the snippets of the output:

```
A laptop was lost by an employee... all employees received
additional security training.
The covered entity's (CE) business associate (BA) incorrectly... BA
to safeguard all PHI.
```

How it works...

We begin by reading the HIPAA dataset into a dataframe and dropping any rows that contain NAs (*step 1*). Next, in *step 2*, we can see that most breaches are relatively small scale, but a small number of breaches are massive. This is consistent with Pareto's principle. In *step 3*, we plot breaches by sector to ensure that the largest breaches occur in Business Associates. Then, we examine which states have the most HIPAA breaches in *step 4*. In *step 5*, we learn that the cause of the largest breaches is usually unknown! In *steps 6* and *7*, we perform a basic NLP on the descriptions of the breaches. This will allow us to extract additional information of interest. In *step 8*, we can see that TF-IDF was able to find some very informative keywords, such as *ransomware* and *driver*. Finally, in *step 9*, we print out breach description containing the keyword *review*. The word, review turns out to be an extremely important word as it appears as part of quality control and as an incidence response tool.

Secure and Private AI 8

Machine learning can help us diagnose and fight cancer, decide which school is the best for our children and make the smartest real estate investment. But you can only answer these questions with access to private and personal data, which requires a novel approach to machine learning. This approach is called *Secure and Private AI* and, in recent years, has seen great strides, as you will see in the following recipes.

This chapter contains the following recipes:

- Federated learning
- Encrypted computation
- Private deep learning prediction
- Testing the adversarial robustness of neural networks
- Differential privacy using TensorFlow Privacy

Technical requirements

The following are the technical prerequisites for this chapter:

- TensorFlow Federated
- Foolbox
- PyTorch
- Torchvision
- TensorFlow Privacy

Installation instructions, code, and datasets may be found at `https://github.com/PacktPublishing/Machine-Learning-for-Cybersecurity-Cookbook/tree/master/Chapter08`.

Federated learning

In this recipe, we will train a federated learning model using the TensorFlow federated framework.

To understand why federated learning is valuable, consider the *next word prediction* model on your mobile phone when you write an SMS message. For privacy reasons, you wouldn't want the data, that is, your text messages, to be sent to a central server to be used for training the next word predictor. But it's still nice to have an accurate next word prediction algorithm. What to do? This is where federated learning comes in, which is a machine learning technique developed to tackle such privacy concerns.

The core idea in federated learning is that a training dataset remains in the hands of its producers, preserving privacy and ownership, while still being used to train a centralized model. This feature is especially attractive in cybersecurity, where, for example, collecting benign and malicious samples from many different sources is crucial to creating a strong model, but difficult on account of privacy concerns (by way of an example, a benign sample can be a personal or confidential document).

In passing, we should mention the fact that federated learning has been gaining more and more traction due to the increasing importance of data privacy (for example, the enactment of GDPR). Large actors, such as Apple and Google, have started investing heavily in this technology.

Getting ready

Preparation for this recipe involves installing the `tensorflow_federated`, `tensorflow_datasets`, and `tensorflow` packages in `pip`. The command is as follows:

```
pip install tensorflow_federated==0.2.0 tensorflow-datasets
tensorflow==1.13.1
```

We will install specific versions of these packages to prevent any breaks in the code.

How to do it...

In the following steps, you will create two virtual dataset environments—one belonging to Alice, and one belonging to Bob—and use federated averaging to preserve data confidentiality.

1. Import TensorFlow and enable eager execution:

```
import tensorflow as tf

tf.compat.v1.enable_v2_behavior()
```

2. Prepare a dataset by importing Fashion MNIST and splitting it into two separate environments, Alice and Bob:

```
import tensorflow_datasets as tfds

first_50_percent = tfds.Split.TRAIN.subsplit(tfds.percent[:50])
last_50_percent = tfds.Split.TRAIN.subsplit(tfds.percent[-50:])

alice_dataset = tfds.load("fashion_mnist", split=first_50_percent)
bob_dataset = tfds.load("fashion_mnist", split=last_50_percent)
```

3. Now, define a `helper` function to cast the data type from integer to float:

```
def cast(element):
    """Casts an image's pixels into float32."""
    out = {}
    out["image"] = tf.image.convert_image_dtype(element["image"],
dtype=tf.float32)
    out["label"] = element["label"]
    return out
```

4. Then, define a `helper` function to flatten the data to be fed into a neural network:

```
def flatten(element):
    """Flattens an image in preparation for the neural network."""
    return collections.OrderedDict(
        [
            ("x", tf.reshape(element["image"], [-1])),
            ("y", tf.reshape(element["label"], [1])),
        ]
    )
```

5. Now, define a `helper` function to pre-process the data:

```
import collections

BATCH_SIZE = 32

def preprocess(dataset):
    """Preprocesses images to be fed into neural network."""
    return dataset.map(cast).map(flatten).batch(BATCH_SIZE)
```

6. Pre-process the data:

```
preprocessed_alice_dataset = preprocess(alice_dataset)
preprocessed_bob_dataset = preprocess(bob_dataset)
federated_data = [preprocessed_alice_dataset,
preprocessed_bob_dataset]
```

7. Now, define a `loss` function for our neural network:

```
def custom_loss_function(y_true, y_pred):
    """Custom loss function."""
    return tf.reduce_mean(
        tf.keras.losses.sparse_categorical_crossentropy(y_true,
y_pred)
    )
```

8. Define a function to instantiate a simple Keras neural network:

```
from tensorflow.python.keras.optimizer_v2 import gradient_descent

LEARNING_RATE = 0.02
def create_compiled_keras_model():
    """Compiles the keras model."""
    model = tf.keras.models.Sequential(
        [
            tf.keras.layers.Dense(
                10,
                activation=tf.nn.softmax,
                kernel_initializer="zeros",
                input_shape=(784,),
            )
        ]
    )
    model.compile(
        loss=custom_loss_function,
optimizer=gradient_descent.SGD(learning_rate=LEARNING_RATE),
        metrics=[tf.keras.metrics.SparseCategoricalAccuracy()],
```

```
)
return model
```

9. Then, create a dummy batch of samples and define a function to return a federated learning model from the Keras model:

```
batch_of_samples = tf.contrib.framework.nest.map_structure(
    lambda x: x.numpy(), iter(preprocessed_alice_dataset).next()
)


def model_instance():
    """Instantiates the keras model."""
    keras_model = create_compiled_keras_model()
    return tff.learning.from_compiled_keras_model(keras_model,
batch_of_samples)
```

10. Declare an iterative process of federated averaging, and run one stage of the computation:

```
from tensorflow_federated import python as tff

federated_learning_iterative_process =
tff.learning.build_federated_averaging_process(
    model_instance
)
state = federated_learning_iterative_process.initialize()
state, performance =
federated_learning_iterative_process.next(state, federated_data)
```

11. Then, display the metrics of the computation by running the following command:

```
performance
```

The output is as follows:

```
AnonymousTuple([(sparse_categorical_accuracy, 0.74365), (loss,
0.82071316)])
```

How it works...

We begin by importing TensorFlow and enabling eager execution (*Step 1*). Ordinarily, in TensorFlow, operations are not performed immediately. Rather, a computation graph is built, and, at the very end, all operations are run together. In eager execution, computations are executed as soon as possible. Next, in *Step 2*, we import the Fashion MNIST dataset. This dataset has become a *de facto* replacement for MNIST, offering several improvements over it (such as added challenges). We then subdivide the dataset 50:50 between Alice and Bob. We then define a function to cast the pixel values of Fashion MNIST from integers to floats to be used in the training of our neural network (*Step 3*) and another function to flatten the images into a single vector (*Step 4*). This enables us to feed the data into a fully connected neural network. In *Steps 5* and *6*, we employ the previously defined convenience functions to pre-process Alice and Bob's datasets.

Next, we define a loss function that makes sense for our 10-class classification task (*Step 7*), and then define our Keras neural network in preparation for training (*Step 8*). In *Step 9*, we create a dummy batch of samples and define a function to return a federated learning model from the Keras model. The dummy batch of samples specifies the shape of input for the model to expect. In *Step 10*, we run one stage of the federated averaging process. Details regarding the algorithm can be found in the paper entitled *Communication-Efficient Learning of Deep Networks from Decentralized Data*.

At a basic level, the algorithm combines local **stochastic gradient descent (SGD)** on the data of each client, and then uses a server that performs model averaging. The result is conserved confidentiality for the clients (in our case, Alice and Bob). Finally, in *Step 11*, we observe our performance, seeing that the algorithm indeed does train and improve accuracy, as intended.

Encrypted computation

In this recipe, we're going to walk through the basics of encrypted computation. In particular, we're going to focus on one popular approach, called Secure Multi-Party Computation. You'll learn how to build a simple encrypted calculator that can perform addition on encrypted numbers. The ideas in this recipe will come in handy in the *Private deep learning prediction* recipe.

Getting ready

The following recipe has no installation requirements other than Python.

How to do it...

1. Import the random library and select a large prime number, P:

```
import random

P = 67280421310721
```

2. Define an encryption function for three parties:

```
def encrypt(x):
    """Encrypts an integer between 3 partires."""
    share_a = random.randint(0, P)
    share_b = random.randint(0, P)
    share_c = (x - share_a - share_b) % P
    return (share_a, share_b, share_c)
```

3. Encrypt a numerical variable:

```
x = 17
share_a, share_b, share_c = encrypt(x)
print(share_a, share_b, share_c)

16821756678516 13110264723730 37348399908492
```

4. Define a function to decrypt, given the three shares:

```
def decrypt(share_a, share_b, share_c):
    """Decrypts the integer from 3 shares."""
    return (share_a + share_b + share_c) % P
```

5. Decrypt the encrypted variable x:

```
decrypt(share_a, share_b, share_c)
```

The output is as follows:

```
17
```

6. Define a function to add two encrypted numbers:

```
def add(x, y):
    """Addition of encrypted integers."""
    z = list()
    z.append((x[0] + y[0]) % P)
    z.append((x[1] + y[1]) % P)
    z.append((x[2] + y[2]) % P)
    return z
```

7. Add two encrypted variables and decrypt their sum:

```
x = encrypt(5)
y = encrypt(9)
decrypt(*add(x, y))

14
```

How it works...

We begin *Step 1* by importing the random library in order to generate random integers in *Step 2*. We also define a large prime number, P, as we will be wanting a random distribution modulo, P. In *Step 2*, we define how a function encrypts an integer by splitting it between three parties. The value of x here is randomly additively split between the three parties. All operations take place in the field of integer modulo P. Next, in *Step 3*, we demonstrate the result of encrypting an integer using our approach. Proceeding to *Steps 4* and *5*, we define a function to reverse encryption, that is decrypt, and then show that the operation is reversible. In *Step 6*, we define a function to add two encrypted numbers(!). Note that encrypted addition is simply addition of the individual components, modulo P. In the *Encrypted deep learning prediction* recipe, the .share(client, server,...) command from PySyft is used. This command is basically the same encryption procedure we have used in this recipe, so keep in mind that these encryption schemes use the techniques we are discussing here. Finally, in *Step 7*, we demonstrate that we can perform computations on encrypted entities.

Private deep learning prediction

In many situations, company A might have a trained model that it wishes to offer as a service. At the same time, company A may be reluctant to share this model, so as to avoid having its intellectual property stolen. The simple solution to this problem is to have customers send their data to company A, and then receive from it predictions. However, this becomes a problem when the customer wishes to preserve the privacy of their data. To resolve this tricky situation, the company, as well as its customers, can utilize encrypted computation.

In this recipe, you will learn how to share an encrypted pre-trained deep learning model with a client and allow the client to predict using the encrypted model on their own private data.

Getting ready

Preparation for this recipe involves installing PyTorch, Torchvision, and PySyft in `pip`. The command is as follows:

```
pip install torch torchvision syft
```

In addition, a pre-trained model named `server_trained_model.pt` has been included to be used in this recipe.

How to do it...

The following steps utilize PySyft to simulate a client-server interaction in which the server has a pre-trained deep learning model to be kept as a black box, and the client wishes to use the model to predict on data that is kept private.

1. Import `torch` and access its datasets:

```
import torch
import torch.nn as nn
import torch.nn.functional as F
from torchvision import datasets, transforms
```

2. Import PySyft and hook it onto `torch`:

```
import syft as sy

hook = sy.TorchHook(torch)
client = sy.VirtualWorker(hook, id="client")
server = sy.VirtualWorker(hook, id="server")
crypto_provider = sy.VirtualWorker(hook, id="crypto_provider")
```

3. Define a simple neural network:

```
class Net(nn.Module):
    def __init__(self):
        super(Net, self).__init__()
        self.fc1 = nn.Linear(784, 500)
        self.fc2 = nn.Linear(500, 10)
```

```
def forward(self, x):
    x = x.view(-1, 784)
    x = self.fc1(x)
    x = F.relu(x)
    x = self.fc2(x)
    return x
```

4. Instantiate the model and load its pre-trained weights, which are trained on MNIST:

```
model = Net()
model.load_state_dict(torch.load("server_trained_model.pt"))
model.eval()
```

5. Encrypt the network between `client` and `server`:

```
model.fix_precision().share(client, server,
crypto_provider=crypto_provider)
```

6. Define a loader for MNIST data:

```
test_loader = torch.utils.data.DataLoader(
    datasets.MNIST(
        "data",
        train=False,
        download=True,
        transform=transforms.Compose(
            [transforms.ToTensor(), transforms.Normalize((0.1307,),
(0.3081,))]
        ),
    ),
    batch_size=64,
    shuffle=True,
)
```

7. Define a private loader utilizing the loader for MNIST data:

```
private_test_loader = []
for data, target in test_loader:
    private_test_loader.append(
        (
            data.fix_precision().share(client, server,
crypto_provider=crypto_provider),
            target.fix_precision().share(
                client, server, crypto_provider=crypto_provider
            ),
        )
    )
```

8. Define a function to evaluate the private test set:

```
def test(model, test_loader):
    """Test the model."""
    model.eval()
    n_correct_priv = 0
    n_total = 0
```

9. Iterate over the private data, predict using the model, decrypt the results, and then print them out:

```
with torch.no_grad():
    for data, target in test_loader:
        output = model(data)
        pred = output.argmax(dim=1)
        n_correct_priv += pred.eq(target.view_as(pred)).sum()
        n_total += 64
        n_correct =
        n_correct_priv.copy().get().float_precision().long().item()
        print(
            "Test set: Accuracy: {}/{} ({:.0f}%)".format(
                n_correct, n_total, 100.0 * n_correct / n_total
            )
        )
```

10. Run the testing procedure:

```
test(model, private_test_loader)
```

The result is as follows:

```
Test set: Accuracy: 63/64 (98%)
Test set: Accuracy: 123/128 (96%)
Test set: Accuracy: 185/192 (96%)
Test set: Accuracy: 248/256 (97%)
Test set: Accuracy: 310/320 (97%)
Test set: Accuracy: 373/384 (97%)
Test set: Accuracy: 433/448 (97%)
<snip>
Test set: Accuracy: 9668/9920 (97%)
Test set: Accuracy: 9727/9984 (97%)
Test set: Accuracy: 9742/10048 (97%)
```

How it works...

We begin by importing `torch` and its datasets, as well as some associated libraries (*Step 1*). We then import `pysyft` and hook it into `torch` (*Step 2*). We also create virtual environments for the client and server to simulate a real separation of data. In this step, the `crypto_provider` serves as a trusted third party to be used for encryption and decryption purposes. In *Step 3*, we define a simple neural network and, in *Step 4*, we load-in its pretrained weights. Note that, in *Step 5*, and, more generally, whenever the `.share(...)` command is used, you should think of the shared object as being encrypted, and that it is only possible to decrypt it with the assistance of all parties involved. In particular, in *Step 9*, the test function performs encrypted evaluation; the weights of the model, the data inputs, the prediction, and the target used for scoring are all encrypted. However, for the purpose of verifying that the model is working properly, we decrypt and display its accuracy. In *Step 5*, we encrypt the network so that only when the server and client are cooperating can they decrypt the network.

In the next two steps, we define regular and private loaders for MNIST data. The regular loader simply loads MNIST data, while the private loader encrypts the outputs of the regular loader. In *Steps 8* and *9*, we define a `helper` function to evaluate the private test set. In this function, we iterate over the private data, predict using the model, decrypt the results, and then print them out. Finally, we apply the function defined in *Steps 8* and *9* to establish that the model is performing well, while preserving privacy.

Testing the adversarial robustness of neural networks

The study of adversarial attacks on neural networks has revealed a surprising sensitivity to adversarial perturbations. Even the most accurate of neural networks, when left undefended, has been shown to be vulnerable to single pixel attacks and the peppering of invisible-to-the-human-eye noise. Fortunately, recent advances in the field have offered solutions on how to harden neural networks to adversarial attacks of all sorts. One such solution is a neural network design called **Analysis by Synthesis (ABS)**. The main idea behind the model is that it is a Bayesian model. Rather than directly predicting the label given the input, the model also learns class-conditional, sample distributions using **variational autoencoders (VAEs)**. More information can be found in `https://arxiv.org/abs/1805.09190`.

In this recipe, you will load a pre-trained ABS network for MNIST and learn how to test a neural network for adversarial robustness.

Getting ready

The following recipe has been tested in Python 3.6. Preparation for this recipe involves installing the Pytorch, Torchvision, SciPy, Foolbox, and Matplotlib packages in `pip`. The command is as follows:

```
pip install torch torchvision scipy foolbox==1.8 matplotlib
```

How to do it...

In the following steps, we will load a pre-trained ABS model and a traditional CNN model for MNIST. We will attack both models using Foolbox to see how well they can defend against adversarial attacks:

1. Begin by importing a pre-trained ABS model:

   ```
   from abs_models import models
   from abs_models import utils

   ABS_model = models.get_VAE(n_iter=50)
   ```

2. Define a `convenience` function to predict a batch of MNIST images using a model:

   ```
   import numpy as np

   def predict_on_batch(model, batch, batch_size):
       """Predicts the digits of an MNIST batch."""
       preds = []
       labels = []
       for i in range(batch_size):
           point, label = utils.get_batch()
           labels.append(label[0])
           tensor_point = utils.n2t(point)
           logits = model(tensor_point)[0]
           logits = [x for x in logits]
           pred = np.argmax(logits)
           preds.append(int(pred))
       return preds, labels
   ```

3. Predict on a batch:

```
batch = utils.get_batch()
preds, labels = predict_on_batch(ABS_model, batch, 5)
print(preds)
print(labels)
```

The result is as follows:

```
[4, 4, 9, 1, 8]
[4, 4, 9, 1, 8]
```

4. Wrap the model using Foolbox to enable adversarial testing:

```
import foolbox

if ABS_model.code_base == "tensorflow":
    fmodel = foolbox.models.TensorFlowModel(
        ABS_model.x_input, ABS_model.pre_softmax, (0.0, 1.0),
channel_axis=3
    )
elif ABS_model.code_base == "pytorch":
    ABS_model.eval()
    fmodel = foolbox.models.PyTorchModel(
        ABS_model, bounds=(0.0, 1.0), num_classes=10,
device=utils.dev()
    )
```

5. Import the library of attacks from Foolbox and select an MNIST image:

```
from foolbox import attacks

images, labels = utils.get_batch(bs=1)
```

6. Select the attack type, in this case, a boundary attack:

```
attack = attacks.DeepFoolL2Attack(fmodel)
metric = foolbox.distances.MSE
criterion = foolbox.criteria.Misclassification()
```

7. Display the original image and its label using Matplotlib:

```
from matplotlib import pyplot as plt
%matplotlib inline

plt.imshow(images[0, 0], cmap="gray")
plt.title("original image")
plt.axis("off")
plt.show()
```

The image produced is as follows:

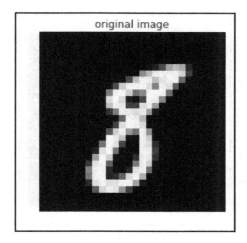

8. Search for an adversarial instance using Foolbox:

```
gradient_estimator =
foolbox.gradient_estimators.CoordinateWiseGradientEstimator(0.1)
fmodel = foolbox.models.ModelWithEstimatedGradients(fmodel,
gradient_estimator)

adversary = foolbox.adversarial.Adversarial(
    fmodel, criterion, images[0], labels[0], distance=metric
)
attack(adversary)
```

9. Show the discovered adversarial example:

```
plt.imshow(a.image[0], cmap="gray")
plt.title("adversarial image")
plt.axis("off")
plt.show()
print("Model prediction:",
np.argmax(fmodel.predictions(adversary.image)))
```

The adversarial image produced is as follows:

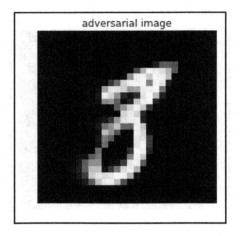

10. Instantiate a traditional CNN model trained on MNIST:

```
from abs_models import models

traditional_model = models.get_CNN()
```

The model architecture is as follows:

```
CNN(
  (net): NN(
    (conv_0): Conv2d(1, 20, kernel_size=(5, 5), stride=(1, 1))
    (bn_0): BatchNorm2d(20, eps=1e-05, momentum=0.1, affine=True,
track_running_stats=True)
    (nl_0): ELU(alpha=1.0)
    (conv_1): Conv2d(20, 70, kernel_size=(4, 4), stride=(2, 2))
    (bn_1): BatchNorm2d(70, eps=1e-05, momentum=0.1, affine=True,
track_running_stats=True)
    (nl_1): ELU(alpha=1.0)
    (conv_2): Conv2d(70, 256, kernel_size=(3, 3), stride=(2, 2))
    (bn_2): BatchNorm2d(256, eps=1e-05, momentum=0.1, affine=True,
track_running_stats=True)
    (nl_2): ELU(alpha=1.0)
    (conv_3): Conv2d(256, 10, kernel_size=(5, 5), stride=(1, 1))
  )
  (model): NN(
    (conv_0): Conv2d(1, 20, kernel_size=(5, 5), stride=(1, 1))
    (bn_0): BatchNorm2d(20, eps=1e-05, momentum=0.1, affine=True,
track_running_stats=True)
    (nl_0): ELU(alpha=1.0)
```

```
    (conv_1): Conv2d(20, 70, kernel_size=(4, 4), stride=(2, 2))
    (bn_1): BatchNorm2d(70, eps=1e-05, momentum=0.1, affine=True,
track_running_stats=True)
    (nl_1): ELU(alpha=1.0)
    (conv_2): Conv2d(70, 256, kernel_size=(3, 3), stride=(2, 2))
    (bn_2): BatchNorm2d(256, eps=1e-05, momentum=0.1, affine=True,
track_running_stats=True)
    (nl_2): ELU(alpha=1.0)
    (conv_3): Conv2d(256, 10, kernel_size=(5, 5), stride=(1, 1))
  )
)
```

11. Perform a sanity check to make sure that the model is performing as expected:

```
preds, labels = predict_on_batch(traditional_model, batch, 5)
print(preds)
print(labels)
```

The printout is as follows:

```
[7, 9, 5, 3, 3]
[7, 9, 5, 3, 3]
```

12. Wrap the traditional model using Foolbox:

```
if traditional_model.code_base == "tensorflow":
    fmodel_traditional = foolbox.models.TensorFlowModel(
        traditional_model.x_input,
        traditional_model.pre_softmax,
        (0.0, 1.0),
        channel_axis=3,
    )
elif traditional_model.code_base == "pytorch":
    traditional_model.eval()
    fmodel_traditional = foolbox.models.PyTorchModel(
        traditional_model, bounds=(0.0, 1.0), num_classes=10,
device=u.dev()
    )
```

13. Attack the traditional CNN model:

```
fmodel_traditional =
foolbox.models.ModelWithEstimatedGradients(fmodel_traditional, GE)

adversarial_traditional = foolbox.adversarial.Adversarial(
    fmodel_traditional, criterion, images[0], labels[0],
distance=metric
)
attack(adversarial_traditional)
```

14. Display the adversarial example discovered:

```
plt.imshow(adversarial_traditional.image[0], cmap="gray")
plt.title("adversarial image")
plt.axis("off")
plt.show()
print(
    "Model prediction:",
np.argmax(fmodel_traditional.predictions(adversarial_traditional.im
age)),
)
```

The adversarial image produced is as follows:

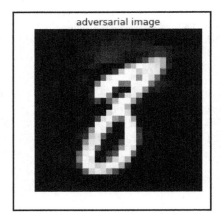

How it works...

We begin by importing a pre-trained ABS model (*Step 1*). In *Steps 2* and *3*, we defined a `convenience` function to predict a batch of MNIST images and to verify that the model is working properly. Next, we wrapped the model using Foolbox in preparation for testing its adversarial robustness (*Step 4*). Note that Foolbox facilitates the attacking of either TensorFlow or PyTorch models using the same API once wrapped. Nice! In *Step 5*, we select an MNIST image to use as the medium for our attack. To clarify, this image gets tweaked and mutated until the result fools the model. In *Step 6*, we select the attack type we want to implement. We select a boundary attack, which is a decision-based attack that starts from a large adversarial perturbation and then gradually reduces the perturbation while remaining adversarial. The attack requires little hyperparameter tuning, hence, no substitute models and no gradient computations. For more information about decision-based attacks, refer to `https://arxiv.org/abs/1712.04248`.

In addition, note that the metric used here is **mean squared error** (**MSE**), which determines how the adversarial example is assessed as close to, or far from, the original image. The criterion used is misclassification, meaning that the search terminates once the target model misclassifies the image. Alternative criteria may include a confidence level or a specific type of misclassification. In *Steps 7-9*, we display the original image, as well as the adversarial example generated from it. In the next two steps, we instantiate a standard CNN and verify that it is working properly. In *Steps 12-14*, we repeat the attack from the previous steps on the standard CNN. Looking at the result, we see that the experiment is a strong visual indicator that the ABS model is more robust to adversarial perturbations than a vanilla CNN.

Differential privacy using TensorFlow Privacy

TensorFlow Privacy (`https://github.com/tensorflow/privacy`) is a relatively new addition to the TensorFlow family. This Python library includes implementations of TensorFlow optimizers for training machine learning models with *differential privacy*. A model that has been trained to be differentially private does not non-trivially change as a result of the removal of any single training instance from its dataset. (Approximate) differential privacy is quantified using *epsilon* and *delta*, which give a measure of how sensitive the model is to a change in a single training example. Using the Privacy library is as simple as wrapping the familiar optimizers (for example, RMSprop, Adam, and SGD) to convert them to a differentially private version. This library also provides convenient tools for measuring the privacy guarantees, epsilon, and delta.

In this recipe, we show you how to implement and train a differentially private deep neural network for MNIST using Keras and TensorFlow Privacy.

Getting ready

Preparation for this recipe involves installing Keras and TensorFlow. The command is as follows:

```
pip install keras tensorflow
```

Installation instructions for TensorFlow Privacy can be found at https://github.com/tensorflow/privacy.

How to do it...

1. Begin by defining a few convenience functions for pre-processing the MNIST dataset:

```
import tensorflow as tf


def preprocess_observations(data):
    """Preprocesses MNIST images."""
    data = np.array(data, dtype=np.float32) / 255
    data = data.reshape(data.shape[0], 28, 28, 1)
    return data


def preprocess_labels(labels):
    """Preprocess MNIST labels."""
    labels = np.array(labels, dtype=np.int32)
    labels = tf.keras.utils.to_categorical(labels, num_classes=10)
```

2. Write a convenience function to load MNIST:

```
def load_mnist():
    """Loads the MNIST dataset."""
    (X_train, y_train), (X_test, y_test) =
tf.keras.datasets.mnist.load_data()
    X_train = preprocess_observations(X_train)
    X_test = preprocess_observations(X_test)
    y_train = preprocess_labels(y_train)
    y_test = preprocess_labels(y_test)
    return X_train, y_train, X_test, y_test
```

3. Load the MNIST dataset:

```
import numpy as np

X_train, y_train, X_test, y_test = load_mnist()
```

The training set is 60 k in size, and the testing set 10 k.

4. Import a differentially private optimizer and define a few parameters that control the learning rate and extent of differential privacy:

```
from privacy.optimizers.dp_optimizer import
DPGradientDescentGaussianOptimizer

optimizer = DPGradientDescentGaussianOptimizer(
    l2_norm_clip=1.0, noise_multiplier=1.1, num_microbatches=250,
learning_rate=0.15
)
loss = tf.keras.losses.CategoricalCrossentropy(
    from_logits=True, reduction=tf.losses.Reduction.NONE
)
```

5. In order to measure privacy, define a function to compute epsilon:

```
from privacy.analysis.rdp_accountant import compute_rdp
from privacy.analysis.rdp_accountant import get_privacy_spent


def compute_epsilon(steps):
    """Compute the privacy epsilon."""
    orders = [1 + x / 10.0 for x in range(1, 100)] + list(range(12,
64))
    sampling_probability = 250 / 60000
    rdp = compute_rdp(
        q=sampling_probability, noise_multiplier=1.1, steps=steps,
orders=orders
    )
    return get_privacy_spent(orders, rdp, target_delta=1e-5)[0]
```

6. Define a standard Keras CNN for MNIST:

```
NN_model = tf.keras.Sequential(
    [
        tf.keras.layers.Conv2D(
            16, 8, strides=2, padding="same", activation="relu",
input_shape=(28, 28, 1)
        ),
        tf.keras.layers.MaxPool2D(2, 1),
```

```
            tf.keras.layers.Conv2D(32, 4, strides=2, padding="valid",
activation="relu"),
            tf.keras.layers.MaxPool2D(2, 1),
            tf.keras.layers.Flatten(),
            tf.keras.layers.Dense(32, activation="relu"),
            tf.keras.layers.Dense(10),
        ]
    )
```

7. **Compiling** model:

```
NN_model.compile(optimizer=optimizer, loss=loss,
metrics=["accuracy"])
```

8. **Fit and test** model:

```
NN_model.fit(
    X_train, y_train, epochs=1, validation_data=(X_test, y_test),
batch_size=250
    )
```

9. Compute the value of epsilon, the measure of privacy:

```
eps = compute_epsilon(1 * 60000 // 250)
```

How it works...

We begin *Steps 1-3* by preparing and loading the MNIST dataset. Next, in *Step 4*, we import DPGradientDescentGaussianOptimizer, an optimizer that allows the model to become differentially private. A number of parameters are used at this stage, and these stand to be clarified. The l2_norm_clip parameter refers to the maximum norm of each gradient computed on an individual training datapoint from a minibatch. This parameter bounds the sensitivity of the optimizer to individual training points, thereby moving the model toward differential privacy. The noise_multiplier parameter controls the amount of random noise added to gradients. Generally, the more noise, the greater the privacy. Having finished this step, in *Step 5*, we define a function that computes the epsilon of the epsilon-delta definition of differential privacy. We instantiate a standard Keras neural network (*Step 6*), compile it (*Step 7*), and then train it on MNIST using the differentially private optimizer (*Step 8*). Finally, in *Step 9*, we compute the value of epsilon, which measures the extent to which the model is differentially private. Typical values for this recipe are an epsilon value of around 1.

Appendix

In this chapter, we offer the reader a guide to creating infrastructure to handle the challenges of machine learning on cybersecurity data. In particular, we provide a recipe for setting up a virtual lab environment to allow for safe and effective malware analysis. We also provide a guide to using virtual Python environments, which allow users to seamlessly work on different Python projects while avoiding package conflicts.

The following recipes will be covered in this chapter:

- Setting up a virtual lab environment
- Using Python virtual environments

Setting up a virtual lab environment

To protect yourself and your network, it is imperative to take preventative steps when handling and analyzing malware. One of the best ways to do so is to set up an isolated *virtual lab environment*. A virtual lab environment consists of one or more **Virtual Machines (VMs)** in an isolated network. Isolating the network prevents malware from spreading through the network, at the cost of less realistic malware behavior.

Getting ready

In preparation for this recipe, do the following:

1. Install a hypervisor.

    A hypervisor is software that allows you to control VMs. One instance is
    VirtualBox, available for download for free at `https://www.virtualbox.org/`:

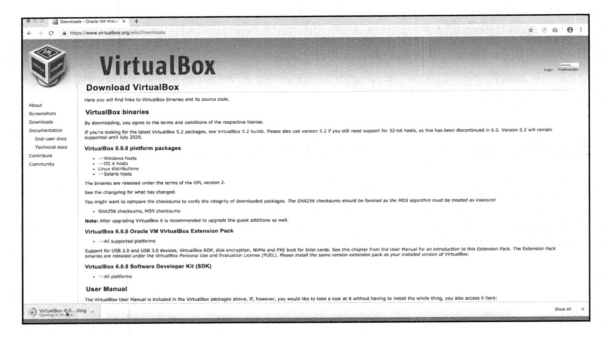

2. Download a virtual image.

    A virtual image is a template for a VM. Several Windows virtual images may be found at `https://developer.microsoft.com/en-us/microsoft-edge/tools/vms/`:

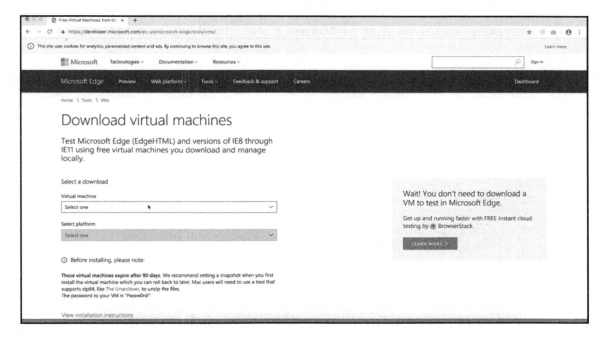

How to do it...

The following steps will guide you through setting up and using a simple virtual lab environment:

1. Create a VM using the virtual image.

    Your screen when opening the VM image should look something like this:

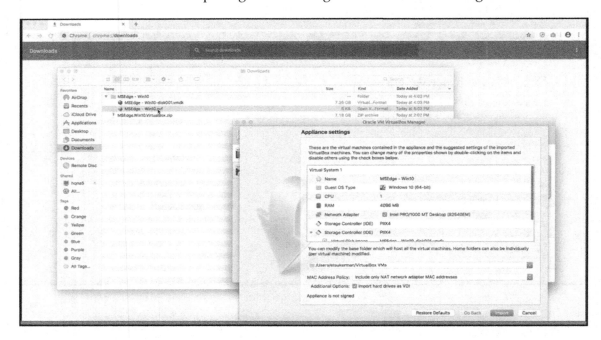

2. Configure the VM for performance and safety. For instance, you may disconnect it all together from the network.

The following screenshot shows how to disconnect your VM from the network:

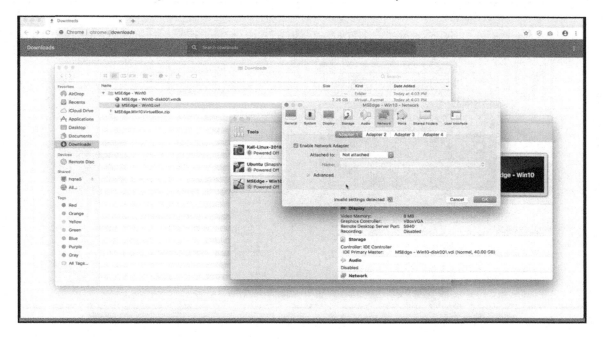

3. Create a snapshot.

You can see what menu option allows you to take a snapshot here:

4. (Optional) Detonate and analyze malware in the VM.

For instance, I ran ransomware in my VM here:

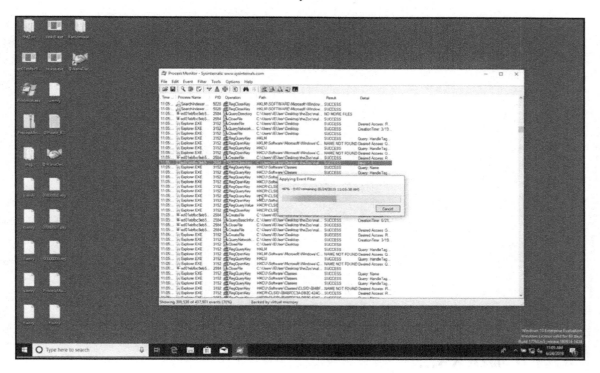

5. (Optional) Revert the VM to your previous snapshot.

   Press the **Restore** button, as shown here:

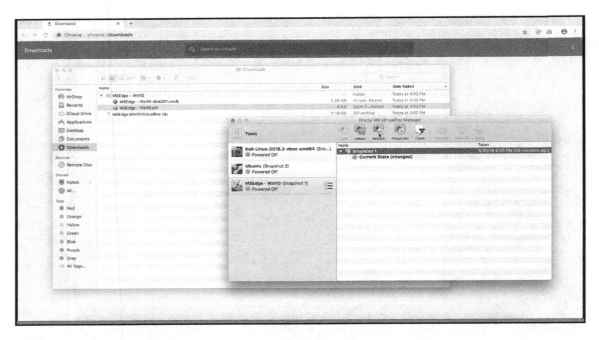

How it works...

We began this recipe by creating a VM from an image (*step 1*). The creation of a VM depends on the format in which the image is given. For the referenced virtual images, double-clicking the `.ovf` file of the virtual image will allow you to set up a VM. Other times, you may need to create a brand new installation of an operating system and then mount the virtual image. Next, in *step 2*, we configured our VM for malware analysis. There are several configuration changes you are likely to want to make. These include setting base memory, the number of processors, video memory, and a virtual optical drive; selecting an appropriate network setting; and creating a shared folder.

Having done so, in *step 3*, we saved a snapshot, which allowed us to save all important state information. The great thing about snapshots is that they allow a user to easily roll back changes made to the VM. So, if you make a mistake, it's no big deal—just revert to a previous snapshot. Next, in *step 4*, we detonated malware in our VM. We recommend exercising caution in this step, and only doing it if you know what you are doing. In that case, you will find a dataset of malware in the repository for this book. Finally, in *step 5*, we clicked the **Restore** button in VirtualBox to roll back our VM to the state it was in when you created the snapshot.

Finally, we note and credit Yasser Ali with the following advice: when installing VirtualBox on macOS, users should make security exceptions for Adobe Software to use the security settings.

Using Python virtual environments

Imagine that you have two projects—project A and project B—whose Python library requirements conflict. For instance, project A needs scikit-learn version 0.21, while project B requires scikit-learn versions >0.22. Or maybe one project requires Python 3.6 and the other Python 3.7. You could uninstall and then install the appropriate libraries or Python as you switch from one project to the other, but that can get tedious and impractical. To solve the problem of conflicting requirements, we recommend using Python virtual environments. You will see how to use a Python virtual environment in this recipe.

Getting ready

The module for virtual environments, venv, is included in the Python standard library on Python 3.3 and later.

How to do it...

To create and activate a virtual Python environment, follow these steps:

1. In a Terminal, run the following command:

```
python -m venv "name-of-your-environment"
```

2. In a Linux or macOS Terminal, run the following command:

```
source "name-of-your-environment"/bin/activate
```

On Windows, run this command:

```
"name-of-your-environment"/Scripts/activate.bat
```

3. Install your desired packages.

How it works...

We began *step 1* by creating a virtual Python environment. The -m flag indicated the module to be used, which, in this case, is venv. Next, in *step 2*, we activated our Python environment, so we can use it and make changes to it. Note that the folder structure of a Python environment is different on Windows than Linux or Mac. An indication that the environment is currently active is seeing the name of the environment in the Terminal, like so:

```
("name-of-your-environment")
```

In *step 3*, you may install packages as usual, as in this example:

```
pip install numpy
```

And rest assured that it will not affect your packages outside of this environment. Sweet!

Other Books You May Enjoy

If you enjoyed this book, you may be interested in these other books by Packt:

Hands-On Machine Learning for Cybersecurity

Sinan Ozdemir, Soma Halder

ISBN: 9781788992282

- Use machine learning algorithms with complex datasets to implement cybersecurity concepts
- Implement machine learning algorithms such as clustering, k-means, and Naive Bayes to solve real-world problems
- Learn to speed up a system using Python libraries with NumPy, Scikit-learn, and CUDA
- Understand how to combat malware, detect spam, and fight financial fraud to mitigate cyber crimes
- Use TensorFlow in the cybersecurity domain and implement real-world examples
- Learn how machine learning and Python can be used in complex cyber issues

Hands-On Artificial Intelligence for Cybersecurity
Alessandro Parisi

ISBN: 9781789804027

- Detect email threats such as spamming and phishing using AI
- Categorize APT, zero-days, and polymorphic malware samples
- Overcome antivirus limits in threat detection
- Predict network intrusions and detect anomalies with machine learning
- Verify the strength of biometric authentication procedures with deep learning
- Evaluate cybersecurity strategies and learn how you can improve them

Leave a review - let other readers know what you think

Please share your thoughts on this book with others by leaving a review on the site that you bought it from. If you purchased the book from Amazon, please leave us an honest review on this book's Amazon page. This is vital so that other potential readers can see and use your unbiased opinion to make purchasing decisions, we can understand what our customers think about our products, and our authors can see your feedback on the title that they have worked with Packt to create. It will only take a few minutes of your time, but is valuable to other potential customers, our authors, and Packt. Thank you!

Index